Carol Lawrence
THE BACKSTAGE STORY

Carol Lawrence
THE BACKSTAGE STORY

by Carol Lawrence

McGraw-Hill Publishing Company

New York St. Louis San Francisco Auckland Bogotá Hamburg
London Madrid Mexico Milan Montreal New Delhi Paris
São Paulo Tokyo Toronto

1 2 3 4 5 6 7 8 9 DOH   DOH8 9 2 1 0 9

ISBN 0-07-036724-8

LIBRARY OF CONGRESS CATALOGING-IN-PUBLICATION DATA

Lawrence, Carol
    Carol Lawrence : the backstage story / by Carol Lawrence, with
Phyllis Hobe.
      p.   cm.
    ISBN 0-07-036724-8
      1. Lawrence, Carol, 1932–   . 2. Entertainers—United States—
Biography. I. Hobe, Phyllis. II. Title.
PN2287.L2894A3   1989
781.42164′092—dc20
[B]   89-12875
                                                                  CIP

Book design by Mark Bergeron

To the spirit in all of us

Acknowledgments

It isn't possible to thank the many wonderful people who have helped me with this book without also thanking those who have helped me in my life.

I am deeply grateful to my sons, Christopher and Michael Goulet, for their love, support and patience; to my manager, Lee Mimms, for prodding me to put my memories on paper and for praying with me for discernment and wisdom in that task; to Phyllis Hobe for her writing expertise in shaping the facts into a readable account; to my dear sister in Christ, Jeanne Blackstone, who anguished with me during the labor pains of the final draft; to my brother, Joseph Laraia and his wife, Mary Lou, for sensing when I needed them so that I never had to ask; to Arlene Hunnicutt, for holding my hand an awful lot; to Leeann Faust, whose shining face was always there in the front row; to Joan Roy, for many years of friendship; to Pat and Shirley Boone, for their guidance over some rough spots; to the many members of Alcoholics Anonymous, Al-Anon and Adult Children of Alcoholics for teaching me what I needed to know about the effects of alcoholism on a family; to Toughlove, for an education in gentleness and strength; to Archibald Hart for his seminars on grief; to my covenant groups at Bel Air Presbyterian Church; to the congregation of The Church on the Way and to its pastor, Dr. Jack Hayford.

Chapter One

September 26, 1957, was the opening night of *West Side Story*, an unprecedented, innovative step forward in the evolution of American musical theater. The show's universal impact has kept it touring and touching young and old all over the world. But the revered legend the show would become was only a possibility to the hopeful unknowns that made up the cast of delinquents, immigrants and establishment figures re-creating Shakespeare's *Romeo and Juliet* as a contemporary tragedy.

I *was* Maria that night. I felt, I loved and I agonized through every moment she existed in the passionate drama. I'd done several Broadway shows in the chorus or as a minor character—but in this gem I was the leading lady and we could all taste that most rare ingredient in a production, the taste of success. Also, we all sensed that this play had potential world-shaking impact—the *real* goal of *theater*!

The audience was glamorously star-studded and prestigious, but foremost on our nervous minds were those seven master critics who could reduce all our months of discipline and dedication to rubble by their sarcasm and smug rejection. We prayed that they and the audience were ready for our strong depiction of one of society's most painful and festering wounds—the loss of our youth to bigotry, racism, lack of tolerance and understanding, resulting ultimately in the violence of gang wars.

An incredible gift from heaven blessed every scene with the perfect electricity and tension that kept even jaded veterans of the theater gasping, guffawing and crying right along with us. As you may remember, the death scene that ends the play reigns supreme in its concise simplicity. Maria's lover, Tony, has been shot and dies in her arms, after which she rises and, in her black, raging sorrow, takes the gun from the stunned murderer and threatens to kill herself and as many of the warriors as the bullets will allow. For, she declares, "We are all guilty—we *all* killed him!" Then she holds the pistol right up to the face of the gang leader, ready to pull the trigger . . . and with a wrenching sob, she recognizes the sheer terror of a young boy as vital and alive as Tony had been a moment before. The compassion in her heart breaks through the hatred and she collapses at his feet. With arms outstretched, she begs and entreats the two opposing forces to help her carry Tony home so that the police officers won't cart him to the morgue. Slowly they come to her side and lift the body to their shoulders. She rises and, weeping and alone, follows the funeral procession off as the death knell peals and the curtain falls slowly.

We scurried to our places just behind the curtain for our bows. The tears were still hot on my face as the curtain was yanked up to reveal a line of eager faces anxious to hear approving applause. This was that life-threatening moment akin to awaiting the bullets of a firing squad. Time seemed to stop as we stared at the audience and they stared back in deathly silence. "Oh God," I thought, "They hated it! They didn't get it. They didn't understand what we were trying to say." All I could hear was my racing heart about to burst, and then, *truly* as if it were choreographed and rehearsed, the entire mass of seated judges leaped to their feet and pandemonium erupted—cheers and whistles, thunderous

applause punctuated with *bravo*s. It was a barrage of unbridled love. Crazy Italian that I am, I burst into new tears
of joy, and as Chita Rivera and Larry Kert and I took our
final bow together, the audience rose to a new height of
hysteria; and the whooping, stamping screams of *bravo*
bathed us in a wave of warm relief akin to no other I had
ever experienced.

I can't remember how many curtain calls we took, bobbing, curtsying and laughing/crying—never letting go of
each other's hands. But when the curtain lay still on the
floor, I turned to see Leonard Bernstein walking to me from
the wings, with arms outstretched and tears running down
that gorgeous beaming face. We hugged each other like
coach and runner just after an Olympic triumph. We were
all winners that night, and I will treasure my place in that
race for as long as I live!

The opening night of *West Side Story* was the culmi-
nation of everything I had ever worked toward and dreamed
about, everything my parents had sacrificed for and encouraged me to be part of ever since I could remember. After
the tumultuous victory hugs and cheers of congratulations
between the cast and creators onstage, we all seemed in-
fused with a second rush of euphoria. We raced to our dressing rooms to bask in the ecstasy with our friends and family
who had been in the audience. Chita Rivera and I shared
the large "star" dressing room suite, created for Hollywood's
Rosalind Russell—a living room, dressing room, and full
pink bathroom—a remarkably opulent space compared to
the regular cubbyholes that actors are forced to call "home"
on Broadway.

The first familiar faces we saw were the ebullient swarm
of Chita's brothers and sisters (by now they were family to
me too). And the pitch of their Latin squeezing, laughing,
pinching, loving was going to be hard to maintain. But all
that was merely a prologue to my mother's entrance. What
a diva she would have made! Still crying from the pathos of
the death scene, she stood—alone—in the doorway, perfectly framed, and wailed, "OOOOOOOHHHHHHhhh,
CAROL . . . I can't believe it!!!!!" All conversation stopped

and heads snapped round in her direction. "You were absolutely gooorgeous onstage . . . Everything was so much more than I could have imagined . . . The exquisite music, the dancing . . . Chita, you are a dynamic marvel . . . and, I can't even catch my breath, it was too much beauty to take in at one time . . . but Carol . . . Carol . . ." and she wrapped those all-encompassing mother's arms around me and we both sobbed the well-earned tears of satisfaction and relief.

She chattered on and on about every nuance of the show. She was instinctively in tune with all of the difficulties, techniques, and sacrifices that went into creating the flawless tale of woe that she had seen on the stage. I felt appreciated and rewarded for the years of struggle I'd weathered. I closed my eyes and savored the warm embrace that was always the safe haven I sought as a child.

When I opened my eyes, my father was walking toward me. He extended his hands, and with both of them shook my hand firmly. He smiled and said, "Carol, it was a fine production." Then he turned to someone nearby and continued a conversation, rejoining the happy din of the crowded room. Somehow all the accolades suddenly meant nothing. The person I most wanted to please and satisfy had remained untouched and unimpressed. Never before had the vast difference in my parents' natures been so vividly delineated. It's an indelible memory I strive to let go of . . . over and over. But it was exactly like a hundred other childhood memories of their opposite reactions to my hopes and dreams.

I was born in the tiny town of Melrose Park, west of Chicago. My family was old-fashioned Italian, where the man is the boss and the woman knows her place. Although my mother certainly knew her place, she had difficulty staying there. When she disagreed with my father—which was often—she let him know it. They would stand screaming at each other until my father lost control and their argument would deteriorate into verbal and physical abuse. Some people saw it as the excitement of Italian passion. No doubt, from the

outside, it sounded like a great and tragic opera. My resulting terror of violence suggests a somewhat more sinister
scenario. So, however much they were into it, I wasn't. Now
isn't it strange that what I most abhorred I re-created in or
attracted into my own life?

My brother Joey and I could hear it coming, and we
would cower upstairs until it was all over. My father never
hit me, and only twice do I remember him striking my
brother. He was a strict man, and he could devastate me
with a look, a word of disapproval or, worse yet, of disappointment. We knew he loved us, because he worked hard
and long to provide for us. But he wasn't the kind of person
who could show affection.

I never spoke back to my father because I saw what
happened when my mother did. I tried endlessly to persuade
my mother to humor him, but she couldn't do it. It seemed
so simple to me. Arguing got you nowhere, so why not just
make someone happy? Was it *that* important to speak your
mind? I figured out later that there was more to my parents'
arguing than a difference of opinion.

My mother came from a family of six girls and two boys,
a home that was always brimming with love, laughter, affection and wisdom. With all the security this situation created, she became the natural center of attention with her
wit, charm and flirtatious beauty. She entertained endlessly
with her hilarious imitations of the Perils of Pauline, her
mimicry of everyone around her and her need to be the first,
the leader of the pack. Her laugh rang out over everyone's
when you told a story—as though you were the funniest
person alive. Everyone wanted to be around my mother.

My father was brought up in an oppressive home, dom-
inated by a tyrannical, abusive father who beat and intim-
idated his wife and children. My grandmother attempted
suicide three times because of his accusations of alleged
incestuous relations with any of their sons if she so much
as ruffled their hair at the dinner table. My paternal grandfather was totally incapable of communicating love, and
couldn't tolerate the expression of it by anyone around him.
He was the role model for my father. I ached over stories

like this: My father had saved hard-earned nickels from all of his ingenious little plans and paid installments on a beloved violin. He proudly brought it home and showed it to his father, who grabbed the violin out of his son's hand and said, "You are not wasting your time on this," and smashed it on the table. The unjust brutality that he inflicted on his family was evident when not one of his six sons and two daughters could muster a tear at his funeral.

Another thing for which my father never forgave his father was refusing to allow him to attend college even though he had won a full scholarship to become the lawyer he had always dreamed of being. I'm sure that shaped my father's obsession with education and his respect for professional careers. His drive was unrelenting for himself and his children. I'm also sure that my father died with countless experiences left unhealed and unforgiven, experiences that throughout his life continued to wound and haunt him and his family. His only priority became going for the best, becoming the best of which he was capable. This explains the lengths to which he was willing to go to win my mother, Rose. In their neighborhood, she was the ultimate "catch."

Before she married my father, my mother had loved another man. My father knew of their mutual attraction. So before he and my mother were even dating, my father went to the other man and told him that he and my mother were going steady. According to old Italian courtship traditions, competition was forbidden. My mother never knew why her true love suddenly disappeared from her life, leaving a clear field for my father's pursuit. However, pursue her he did, and she fell totally in love with him. Nevertheless, crime doesn't pay. My father could never believe that my mother really loved him. He was a jealous husband. If my mother even laughed at something one of his friends said, my father accused her of having an affair. My father denied my mother access to his true feelings. She always yearned to hear him say that he loved her. Sadly, he never did in a way that could satisfy her. That was their relationship.

But my father did love my mother. Every day for years, he would come home for lunch, and they would retire to the bedroom for an hour. He was proud of her and enjoyed her enormously. We could tell that, but he couldn't tell *her*. How could he have learned to do that from the family in which he was raised? So they kept their marriage volatile. Instead of praising her for something, he would find fault with her simplest expression.

I've always felt that inside that rigid man was a softness, a warmth that no one was ever allowed to reach. I was convinced that his feelings ran deep. His personal goals had been thwarted, but he would not allow that to happen to his children!

I heard the violin story many times while growing up. But as for *my* personal goals and when they began to take shape . . . I suspect that at birth, when the doctor slapped me, I probably broke into an appropriate song, something like "Mean to me . . . Why must you be mean to me?"

My mother always said that as soon as I could stand and walk, if there was music playing, I was *dancing*, and if there was no radio on, I'd be singing my own accompaniment. What special genes combined to produce this gift of heredity I do not know; but I do know that my maternal grandfather was the saluted dancer of his village in the mountains of Italy and that my son Michael exhibited sheer ecstasy in whirling and creating his own unique routines to the music of "Sesame Street" long before he *understood* the word "dance."

When I was around three, sitting in a movie house, I watched the luxurious splendor of the golden age of Hollywood musicals and wanted desperately to make that special-tinkling music that sprang from Fred Astaire's feet! I'd go home and mimic the dancers' every move, to my mother's smiling delight, but those rhythmic sounds were missing. Finally I was given my first patent leather tap shoes and lessons at the local dance studio like every other little girl in the neighborhood. Wow, was I hooked. I took the shoes off only to take a bath or go to bed. The rest of my time I tapped the tedium of all those shuffles, flaps, and ball changes into the very sinews of my body.

How my mother put up with the incessant noise in our

tiny flat is a tribute to her loving patience. Because my shoes made terrible marks on the linoleum, she did insist that I limit my practice to one corner of the kitchen, and, believe it or not, I wore that pattern completely away—right down to the black asbestos base. I still have those little black Mary Janes in my curio cabinet, and the trade name "Mac's Taps" imprinted on the steel plates is also worn to a whisper.

At first the dancing afforded me one more means of approval from my parents. They loved having me entertain their many friends before I hopped off to bed, and that led to performing for my dad's Kiwanis Club, Elks Club, Chamber of Commerce, and church affairs. I'd accept any excuse to perform.

By the time I was nine we had moved to a new home with a beautiful, modern kitchen, carefully designed to utilize every corner with cabinets and appliances. There were no "wasted corners" in which I could polish my tap steps— besides, they had just laid a new, shiny floor and big black patches of worn-off patterns could not be tolerated. I had progressed to dance routines that demanded more space for the grand jetés (flying leaps) and circles of whirling piqué turns, and whole sequences that kicked and flapped "Shuffling Off to Buffalo" from one side of the stage to the other.

The only available alternative was the concrete floor of our one-car garage, once Dad left for work. Mindless of the ravages that dancing on concrete wrought on a dancer's legs, I was grateful for this new arena. Before you knew it, I had mopped the floor and hung everything on the walls. Leaving the automatic garage door half open for fresh air, I could hear any approaching footsteps on the sidewalk outside. With a flick of the switch the door would roll up like a main drape in a theater, and I worked my way to the open door, singing and dancing at *full* power—hoping any passersby would stop and become my enraptured audience.

They were always startled by the moving door and the funny little kid in tap shoes, top hat and cane pouring her heart out. They usually paused or froze with a quizzical look of surprise for a second or two. My favorites were the warm-hearted, sympathetic dears who stood and smiled at least until the end of the chorus, and then applauded or patted me on the head before they continued their journey. I must say there were a few who barely slowed up, even when I sang louder, tapped harder and leaned *way* over the imaginary footlight to keep them entertained. Lincoln was right about not pleasing all the people all of the time—but he was better at dealing with rejection than *I* was at nine.

I had worked my way to the most advanced classes in our local studio and was advised to study in the Big City at the best dance academy, the Edna McCrae School of Dance. I was twelve years old and in tap class with professionals working the Chicago theaters and various nightclubs.

Almost every weekday afternoon after school, I'd take the bus from Melrose Park to Chicago and spend several hours in dance classes at Edna McCrae's studio. Then I'd take the elevated train home, eat dinner around eleven, and sit up half the night doing homework. Good grades meant a lot to my father, so I worked hard to become a straight-A student. After a few years, the strain affected my health, so my mother began driving me to school in the morning and picking me up at the train station at night. She even excused me from helping her clean the house.

I began performing professionally at age thirteen because Miss McCrae believed that no matter how well you danced in the classroom, you never knew how good—or bad—you were until you performed in front of a real audience that paid to see you work. She was absolutely correct. Naturally, we didn't tell anyone I was only thirteen. I piled my hair high on my head so I looked older, and I lied about my age to get a work permit.

September of each year was a difficult time for me. That's when I would compete for a full scholarship of dance classes at the McCrae School, which included an intensive summer schedule of daily classes from 9 A.M. until 6 P.M. or later. I was awarded a scholarship each year and that was my proudest achievement because I knew it relieved my father of the burden of paying for so many lessons.

It wouldn't be fair to say that my father didn't encourage me. After all, it was he who paid for my shoes and costumes.

And it was he who rubbed my legs with hot camphorated oil. It was his strong fingers that sought out the charley horses and released the knots of spasms from hours of study and rehearsal. I didn't realize the wisdom doing this, but he knew that it would relieve my pain and allow the muscles to grow smooth and well proportioned. Thanks to him, I don't have the typical knotted "dancer's legs." And it was *he* who persuaded me to change my name when it was time for me to sign my first professional contract. Until I was thirteen, I was Carolina Maria Laraia—Carol Laraia, for short—and then I became Carol Lawrence. "People can't read Laraia," my father told me. "So they won't remember it, too many vowels in a row. And if you're going to sing and dance in front of a lot of people, you want them to remember who you are."

My father knew whereof he spoke. He was an elected official, and he was often asked to speak at political meetings because he was so persuasive, articulate and able to communicate his trustworthiness and genuine concern for the town. His patience and wisdom in quelling arguments and solving problems was well known. It was a part of him I loved proudly. But he knew how embarrassing it was to have someone say, "And now I want to introduce Mike Lar—uh, um, Mike La—anyway, here's Mike from Melrose!" "Carol Lawrence" was his idea. He liked the way it sounded. So did I, although I felt somewhat uncomfortable with it at first. It just wasn't *Italian*.

While I went to school, I performed only on weekends, mostly in local clubs and private halls on Chicago's South Side. Some of them were pretty rough, and most of the customers were men. I'd come out and sing "Sorrento" or "Siboney" and do a tap dance. The money wasn't much, but I was one step closer to Broadway, and Broadway was where I wanted to go.

Some people say you shouldn't pursue a dream because you chance living a life of disappointment when it doesn't come true. I don't agree. Of course, you have to want it desperately, and be willing to work relentlessly to get it. But I once heard that it was better to hitch your wagon to a star

and land on a mountaintop than to spend your life struggling up a hill. What I've noticed is the inner joy and excitement that flows out of people who spend their time doing
what they love. Every minute to these people feels like a
success. And you know what? They usually are a success,
because everyone else believes in them and wants to be
around them. (The trick for grown-ups is to make the effort
to recapture what we knew automatically as children. We
must take the psychological and aptitude tests that tell us
our strengths and abilities, the ones that set our hearts on
fire, so we can be reconnected to the master plan for which
we were designed. Never was anything created that didn't
have a purpose, I'm convinced. Just read Brian Swimme's
book, *The Universe Is a Green Dragon*, or Lewis Thomas'
Lives of a Cell.)

I think I got some of my determination from Miss
McCrae, who was a strict disciplinarian. She was a tall, thin,
Scottish woman who spoke with a burr and didn't waste
words. "Does that hurt?" she would ask, as she demanded
impossible things of our young bodies at the ballet barre.

"Oh, yes!" I would say, expecting some sympathy.

"Well, it's *supposed* to," she would announce, drawing
herself up to her considerable height and moving on to the
next student, If we didn't execute our steps precisely, she
would whack us with the cane she carried more for ad-
monishment than support. She was a tough cookie—and I
adored her.

When I was thirteen, Miss McCrae thought it was time
I had an agent, so she made an appointment for me to
audition for one. The man didn't ask me to dance. He didn't
ask me to sing. He just looked at me and said, "You know,
you've got a real natural beauty, so why don't you go home,
grow up and get married?" It was the kind of put-down a
woman hears, often in more subtle forms, throughout a
theatrical career, and I'm glad I didn't take it seriously. When
he turned me down, I thought, "That's what you think,
mister! But it's not what I AM!" I knew I had a lot more
growing to do and so much more to learn. Besides, my
teacher wouldn't have sent me to an agent unless she

thought I showed promise. The next agent who auditioned me agreed.

My greatest asset was my mother. If you're going to pursue a dream, it's important to have someone who keeps saying, "Yes, you can! Yes, you can!" Especially when you get turned down. You need someone willing to go all the way with you and be there for you no matter what happens. That was my mother. She thought I could do anything.

My father was a different story. As much as I loved him, I couldn't become the person he wanted me to be, which was another version of himself. Throughout my father's life, he tried to behave like a lawyer. After he'd graduated from high school and got a job as a bank teller, he dressed as if he owned the bank. And somehow there was a little bit of a British clip to his Midwestern accent. He would have made a great judge.

When I was a child my father had three jobs. He was both the village clerk and controller of Melrose Park, and on the side he was an insurance broker. All day long he'd listen to people complaining that their water bills were too high, or their garbage wasn't picked up, or the streetlights were too bright, or not bright enough. Then at night—always at dinner, because my mother was famous for her cooking—people came to talk. They'd say they wanted to pay their premiums and discuss their insurance policies, but most of the time they just talked to my father about their families and their troubles. He was such a good listener—to strangers. I used to resent having so many people at our table every evening, because I never got a chance to talk to my father the way those strangers did. My brother and I had to be on our best behavior, which meant we had to be quiet and let the grown-ups talk. I decided then that when I had a family of my own, dinner would always be a private time for us.

I suppose you could call my father a workaholic because even when he wasn't at work he was always doing something. He was wonderful around the house, and there wasn't anything he couldn't build or repair. But whenever he did anything—from installing a beamed ceiling in our living room to fixing a leaky faucet—he was like a chief surgeon. Someone, usually my mother, always had to stand close by and hand him the tools as he called for them.

"Wrench."

"Here, Mike."

"Washer."

"Here, Mike.

"No, not that one! The next bigger one!"

"Okay, Mike, okay—here's the one you want."

In later years my son Christopher took my mother's place beside my father when repairs had to be made, and I marveled at Chris's patience. My younger son Michael was more like the rest of us—when Grandpa went for his toolbox, Michael knew that was a good time to head for the bathroom!

My brother Joey is four and a half years younger than I am, which I'm told is a favorable birth order for siblings because an older sister is likely to mother a younger brother instead of competing with him. While that may be true, I think the reason my brother and I have always been so devoted to each other is that my mother took care to give both of us a lot of her attention. She told me that when Joey was born, she was like any new mother and fussed over him to the exclusion of everyone else. But one day, while she held Joey in her lap, lavishing him with kisses, I tried to climb up alongside Joey, and taking her face in my hands, said, "I want some too!" That's when she realized that she had been ignoring me. From that moment on, if she hugged my brother, she hugged me too, so I never felt that Joey had replaced me in her affections.

In the lives of children, four and a half years is a major age difference, and ordinarily Joey and I wouldn't have done many things together. But in our case, we spent a lot of time with each other. My parents couldn't afford babysitters, so wherever my mother went, we both went with her. My mother spent a great deal of her time helping me to become a dancer. She took me back and forth to performances, and sat through the long hours while I was rehearsing and waiting to go onstage. Joey was always with her, so from an early age I had the feeling that not only my mother, but also my brother, was there for me.

When I was in the ballet corps of the Lyric Opera of Chicago, we would rehearse three or four nights each week. Joey would sit up in the balcony where it was dark and no one could see him, because he wasn't supposed to be there. After a while, he learned all the singing parts and could sing along with the entire cast. Silently, of course.

Joey had, and still has, the most loving and patient nature. My mother used to take him along when she went to buy fabric for my costumes. Joey and I had exactly the same coloring, so my mother would sit him up on the table while she held swatches of cloth against him. She was so intent on her selection that she didn't realize people were smirking at Joey and whispering. Finally he would say, "Hey Ma, can you hurry a little? They think this is for me!"

In the summer Joey and I spent more time together, especially during our family's two-week vacation. My father used to spend all year planning that trip, and he insisted that it had to be something educational for us. We'd drive along the entire Eastern seaboard, stopping at Washington, New York, and Boston. We'd visit every museum, every courthouse, every historical site that offered a tour. I remember always carrying a pad and a pencil so I could take notes, and I kept a diary of our trips. So did Joey. They always came in handy for extra-credit reports at school.

As a family we were very close. We worked, played and traveled together whenever we could—and that became the pattern for me to follow when I married and had children of my own.

As Joey often recalls, my mother had "the quickest hands in the Midwest," because the moment we did anything wrong we got slapped. Not hard, yet enough to let us know what the rules were. But my mother was even quicker with her love. To her, hugging us was as natural as breathing.

From the very beginning I had a hard time with childhood illnesses. When I was eighteen months old I got whooping cough and then double pneumonia at one time. My lungs were filled with fluid and I couldn't breathe lying down in my crib. My mother held me upright in her arms, rocking me to sleep. She did that day and night for weeks until I got well. She even continued to nurse me because I refused any other kind of nourishment.

When I started school I came down with a bad case of scarlet fever and had to be quarantined for six months. My brother and father stayed with relatives, but my mother took care of me. The only other person brave enough to risk exposure was my maternal grandmother, who came to make me laugh and sing. She was the only one who could beguile me into taking my medicine, which resembled a cup full of blood and tasted vile.

"Carolina, here's your *medicina*," my grandmother would sing. "Nuncha say no! Waita you see how many times I coulda say 'gotarrotta' before you finisha si?" And before I realized what was happening, she'd be singing, "Gotarrotta, gotarrotta, gotarrotta" as fast as a machine gun firing—and I'd have downed the whole mess! She and my mother were wonderful examples of love and sacrifice. When I became a working mother, any comparison of me to the role models they set made me feel inadequate and guilty.

Those early diseases left their mark on me. I missed out on so much nourishment that I became a chronic undereater, and that led to rickets and anemia. What a skinny, funny-looking waif I was. But Mama still loved me!

And yet, although I knew I was loved, I always had the feeling that I was not enough for my parents. I loved my mother and father, and did everything I could to prove it. Still, I always seemed to fall short of their expectations. I couldn't give up dancing to please my father by becoming a lawyer, and although I pleased my mother with my dancing, she let me know that I failed her in other ways. She complained when I was a child that I didn't hug her enough; when I was older, that I didn't call her often enough. Sometimes I used to think if only they could see inside me, they would know how hard I was trying to measure up.

Just recently I read in Stewart Emery's marvelous book, *The Owner's Manual for Your Life*, the clearly stated reason for my frustration.

> Children, poets, and great scientists have in common the ability to look at the world and to be filled with wonder . . . the very qualities about us that are magical as children . . . The ability to wonder, to love, our passionate curiosity, all fade unless we are given the opportunity to contribute them to others.
>
> Self-esteem accrues out of our on-going experience that who, and what, and the way we are, make a real and positive difference. If that's not forthcoming, even if all our needs are met, even if we are given "love," we can grow up with no self-esteem at all.

I would search frantically for someone to let me contribute, someone who would acknowledge that I had made a difference in his life. From my parents I really needed approval, but perhaps they were afraid it would lead to complacency—or maybe they didn't have it to give me because they didn't have it themselves.

I think my mother wanted my success at least as much as I did. I know that deep in her heart she lived out her unfulfilled dreams of being "in the movies" through my efforts and study. And she wasn't easily satisfied. She was always suggesting ways I could improve my performance (and she would break me up when she tried to demonstrate what she meant). Seeing me struggle to pull my body into difficult ballet positions, she would hold up her flour-covered hands and exclaim, "That's beautiful! Beautiful! I can't believe you came out of my body, you're so beautiful!"

Many years later, I realized how little my mother thought of herself—and that was a shock to me. "I can cook, that's all," she said to me one day.

"But you can do more than cook, Mom!" I protested. "You could be a diplomat with how well you understand people and what they need to bring them together, and you could be an interior decorator, look how you've turned our

house into a beautiful home. You have exquisite taste—
better than anybody I know! And you know how to make
people laugh and have a good time."

"That's nothing," she said, not with bitterness, but
simply stating what, to her, was a fact of life.

I think a lot of women, not only then but now, diminish
their own sense of worth and value because they don't feel
sufficiently validated and appreciated. (Wouldn't it be great
if we taught and encouraged each other to look for and
magnify the positives as proficiently as we do the negatives?
How changed our lives and our world would be!) Take my
mother's cooking, for example. It was one of the tangible
proofs of her talent, and it had helped build my father's
business. Yet my father wasn't much of an eater, so although he acknowledged her culinary expertise, it was easy
to take for granted something that was always there for him.

Unfortunately, my mother ate too much, maybe because she was frustrated at being unable to win my father's
praise, or maybe because everything she cooked tasted so
good. I'm told that she was quite slender until she became
pregnant and all her relatives urged her to "eat enough for
two." But after I was born she just kept on eating, and as
far back as I can remember she was overweight. Sadly
enough, this was way before Weight Watchers and the current awareness of the need for low-cholesterol, sugar-free
cuisine and regular exercise regimes. Then she was diag-
nosed as diabetic. She was put on insulin and a very strict
diet. "It's got no taste!" she'd always say. Even after several
alarming trips to the hospital to correct her high sugar
count, she couldn't resist sampling the cooking she did for
everyone else. And she absolutely refused to change the way
she cooked.

That made me angry. I was aware, early on, that diabetes is a dangerous disease, and I was so afraid that it was
going to take my mother away from me.

As for my mother's "heart attacks"—they were something else! She was copying her sister's mother-in-law, who
would pretend to have a heart attack every time she didn't
get her own way. And it worked. So when Joey or I, and

sometimes my father, gave my mother a hard time, she would suddenly collapse, gasping and clutching at her chest. At first we used to call for the doctor, but while she was lying stretched out, she would "come to" and play a death scene straight out of *Camille*.

"Remember," she would tell me as she held on to my hand with all her might, "that I love you. I know I said some terrible things to you, but promise me you'll forget them. Just remember, I love you." Then the doctor would arrive and prescribe a little rest and some whiskey, which my mother swallowed as if it were poison, and a few hours later she would be fine. The doctor never found any evidence of heart trouble, but of course he didn't tell that to my mother. Only to my father. But Joey and I caught on. We never called my mother's bluff after that. We'd let her go through the whole scene, last words and all, every time.

We couldn't help admiring her dramatic talent. But the ravages of diabetes and her stressful nature led to cholesterol problems, ulcers, a gall bladder removal and an eventual weakening of her heart. Ironically, the malady she invented to cover up her inability to deal with her problems turned into the reality of heart disease, which killed her at the age of sixty-one.

My mother had so much joy and drive, she could have accomplished anything. She was an excellent dancer, and that was something she and my father enjoyed doing all their lives. Perhaps she could have gone on the stage. But in her day, and the tradition in which she was raised, a woman went from grade school into a factory and, hopefully, into marriage. Then she stayed home. Maybe she dreamed dreams, but she certainly never dared try to make them come true. And maybe she passed those dreams on to her daughters, knowing they had a better chance with a new generation.

In spite of my mother's insistence that I was beautiful, I knew I wasn't. I knew what I saw in the mirror. I wasn't a pretty child, and I can confirm it when I look at old snapshots of my brother and me. I wasn't homely, either, but when you have your heart set on Broadway, you want to look special.

I remember one day when my Aunt Josephine, my father's sister, was visiting us and I started to cry about something my aunt considered insignificant. "Will you stop crying!" my aunt shouted at me. "Don't you know that you're ugly enough without crying?"

That ended my tears, all right, and not only then, but for many years to come. I absolutely refused to cry, no matter what happened to me. I was so afraid that Aunt Josephine was right, and that I would never get on the stage because I was ugly.

To make up for what I felt I didn't have, I worked twice as hard. I tapped faster, leaped higher and smiled more often than anyone else in my dance classes, which pleased my teacher but didn't exactly win me friends. I didn't care, though. I wasn't dancing to win friends. I wanted to win scholarships and, eventually, audiences.

In school it was the same story. I was the teacher's favorite, the girl who got A's, who never talked in class except to answer a question, and the one who always volunteered for extra projects. That didn't endear me to my classmates, either. But then I didn't see much of them after school anyway, because I headed straight for Edna McCrae's studio even before the bell rang. I forfeited all my free study periods to get excused early enough to make my dance class an hour away in the Loop.

I didn't start out as a model student. In fact, I got through third grade by cheating. I had missed a lot of school during first and second grade because I was sick with scarlet fever, plus the usual mumps and measles. Probably I should have repeated one of those grades, but I would have died rather than do that to my father. I wanted those A's and Excellents to make him proud of me. So when I realized that I couldn't read as well as the other kids could, I faked it. I had friends then, mostly boys from our neighborhood, who would always oblige when I needed some whispered help during a test.

Then we moved, not far actually, but far enough to put me in another school district. And I'll never forget the first test I took there.

"Psst!" I hissed to the girl sitting at the desk to my right. "What's the answer to the second question?"

I leaned a little her way and was almost deafened by her answer. "*We* don't *cheat* in *this* school, the way they do over in Melrose Park!" she screamed at me, clutching her paper to her underdeveloped bosom. In an instant, the teacher was towering at my desk side. "Yes, Carol, we don't do anything dishonest here, so don't let me catch you doing that ever again."

My face was hot and I could feel my heart pounding all over my body. I was mortified. Somehow, asking for help from other kids hadn't seemed like cheating, but now that I knew it was, it would never happen again. I'd show them. I was going to learn to read better than anybody else in the class. My academic record, when I graduated from high school, was the best in the school's history—all A's for four years.

If I've painted a picture of oppressed childhood, I want to sing out loud and clear that I was as happy as I knew how to be—and never did I feel deprived. My brother and I were disciplined but safe, and we knew the most important priority was family. In the enormous family of uncles, aunts and cousins, the fierce loyalty of my ethnic roots was demonstrated over and over. Whenever a relative was in crisis, or need, everyone flocked to his side and together took care of what was necessary.

Without a doubt my favorite example of Italian tradition was always abundantly evident at the religious holidays. Literally weeks before Christmas or Easter, my mother would begin the elaborate, time-consuming and intricate preparations for delicacies reserved only for those specific days. She could have cooked them in July, but that would take the edge off walking in from the freezing snow on Christmas Eve and catching the unique aroma of calamari being sautéed, lemons and garlic being tossed into a mixed fish salad, artichokes stuffed with raisins and cheese baking in the oven, a scrumptious spaghetti/lobster sauce simmering on one burner and succulent raviolis gently boiling on another. Her caramel tapioca pudding was thickening as she stirred it, and somehow she was able to juggle each complexly timed delight so that everything arrived at the beautifully set table at the peak of its flavor.

All the shapes of frosted, cherry dotted or chocolate layered cookies you could imagine had to bake and be tightly stored in cookie tins. The most difficult and prized of all my mother's feats of culinary glory were her "crustels," a paper-thin dough that was hand rolled until you could read through it. Then with a pastry wheel, one-inch-wide strips were cut into fifteen-inch lengths and carefully pinched and turned and sculpted into a flat lacy rosette. These fragile flowers were then nimbly placed into a deep fryer where they would inflate to a more intricate shape. After turning a golden color, they were carefully drained of excess oil on paper toweling and allowed to cool. Then the pièce de résistance (and I don't know anyone who could resist them anyway): Mom would take her prettiest platter and overlay it with delicate paper doilies, on which she'd arrange the crustels like flowers in a bouquet, then dribble hot honey over them and sprinkle them with powdered sugar. Their airy crispness combined with the hot honey and the fragility of it all had people begging her for the recipe, but never would she give anyone the secrets on which she built her reputation as the best cook in Melrose Park.

My father wanted me to go to college, and although it would be difficult, he would have paid my way through law school—gladly!—even if it meant getting a fourth job. I enjoyed school and wanted a good education, but I knew that if I wanted to work in the theater, I had to start soon. I also needed the competitive edge that comes only with youth. So I tried to compromise.

My grades were high enough to get me a scholarship to Northwestern University. It was the last thing in the world I wanted, but my father was thrilled. Miss McCrae was not.

"You sold out," she said the afternoon I told her about the scholarship.

"No, I didn't!" I said. I felt as if she had struck me across the face with her cane. "I didn't ask for it!"

"Then don't accept it," she said, turning her back, but I could see her face, tight-lipped and fierce, in the mirrored wall behind the ballet barre.

"I have to," I told her. "My father expects me to!"

"You're a fool," she said. "You should be going to New York, and you know that."

From that moment on she allowed me to continue in her classes, but she refused to speak to me. My heart was broken and I felt betrayed, because she had been my professional mother.

⁓ Chapter Two

The story of how I got to Broadway is like an old-fashioned movie musical—call it *Carol Hits New York*. Nevertheless, it's true. I went to Northwestern, but I told my father that I wouldn't study law. He didn't try to change my mind. I think he hoped that an academic environment would do that for me. It didn't. After one year and more A's, I came home for the summer knowing I couldn't go back. I had been in a few school productions, but they were simplistic compared to the work I had already done professionally in those nightclubs and theaters around Chicago. Ironically, as a result of being in a university production, I was named "Freshman of the Year in Drama" and awarded another scholarship—the last thing I wanted. My father was thrilled and I was miserable. The only school where I felt I could learn what I needed to know was Broadway.

Every summer our family went on vacation for a few weeks. That year, as we were trying to decide where to go, I took a deep breath and asked my father if we could go to New York.

I knew I had surprised him. He didn't answer right

away, and then he said, "It's hot in New York. Why should we go there?"

"Because," I said, "I want to get a feeling for it."

"Why?"

"Because all I really want is to investigate what it's like to try out for a show: what goes into an audition, and what I need to compete."

"That's crazy."

"I know. But if I don't find out, *I'll* go crazy."

He never said yes in so many words. He just nodded his head sadly. And I was ecstatic.

So my mother, my father, Joey and I went to New York, and before we even checked into our hotel I bought a copy of *Show Business*, a trade paper that listed auditions. I didn't have an Actors Equity card yet, because you have to be in a show before you can get one, so I had to look for "cattle calls"—auditions that were open to anybody. I found one for a show called *Borscht Capades*.

"I'm not actually going to try out for this one," I told my parents. "I think I'll just ask if I can sit in the theater and watch."

At the theater I told the stage doorman the same thing. "Could I please come in?" I inquired.

"Are you kidding?" he snarled. "Go put on a leotard and get up on that stage—or get lost!"

I went back to our hotel, got my leotard and joined a lot of other young hopefuls on the stage. As a group we were asked to do basic dance steps, and gradually some of us were eliminated. By the end of that day I had a job in a Broadway show.

My mother was enthusiastic.

"It's only the chorus, Mom!" I tried to explain to her, but she was seeing my name up in lights. "You're gonna be great!" she kept saying. My father said nothing.

"Now I can get my Equity card," I said.

"Where are you going to live?" he finally said.

"Here," I told him.

"You can't afford to live in a hotel," he said.

"No, I mean New York. I'm going to live in New York. Dad, I'm in a *Broadway show!*"

"Who are you going to live with?" he insisted. "You can't live alone on what you're going to make—and I'm not going to support you."

I wasn't surprised. In our kind of Italian family, when you leave home, you're on your own.

Fortunately, Miss McCrae, who'd begun speaking to me again when I told her I was going to New York, had given me the name of a former student, Darlene Traynor, who was a Rockette at Radio City Music Hall. Darlene got me a room at her hotel on 79th Street and Riverside Drive for around $28 a week, if I remember correctly. I had a tiny room with a twin-sized bed, a dresser and a small fold-down table. The bathroom was down the hall. So was the telephone, but there was a switchboard operator who took incoming telephone messages. My mother was very unhappy with my accommodations, and later Joey told me that she cried all the way home. But I was in heaven.

While the show was in rehearsal I made $25 a week, which wasn't enough to pay my rent and feed me. (And that salary was only because Phil Harris, one of the stars, found out we were getting paid nothing, and said, "You pay them and take it out of my salary!" See why I love this business?) But I used my old South Side Chicago nightclub act to audition for a job at Leon and Eddie's, and I got it. Even with two jobs I had to live frugally, but I never found that a problem. Money was only something that made other things possible.

In *Borscht Capades*, which was a Catskills kind of revue, I worked with Joel Grey and his father, Mickey Katz, who was the star of the show. Phil Harris and the Barry Sisters were in the cast too. I didn't get beyond the chorus, but another girl and I spoke the opening lines of the show's prologue, and to this day I remember every single word of them. We were dressed in white ten-gallon hats, short skirts with fringe, and white cowboy boots, and as we burst through the curtain we gushed:

Shalom from California
Land of palms and dates.
Home of the misha goyim
You'll see in *Borscht Capades* . . .
The borscht is boiling over—
Hold onto your hats—
Here comes that little *mahzick* . . .
Presenting: Mickey Katz!

The show was a hit, so I knew I was going to be in New York for a while. "I guess I can't fight you," my father said, and I knew that as one of my dreams was coming true, one of his was ending. It was my brother Joey who became the lawyer in the family, and even though I think it wasn't what he really wanted to be, he is a great one.

With the show open, I had to give up working at Leon and Eddie's, but I still needed another job. I began looking into television commercials because I could do them during the day. I also moved in with three other girls, two dogs and three cats, who lived in a fifth-floor walk-up at Sixth Avenue and 54th Street, where the rent was cheap. Food wasn't a problem; I could eat on fifty cents a day if I had to.

I was very happy then. I always had work and I loved what I was doing. I continued with dancing lessons and vocal training, and began going to acting classes as well. I was moving up out of the chorus into small parts and some of the reviewers were beginning to notice me. I wasn't in a hurry, but I could feel myself growing.

New Faces of 1952 was an important break for me. I was working with many young, talented people—Eartha Kitt, Ronny Graham, Robert Clary, Alice Ghostley and Paul Lynde. The show was a hit and it played for a year on Broadway. Then we went on the road for another year.

I was nineteen. And that's when I began to feel lonely.

My mother and father used to be so proud of me when I was growing up because I wasn't interested in boys. I knew they were around, but I thought they were silly, and I thought the girls who fussed over them were even sillier. I didn't have time to be silly. I was too busy studying. And if a boy even suggested a date, I felt offended because he thought I was the kind of girl who indulged in *that* sort of thing—whatever *that* was. What little knowledge of sex I had I had learned from my mother, who was tragically misinformed by her mother. Sex, to those ladies, was something men required and women endured. "It's terrible," my mother told me, "but you have to do it." I realized my mother's world was very different from mine, and there were some things I had to find out for myself.

I was a passionate, imaginative child, and I saw life in terms of black or white, good or evil, allowed or sinful. The pomp and pageantry of Old World, Italian-Catholic ceremonies were etched deep into my soul. When I was six, I saw the movie *The Song of Bernadette*, and wanted to become a nun. In my mind I played the poignant death scene over and over—until someone told me that if I became a nun I wouldn't be allowed to sing and dance. Reluctantly, I let that dream go.

But there was a strong religious influence in my life. I tried to be the virginal maiden my cultural background demanded I be, and when I entered Northwestern University I had yet to be kissed. Naturally, being in show business at such an early age, I saw things—hookers, sugar daddies, lecherous drunks wanting me to go out with them after the last show—but Mom had been there to gloss it over. But I had never before felt that something was missing from my life because I wasn't in love. I'd always thought I was young and there was plenty of time for love later. In retrospect, I was totally inexperienced in even the dating process as a teenager. Social graces and the sophistication to fend off male advances were not in my makeup. I was a naive child in an adult body and entering the fast lane in America's toughest flesh-peddling arena—glittering Broadway.

By the time I was living and working in New York, I still had no social life or "dates." Most of the guys in the chorus line were gay. They were witty, fun friends and loyal confidants. I was hardly a sex object to them! I had had a giant crush on the only straight dancer, but his family helped Max to get over me quickly by pointing out the differences in our religion. So our dream of working as a choreographic team faded with the closing of the show. Then there were the few men who wanted to take me out just for the conquest. I decided early not to waste my time being conquered.

While I was at Northwestern, I had been infatuated with a young man who was a theater major, but I wasn't there long enough to get to know him better. I saw him again when he came to New York, hoping to get a part in a play, and immediately I felt the old attraction. I used to cook for him in the little one-room apartment I had gotten, and one night we made love. It was awful. He kept watching me, asking me how I felt. I finally told him, and he wasn't exactly pleased with my answer. I never saw him again.

Being on the road with *New Faces* was exciting and demanding, but it left me with a lot of time to myself. And I began to realize that like any other girl, I wanted to belong to someone. I wanted someone to care what happened to me, to feel alive when I walked into the room. I wanted to do more than think about the next performance or the next show. I wanted to imagine a lifetime with someone who could make each day, each hour, important.

I was ready for Ken Trevor (or so we'll call him).

I met him through Lee Winters, an actress and friend of his family. Ken was twelve years older than I. He was completely bald, very handsome, and he loved to laugh. Right away I sensed that he was different from the men I usually met. He was interested in people, politics and philosophy, and I felt I could talk to him about anything.

I was still living in New York when we met, but Ken lived in Los Angeles, where he was a stockbroker. It was a long commute for him, but he came to New York often. Then *New Faces* went on the road.

We played San Francisco for about six months, and every weekend when I wasn't onstage I was with Ken. We stayed in a house on Belvedere Island that belonged to a friend of his.

Love may have been a little late getting around to me, but I certainly made up for lost time. And if Ken didn't feel the same way, he was very good at pretending. Being with him, talking to him, cooking for him, making love to him, thinking about him, became my whole life. We never discussed getting married, but I began to put a trousseau together. I didn't have much in the way of furniture, but I began to browse through antique shops looking for the kinds of pieces we might want in our home. Don't forget, even though I was in show business, I came from an old-fashioned family. Love was anything but casual.

It never occurred to me—and probably not to Ken either—to discuss religion. And we should have. Ken was Jewish and I was Catholic, which doesn't mean that we couldn't have built a good life together, but at least we had to begin acknowledging the differences in our religious backgrounds.

One night, shortly before *New Faces* was about to end its San Francisco run and move to St. Louis, Ken said to me, "I suppose you'd want a Catholic wedding, wouldn't you?"

We were in bed. His arms were around me and my head was on his shoulder. I was falling asleep. "Sure," I said drowsily—I didn't know any other kind of wedding. I took his silence to mean that he was as contented as I was.

Another thing we hadn't discussed was the distance between Los Angeles and St. Louis. Since it wasn't as great as the distance between Los Angeles and New York, I was disappointed when Ken said he wouldn't be able to see me as often. He said he had to put more time in at his office. "But I'll call you," he said, before I got on the plane. He never did. I never heard from him again.

I called and never got through to him. He didn't return my calls. Or answer my letters. I was confused and heart-broken. I kept going back over my memories, looking for something I had done wrong that I could try to make right. Nothing—except perhaps the way I answered his question about a Catholic wedding. But if he didn't want a Catholic wedding, why didn't he tell me? We were always so open with each other.

It was months later when I found out what had happened. Lee Winters came to Chicago to play the part of Julie in a summer stock production of *Show Boat*, and I was playing Ellie. We were happy to see each other and catch up on news, but I waited for her to say something. Finally I did.

"Lee, how is Ken?"

"Fine, I guess," she said. "We haven't seen him lately." Then she caught the expression on my face. "Wait a minute," she said. "You don't know, do you?"

"Know what?"

"Oh, honey—Ken's married. I thought you knew."

"No. When?"

"A few months ago. It was very sudden."

When I told her what had happened in San Francisco, she nodded emphatically. "Ken never could have married a Catholic," she said. "It would have killed his mother."

So many things went through my mind. He could have told me. Who knows? maybe I would have converted. I was brought up in the Catholic Church, but in many ways I wasn't happy there.

For a long time I hadn't wanted to think about the spiritual part of my life. I was breaking every important rule in the book and I felt terribly guilty. I had no buffers against the sophistication of life. I wasn't educated in psychology, philosophy, human relations or social norms. But, worst of all, I had no comforting spiritual foundation to fall back on. The simple catechism "You are born to love and serve God" was drilled into my head from childhood, but never did I hear that God loved *me*. How could God, after what I had done? How could anyone?

I felt lonelier than ever before in my life, because I couldn't share my pain with anyone. The people in the summer stock company were strangers. If I told my family, they would have disowned me. Why did Ken have to deny both of us the happiness we might have had, without even a chance to discuss my feelings or search for an alternative?

But there was another possibility I began to consider. Perhaps what I thought was love had been just another conquest for him, one that was far more skillfully accomplished than most. I hadn't even seen this one coming.

Deliberately I began to make sure that I wouldn't risk

that heartbreak again. I grew up believing that people were good and wouldn't hurt me. In spite of the conflict between my father and mother, I never doubted for a moment that they loved me and cared what happened to me. I thought I could trust everyone else the same way I trusted them. Well, I was learning that I couldn't. In fact, it seemed to me that caring for somebody was the easiest way in the world to get hurt. So on my way back to New York after *Showboat* closed, I decided that I wasn't going to let anybody get close enough to hurt me again. Ever.

My father was still hoping that I would find it too hard to stay in New York and would come home. But I was never without work. I did industrial shows, and some TV roles, and usually something on Broadway. When New York slowed down in the summer I did summer stock in Highland Park outside Chicago, where I was the resident ingenue. That was a valuable experience for me because we did a different show each week, going from *Guys and Dolls* to *Oklahoma!* to *Anything Goes* to *Finian's Rainbow*. I became a quick study.

It was obvious to me that although I thought of myself primarily as a dancer, I was doing a lot more singing. While singing comes naturally to Italians, I didn't have any formal training. I decided it was time I did, so when I returned to New York one fall I began taking lessons from a fascinating woman named Sue Seton.

Sue had a fine voice, but she also had a lot of phobias. She was afraid of elevators, afraid to fly, sometimes even afraid to leave her house. When she was younger, she was invited to audition for the Metropolitan Opera Company but at the last minute she became so nervous, she never got there. Nevertheless she had a successful career as a teacher, and it was she who trained Audrey Hepburn for *My Fair Lady*, Katharine Hepburn for *Coco* and Melina Mercouri for *Illya Darling*, the musical version of *Never on Sunday*. I hadn't thought of my voice as operatic, but when you're young and your vocal cords are flexible, it's easy to reach the high notes. Also, I was a born mimic, so all Sue had to do was show me how to sing and I could imitate her. Consequently, although I became a better singer, I never learned enough about technique or proper vocal production.

I thought my big break had come when I tried out for the lead in *Pipe Dream*, a new musical by Rodgers and Hammerstein, and got the part. It was 1955, and everything by Rodgers and Hammerstein was a hit.

But . . .

The summer before, when I was back home and working in Highland Park, I had agreed to spend the next fall at the Lyric Opera as a soloist in the opera season ballets.

"Of course, if I get a part in a Broadway show, then I can't do it," I remember telling the management. And the management smiled and said, "We understand. That's fine with us." But such a clause was never written into my contract.

When push came to shove, it wasn't fine with the management, and they held me to my agreement. That meant I was out of *Pipe Dream* because I couldn't start rehearsals in September and be in Chicago as well.

I was very resentful about going back to Chicago, not only about the loss of *Pipe Dream*, but because each time I went home my father put more pressure on me to leave New York for good. Even my mother began to side with him.

"It's not right," my mother kept saying. "You're a young girl all alone there. People ask me what you're doing. They make jokes and say, 'How does she make a living? As a streetwalker?' "

"You should be getting married," my father said. "What kind of man are you going to meet there?"

"Maybe you should've taken a secretarial course or something like that," my mother said once, and I felt all the hope go out of me. Up until then I'd thought I was doing well. Now, with *Pipe Dream* gone, and another three months of pressure ahead of me, I wasn't so sure. If only I could find a way to assure my parents that I was safe and secure in New York, I knew it would be all right.

A few weeks before I was to leave for Chicago, I was rehearsing for a television show, and I met Gus Allegretti. He was the charming, talented puppeteer on "Captain Kangaroo," which was in preproduction at CBS. The show's concept was unorthodox and innovative compared to the other programs for kids, and rumor had it that the soft-spoken Captain would not survive on television. After all, who'd ever heard of a show for kids with grown people singing children's songs and doing crazy things, and in a gentle, educational manner? No one I knew.

Gus was about eleven years older than I, darkly handsome and very suave. He was Italian and Catholic and it was fun to talk to him because we had a lot in common. But that was as far as it went. In fact, when Gus began to show a more serious interest in me, I was quite rude. If he invited me to dinner, I'd say I was busy and walk away. But he was persistent. One day while I was taking a break with some other members of our cast, Gus came into the rehearsal hall.

"How about a cup of coffee?" he said to me.

"I can't do that," I snapped. "Can't you see that I'm with my friends?"

He wasn't offended. He smiled and said, "Well, suppose I buy them all some coffee?"

"Hey!" I called to the others, "Want some coffee? He's buying!"

Sitting at the counter, laughing and talking about the show and our work, I realized how comfortable it was to be with a man who was in the same business. Who else would understand the way show people are?

I guess that's what really drew me to Gus—he was comfortable. When I told him how my parents felt about my living in New York, he said, "Oh, they're just being silly. They should leave you alone." Naturally, that's what I wanted to hear. We went from coffee to having dinner together, always at the best restaurants. Gus knew them all.

We had been seeing each other for about two weeks when it was time for me to go home. Gus wanted to take me to the airport, but I said no. Another friend was already planning to.

"If we were engaged, *then* would you let me?" He laughed, but he was serious.

I was about to say something funny back. Then I thought, *Wait a minute!* Gus could very well be the answer to all my problems. If I were engaged—especially to a successful, older Italian man—my parents would have no reason to object to my staying in New York. What could possibly happen to me? My mother could tell all her friends that I was respectable and my father could stop worrying about the kind of men I was meeting. Besides, getting engaged didn't mean I had to get married right away. Some people were engaged for—five years!

"Okay," I said. "Sure, we can get engaged."

As Gus started to put his arms around me, I told him that I couldn't get married for at least another two years. I still wanted my crack at stardom.

"That's okay, that's okay," he said. "Anything you want."

We were married four months later. Gus insisted on it. "I know what'll happen," he said, when he came out to Chicago to meet my parents while I was working at the Lyric Opera. "You'll find somebody else, somebody handsome, and you'll get a show and become a big star, and I'll lose you."

I tried to tell Gus that nothing of the sort was going to happen. As a matter of fact, Gus was a handsome man. He was not very tall, but lean and wiry, with dark wavy hair like my father's. Actually he looked very much like my father. They both resembled Bogart.

I had no interest in falling in love—with anybody. It hurt too much. It was enough for me that I liked Gus, and I had every intention of marrying him—eventually, that is. He wrote such tender, witty letters all through the fall, and at least my parents approved of him. So when he insisted that we get married before I returned to New York, I couldn't think of any reason to object.

We were married in January 1956. We had a big Italian wedding in Melrose Park and the church was filled with our relatives and most of the town. It was almost a circus of pushing, curious strangers, but very exciting! And I was assuring my parents that I had everything under control. I was trying to make my life play like the last reel of a movie.

By then I had persuaded myself that I could handle marriage and a career, could have a real home and, someday, children. I wanted children, but not right away. I wanted to give my attention to my career, and I knew I could not do that if I had a child. But Gus, being in the theater, didn't object. He said he could wait to be a father—as long as he didn't have to wait too long. "I'm not a young man," he used to remind me.

"That's one of your greatest charms," I told him. I meant it. Although he wasn't old enough to be my father, being with him felt similar. I trusted him and enjoyed our time together when he was in a good mood. And sometimes he even approved of me when I was sitting on the floor making his puppets (they were cute too!) or cooking his favorite meal. But as in many marriages, things started to change after the wedding—and not for the better.

I had my work, and that was what saved me. Contrary to everyone's expectations, *Pipe Dream* had flopped, so I didn't actually lose ground by being out of it. I was in the chorus of *Plain and Fancy*, which ran a long time, and I was the understudy for the ingenue.

The first year Gus and I were married, two things happened. I got a big role in *Shangri-La*, the musical version of James Hilton's *Lost Horizon*, and I began auditioning for a show that didn't yet have a title, but would eventually be called *West Side Story*. Each one turned out exactly the opposite of what I'd anticipated.

Shangri-La had a lot of what we would call "special effects" today. It began with a plane crash, which was marvelously re-created with sound and lighting that made the audience feel as if the plane were coming down right in front of them. That part of it worked beautifully, but the show had a lot of other problems. All shows do, and the reason we have tryouts is to give everyone a chance to come up with solutions. We weren't worried. We expected success.

Originally Lew Ayres played the lead role. The character's name was Conway. He was a man of deep spirituality, and Lew was perfect for it. If ever I have met a man of God, it's Lew. His philosophy and his faith don't seem to fit into any category, but when you're with him you know that something about him reaches beyond this world.

When World War II started, he was at the height of his movie career. He lost all that success because he refused to carry a gun. He avoided military service on the grounds that he was a conscientious objector, which, in those days, was met with scorn. "Yellow," they called him. Some even said "traitor." Lew never attempted to correct those impressions. Quietly, with no publicity whatever, he did something that took at least as much courage as carrying a gun, and perhaps more. He was a medic and stretcher-bearer during the war, and he would go out into the battlefield, under fire, to bring back the wounded. There are men alive today who remember what he did to save them. So often when we were on the road with tryouts of *Shangri-La* and would stop to grab a quick dinner in a local restaurant, someone—sometimes a man, sometimes a woman—would come over to our table and apologize for interrupting.

"Excuse me, Mr. Ayres, you don't know me, but my son"—and they would tell us the young man's name—"would want me to say hello for him." And Lew always remembered. "Yes!" he might say. "How is his leg now?" Or his arm. Or his eyes.

Lew left the show before we opened. Too many changes were made in the script, along with clumsy attempts to add contemporary references, such as Communists threatening to overrun the Tibetan mountains. Somewhere along the line the basic profound philosophy of the novel had been lost, and Lew wasn't comfortable with what was left. He was replaced by Dennis King.

We were to open in New York in two weeks. The part of Conway included several long soliloquies, which was a lot to learn in a hurry, even for a pro like Dennis. In rehearsal he kept missing cues and forgetting whole lines. Now that's the sort of thing that happens all the time in a show, and it means that the other members of the cast have to think of ways to help the forgetful member recall his lines so that everybody else can then get on to theirs.

Dennis had the first lines in the show. After the plane crashed, he came out of the wreckage looking for his friend, calling, "Mallinson, Mallinson, are you all right?" Well, in the last preview before we opened on Broadway, Dennis came on and shouted, "Conway, Conway—oh, no, that's me! I'm Conway!" Then he went on with: "Mallinson, are you all right?" The audience was somewhat puzzled, but then they laughed, settling back in their seats for what they thought was going to be a comedy.

The usual way to help an actor who forgets his lines is to ask him a question that will lead him into what he was supposed to say in the first place. But during a critical scene in the first act, it wasn't easy to come up with a question. Dennis, as Conway, was supposed to follow Mr. Chang up a mountain and stop at a rope bridge, amazed by the panorama he saw before him.

"My God, I've never seen such a magnificent vista!" he was supposed to say to Martyn Green, who was playing the Tibetan monk, "Tell me, Mr. Chang, what do you call this paradise?" At which point Martyn was to pause and then say, "We call it Shangri-La!" That was the cue for the orchestra to come in with a tremulous crescendo as a huge chorus sang, "Shangri-La, Shangri-La!" from the orchestra pit.

Knowing that Dennis King was having trouble remembering his character's name, Martyn Green kept trying to think up ways of jogging Dennis' memory in case he forgot to ask the name of the magnificent vista. Perhaps he could say something like, "Is this not the most beautiful vista you've ever seen?" Or whatever. Anything to enable Martyn to finally say, "We call it Shangri-La!"

Dennis climbed the mountain, stopped in amazement, and said, "My God, I've never seen such a magnificent vista! Tell me, Mr. Chang, what do you call this paradise?" Perfect!! And Martyn, in his absolute consternation, stammered, "Shinga-Rang! I mean, Shanga-Li. No—Shina-La!" We all broke up. Porters carrying the plane's luggage fell off the mountain. The orchestra did its best, but the tremolo dissolved into windy blasts. The chorus couldn't hit a note

on target, and the audience now decided, for sure, this really
is a farce!

Opening night wasn't much better. There were only six
more performances after that. Fortunately for me, I immediately went into *Ziegfeld Follies*, with Bea Lillie and Billy
DeWolfe.

The other show for which I was auditioning had orig-
inated in the incredibly brilliant mind of Jerome Robbins
ten years earlier. He'd meant it to be a musical version of
Abie's Irish Rose, an old classic about two young lovers from
totally different cultural backgrounds. Leonard Bernstein
was also interested in it, but both men always had something else going on in their professional lives. Over the years
the concept of the show changed, so that when I learned
about it, the young lovers were poor kids—teenagers—one
Hispanic and one white. It was a modern version of *Romeo
and Juliet* with gang fights instead of swordplay. By then
there were other wonderfully creative people involved as well,
Arthur Laurents and a young man named Stephen Sond-
heim. Cheryl Crawford was producing it. With talent like
that, how could the show miss?

In any number of ways—at least, that's what some
pros thought. As Cheryl Crawford said when she backed
out, "It's got an operatic score, four ballets . . . It's about
a bunch of teenagers in blue jeans, and people are reading
enough about them in their daily papers without paying
good money to see a show about them. It's got a cast of
total unknowns, and it ends tragically. Sorry fellas, it will
never work."

Over quite a long period, I auditioned thirteen times
for the role of Maria in what they finally called *West Side
Story*. Even then, thirteen auditions was a lot, and today
Actors Equity would not permit it. But I was working in
other shows and I could be patient. Besides, maybe people
were right—maybe *West Side Story* would never happen.

When I was called back for the thirteenth time, Larry
Kert was there to audition for the role of Tony. We had read
for the roles together before, but this time I had asked if we
could take the scenes home and memorize them. Jerry Rob-

bins had agreed. But instead of asking us to sing a few songs, Jerry told Larry to go backstage and wait there. Then he said "You," pointing to me but calling me "Maria."

"See that scaffolding up there over the stage?" he said, "Look around, find out how to get up there. Then stay there, out of sight."

It was an unusual request, but I would have found a way to get up there even if I'd had to grow wings. Instead, I found a narrow metal ladder leading up to who knows where, and up I went.

Jerry called Larry onstage and told him to find me and take it from there. Up where I was, I began to feel as if I really were Maria, watching Tony search for me, but afraid to call out for fear of alerting my family. And Larry/Tony was genuinely desperate to find me. By the time he saw me and climbed up to where I was, the two of us were almost breathless. We did the balcony scene from there.

When we came down, Jerry said, "You've both got the parts," and then went on to other things. He was like that.

I burst into tears of relief. The producer, Hal Prince, said "No, really—you're Maria!" Then I cried for pure joy.

Chapter Three

We worked long hours rehearsing *West Side*, and when I went home to my apartment, I worked at being a good wife. Regardless of when I came home or how tired I was, I cooked Gus a big Italian dinner. I didn't feel it was unreasonable. I thought that's what a wife ought to do, and I wanted to please him. But it was difficult to get up early in the morning to watch him on "Captain Kangaroo," which he insisted I do.

When we were first married, I used to get up *very* early and make a gourmet breakfast by 5 A.M. like eggs Florentine or a western omelet, with all the trimmings. That was the only way I could share some time with my husband in the morning because he had to be at the studio for rehearsal two hours before the live broadcast at 8 A.M. For a while Gus ate everything as quickly as possible, but when he got to the studio, the stress and pressure of TV got to him and he struggled with nausea as he crouched behind the counters from where his puppets appeared. Finally, he mustered the courage to ask me to stop cooking breakfast. He preferred to reheat last night's coffee and be on his way.

Sometimes I'd get up in time to see him off. Then I'd go back to bed until the alarm told me it was time to watch the show. I'd get up, turn on the TV, settle down in a comfortable chair, and fall asleep after the first few minutes. If Gus was on in the beginning of the show, I got to see him, but after watching Bunny Rabbit go through several verses of "I'm a little teapot, short and stout," I couldn't stay awake, no matter how hard I tried.

Gus used to play tricks on me. He'd always come home and ask me if I had seen the show, and I'd say yes because I didn't want to hurt his feelings. But sometimes he'd say something like "What did you think of my Cinderella routine?"

"Oh, that was terrific!" I'd say. "I really thought that was clever."

"I thought so," he'd say, frowning and shaking his head. "We didn't do Cinderella today. You didn't watch me, did you?" It was hard for me to give the same concentration to watching "Captain Kangaroo" that I was automatically giving to rehearsals of *West Side*. There, we knew we were breaking new ground in the theater—and Jerry Robbins was breaking us!

One of the thrilling aspects of working on Broadway with the greats is to be in a position to watch the various ways genius draws the best out of people. And what's interesting is that whether they love or beat your best out of you doesn't matter; in either case the results are so exhilarating, you'd do it all again in a minute. *West Side Story* is a perfect example. Never have I worked with anyone more tyrannical than Jerome Robbins. When he is working, it is the work that matters and not any of the people involved in it. (This applies to his working style only, because offstage he is warm, thoughtful, generous and a most engaging host.) We learned, very quickly, that he demanded more of us than we ever thought we could give—and that if we didn't meet those expectations, we were out.

We rehearsed and lived by strict rules. We had to literally *become* our roles. We were not allowed to call ourselves or each other by our real names. We had to use the names of the characters we played. I was Maria, never Carol. The actor playing my brother was Bernardo, not Kenny. To keep us from slipping out of character, Jerry would suddenly ask us questions about our parents—not our real parents, but the parents of the characters we were playing, even if those parents weren't mentioned in the show. He trained us to imagine what it would be like to *be* the characters we played, and to discover why we were the way we were. The result of this was as fascinating a study as Golding's *Lord of the Flies*. We humane, civilized actors were becoming the hate-filled, violent street gangs we were portraying. If you think onstage was exciting, it didn't compare to backstage! The Sharks and the Jets lived! Violence and sexual intimidation, fights and injuries, you name it—it was going on and getting worse. So when the audience thought the acting was amazingly realistic—that's only because it was!

These backstage rumbles were carried onstage so that the animosities culminated in bloody noses, wrenched backs, concussions, broken teeth, torn ligaments and fractured bones. One night at the end of the rumble, Bernardo (George Marcey), who was supposed to be killed, was writhing on the stage screaming, "Get me off this fucking stage —my leg is broken!" And it was! in three places. He said he looked up to see his heel facing him and his thigh bone poking through his trousers. As he was dragged offstage and carried out, he actually found the wild humor to sing the opening line of Ellington's "Do Nothin' Till You Hear From Me." Just recently I spoke to George, only to find that the horrible injury he sustained that night terminated what probably would have been a brilliant career.

In rehearsal, Jerry was unmerciful in his pursuit of perfection. The slightest mistake in a dance step, gesture or word met a fate worse than death. Almost daily, Jerry would single someone out for criticism—for the entire day! "You don't know what to do with your hands!" he would shout at that person. "Keep them in your pockets, damn you!"

In one of the most dramatic moments in the show, when Maria is told that her brother was killed by Tony, and then Tony climbs in her window, I was supposed to beat my fists against Tony's (Larry Kert's) chest and then drop to the floor. For the longest time Jerry wasn't convinced that Tony looked properly guilty about what he had done, so he told the two of us to come onto the balcony with him where he could work on the scene without holding up the rest of the cast. He had us go over it for hours, whispering to me to hit Larry harder and make him *feel* the guilt and pain. So I beat Larry's chest with all my might. Finally, Jerry was satisfied, and we broke for dinner.

Later, when I was back in my dressing room, Larry knocked on the door and came in. He wasn't wearing a shirt, and his entire chest was heavily taped. He told me he had gone to the doctor during our dinner break because he had such pains in his chest. The doctor, after taping him, said that I must not hit him on the chest again because I was loosening his lungs from his rib cage. I knew I was strong, but not that strong! I started to sob with guilt for what I had done to my dear comrade-in-arms.

"What'll we do?" Larry said, and I understood what he meant. How would we tell Jerry?

"We have to tell him," I said. "I'll go and talk to him right now."

When I told Jerry that I couldn't hit Larry's chest again, at least not in the near future, Jerry answered immediately: "Hit him in the head—you can't do any damage there." He wasn't joking.

Originally, the parts of Maria and Tony called for singing but no dancing. Dance-ins would substitute for us, even though I kept saying to Jerry at the end of each rehearsal, "Mr. Robbins, I also dance."

"Yes, dear," he would answer, having heard the line a hundred times before.

Eventually, however, Larry and I were allowed to learn the big romantic second-act ballet, and out of that decision came one of the loveliest moments in *West Side*. It was a major departure from the traditional musical for the leads to have no dance-ins. We portrayed our characters in both song and dance.

As the choreography evolved during rehearsals, the dancing became more athletic and demanding. And here, too, Jerry Robbins kept reminding us that we were not people, but the human embodiments of his creative ideas. For instance, in one scene, Maria was supposed to be picked up by one group of boys, carried high over their heads, and then cast through the air into the arms of another group. Now that was difficult enough to do, but we also had Jerry calling out orders to us as if we were a military unit. There were the "Maria Catchers," the "Maria Throwers," and "Maria."

"Now—the Maria Throwers, pick up Maria, that's right—no, no, put her down and do that again . . . You're too slow . . . The Maria Throwers, pick up Maria . . . *Now*, you Maria Catchers, *catch* her!"

We repeated the routine many times before he was satisfied, and then he said "Once more!" And once more I was picked up and pitched into the air. But at that moment Jerry was distracted by something and didn't tell the Catchers to be ready for me. And the Catchers, poor guys, were so terrified of Jerry that they wouldn't dare make a move unless he gave the command.

I went crashing to the floor, landing on my stomach with the wind knocked out of me. All action stopped. I think everyone—except Jerry, who doesn't fear anything—was afraid I was dead. I lifted my head, and I remember seeing my three understudies leaning out from the wings with that terrible look of hopeful anticipation on their faces. That was enough to revive me.

"I'm fine, Jerry!" I said quickly.

"Well, then, do it again!" he said. "And this time, do it with the Maria Catchers"—as if it were my fault they hadn't been there. We did exactly what he asked without a moment's delay.

I ached for a long time after that, but I never let Jerry see it in my performances. That's where the discipline and dedication I learned as a dancer helped me.

This was Jerry's first directorial effort. He had lived all his life in the ballet world where the choreographer and

dancers played "master and slaves." It was his modus op-
erandi to berate and belittle us into anger so we would prove
him wrong by jumping higher or turning faster or hitting
each other harder in a fight sequence. He drove us to fear
or hate him—sometimes both. But the result permitted us
to experience a potential in ourselves that we would otherwise never have known existed. What a gift! I have been in
undying awe of the man's talent ever since.

The opposite style, and in this show the balance to
Jerry's, was Leonard Bernstein's. Here, too, was a genius,
but one who was sensitive to the feelings, needs and anx-
ieties of human beings. Very often after Jerry took us apart,
Lenny would put us back together again. None of us was an
opera singer, and we knew it, yet we were singing opera. If
Lenny saw that we were having difficulty with a passage in
a song, he would say, "Tell me, how does that note feel in
your mouth? If it doesn't feel comfortable, I'll change it." He
would work with each of us on an individual basis for hours,
and we couldn't take our eyes off his face, because so many
emotions were written there. He never lost his temper or his
good manners. He didn't drive us; he led us by believing in
us. He is one of the gentlest, most thoughtful men I have
ever known, and we knocked ourselves out for him because
we loved him. Performers still do.

One day while we were in rehearsals, Lenny asked Larry
and me to go with him to see Mitch Miller, whose TV show,
"Sing Along With Mitch," was very popular. In those days,
if a well-known artist recorded a song from the score of a
musical just before it opened, it could be a tremendous boost
for the show, so we were ready to do our best.

We were shown to a piano in Mr. Miller's office and,
with Lenny accompanying us, Larry and I began to sing our
way through the score. The bearded maestro sat puffing on
a big, black cigar, expressionless and without a word, until
we sang "Somewhere," the triumphant song of hope for the
future. Then he came to life.

"Now that one can work," he said, "if you just put a lot
of hard triplets behind it. Like this."

There's (da-da-da, da-da-da)
a (da-da-da, da-da-da)
place for (da-da-da, da-da-da)
us (da-da-da, da-da-da)

Thank God that Lenny stood up, offered his hand politely and said, "Thank you, Mr. Miller, for giving us so much of your time." Larry and I quickly gathered up the music and followed him out.

Today, any mention of playing in *West Side Story* floods my brain with speed-shutter images of the parade of celebrities that came backstage at the end of a performance. It was awesome. Everyone from Fred Astaire to Elizabeth Taylor, diplomats from afar to the entire companies of the Russian Bolshoi and Moiseyev ballet troupes. And, most probably, we would all still be sharing the tears of the death scene when our visitors arrived.

Up until opening night, no one in the cast had a name or notoriety of any import. We had been privileged actors chosen painstakingly by the geniuses at the helm of this adventuresome journey.

Chita Rivera was like the sister I'd always wanted, and we became very good friends. That was a new experience for me. It's almost impossible for women in the theater to form friendships because we're all competing for the same roles. We're afraid to share our hopes and fears because someone might take advantage of us.

Before I met Chita, I had heard about her—about what a great dancer she was and how tough she could be if anyone crossed her. We were going to be sharing a dressing room for a long time, and if we didn't get along, it might adversely affect our roles in the show. Anita and Maria, the two women we played, had their differences, yet they were extremely close.

We surprised everyone. We got along famously from the instant we met. We laughed at many of the same things and enjoyed playing practical jokes. Because we had both grown up in the unique world of training that only dancers understand, we could appreciate each other's stamina and dedication to her work. We also had the Latin passion so necessary to the blood and guts of our roles. Onstage we were family, and that carried over into our real lives as well.

Ties that are deep aren't forged overnight. With us they evolved during a long period of rehearsals under a director who was more demanding than most. Mastering a role is not a matter of memorizing lines and behavior, it means bringing a whole new person into existence. In *West Side Story*, each of us had to create a character with an emotional range that matched the magnificence of Leonard Bernstein's music, and in the final death scene we had to lay our hearts and souls bare. Anyone who is with you in those moments stands as naked as you are. Perhaps that is why actors so often fall in love, or learn to hate each other, during a show's run. You're like soldiers in battle, and the bonds last a lifetime. Chita and I could tell almost viscerally—by a look or a turn of the head or a gesture—what was going on in each other's mind.

Our favorite memory from *West Side* was a glitch in our climactic second-act duet, "A Boy Like That." In the scene, Anita bitterly berates Maria for loving Tony, the young man who killed Maria's brother Bernardo—who'd been Anita's lover. But Maria interrupts Anita's vicious attack by declaring how deep and tender her love for Tony is. At that poignant moment Maria collapses to her knees and, like a wounded child, places her head in Anita's lap, begging for comfort and forgiveness. Anita succumbs and gently takes hold of Maria's shoulders, lifting her head so that their eyes are just inches apart. Then Anita warns Maria that Bernardo's friend Chino has sworn to avenge the death. "Maria," she says, "Chino has a gun. He's sending the boys out to get Tony!" That was a turning point in the script and the climax of our scene together.

One night, as we came to Anita's final line to Maria, disaster struck. Chita began as usual: "Maria, Chino has a gun . . ." From there on it was as if the needle on an LP had gotten stuck in a ruptured groove. "He sending the boys . . . he's sending the boys . . . he's sending the boys . . ." she kept repeating.

An actor's greatest dread is to stumble over an all too familiar word or line, and know that you must correct it or die—only to find that your tongue has become a rebel without a cause. It torpedoes your every effort to solve the problem, and leaves you drowning in futile repetition. There we were, nose to nose, fully aware of what was happening, yet helpless to do anything about it. My instinct was to slap Chita, as I would any person out of control, but you don't do that to Chita. And by then the tension and agony of our situation had to find some release. It took the form of hysterical laughter, which I hid by burying my face in her lap as if I'd relapsed into sobbing. Chita had no such refuge, and I could feel her body shaking with repressed laughter.

Fortunately, a knock on the door brought in the police to interrogate us about Bernardo's death. At least they were new blood and were unaware of our dilemma—but we couldn't stop laughing! We didn't dare look at each other. We answered our cues with catches in our voices, praying that the audience would interpret them as sounds of sorrow. The short scene ended in a blackout and we were mercifully reprieved.

Reprieve means temporary relief, and that's all it was. That was the night of Chita's surprise wedding shower, and all through the party our spastic scene was reenacted by everyone in the cast, with every imaginable variation.

As we prepared for the next performance in our dressing room the following evening, Chita asked, "You wanna go through the dialogue after our duet, before we do it on stage?"

Without a second's delay I said, "No! I really don't *ever* want to hear it again after last night's marathon!"

"Okay," she sighed, "only don't worry. I promise I won't louse it up. Trust me."

Unfortunately I couldn't trust myself. From the moment the curtain went up that night, all I could think of was facing Chita and hearing the words, "Chino has a gun." Just the thought of it made me chuckle deep inside where I had no control. My only defense was to immerse myself so deeply in the tragedy of that scene that nothing could possibly make me smile, let alone laugh. I imagined my mother had been slaughtered, my father run over by a train, my brother gunned down by the Mafia—and all the while Chita and I were singing our hearts out. By the end of "A Boy Like That" we were exhausted and drenched in tears.

When the music stopped, I buried my head in Chita's lap. I'd have given anything to play the rest of the scene from there—but no, right on cue, Chita grabbed my shoulders, looked straight into my eyes and spoke as if in slow motion. With each syllable she opened her mouth as far as it would reach to ensure perfect enunciation: "Chi . . . no . . . has . . . a . . . gu-u-un!"

I was dumbstruck. With each syllable I could see all the way down her esophagus. That was all I could take. I collapsed in her lap, more hysterical than the night before. She was gone, too. We wrestled with our lines until the police arrived to rescue us.

In the theater's unwritten code of honor, breaking up repeatedly at the climax of a tragedy is tantamount to treason. And in a Jerry Robbins company, there were no pardons. By the following night the wings were full of onlookers tittering with glee at our disgraceful behavior. Chita and I were devastated, but could find no solution to our agony. Though we tried to bolster each other's courage and prayed for a miracle, Chita didn't make it past "Chino" before I fell off her lap *and* my knees, lying convulsed on the floor.

The next night found us pacing nervously in our dressing room, trying to think of alternate staging—or a double lobotomy or a suicide pact. Ruth Mitchell, our stage manager and Jerry's right arm, poked her head in and asked to speak to us for a minute.

"Please, Ruth," I began, "You don't have to reprimand us. No one is more eager to do it right than we are. This is our favorite part of the show—it's killing us to laugh."

"We've tried everything to stop," Chita chimed in. "We're in agony."

Ruth raised her hand and smiled. "No, no, I'm not here about that. You'll work it out, so stop worrying. I'm here to warn you that the second part of the bedroom set has a

problem rolling in the track and may not be fastened together. So be careful on the platform at the door because
it'll be shaky. That's all."

Chita and I were so relieved. Then Ruth looked at her
watch. As stage manager she had to call the half-hour warning from the microphone at her desk. "Have to go now, it's
half-hour," she said as she opened the door to leave. "Oh,
yes, Jerry Robbins will be in the audience tonight. See you
after the show."

Chita and I froze in our shoes, and, without a word,
we hugged each other hard.

That night the crucial scene took on a menacing yet
mesmerizing reality for both of us. It was charged with excitement and danger as Chita held my shoulders and I lifted
my head. With poignant tears, she said, "Chino has a gun.
He's sending the boys out to get Tony," as perfectly as Rex
Harrison extolling "The Rain in Spain." I was so proud of
her. I wanted to kiss her, but I obediently said my next line.
We were home free.

Months after, we found out that Jerry Robbins was not
in the house that night, and that Ruth Mitchell was a brilliant, sensitive captain who knew how to put us back on
course.

My attention was primarily focused on this kind of
larger-than-life crisis, plus the excitement of my being in
such a celebrated Broadway production. It began to intim-
idate Gus. His charming and equally successful role as a
puppeteer on a popular TV show may have seemed pale by
comparison. Sure he was the voice behind Mr. Moose,
Grandfather Clock and the mischievous Bunny Rabbit. He
even cavorted inside a bear costume as the Dancing Bear.
But none of the millions of "Captain Kangaroo" fans knew
what Gus Allegretti looked like, and that was hard to take,
especially when he was married to a brand-new overnight
star of the biggest show in the history of Broadway. At public
functions, which we always attended together, he would
cringe every time someone referred to him as "Mr. Lawrence." I cringed too, because I hurt for him—and because
I knew that later I'd have to deal with his frustration. The

more he withdrew, the more moody, sensitive and jealous he became.

Although our marriage was in trouble, I was busy doing everything I loved, surrounded by dedicated, wonderful people. The show was an enormous success and suddenly some of its unknown players became stars. A few nights after we opened in New York, I arrived at the theater and saw my name up in lights. "Wow!" was all I remember thinking, because I was too startled to be articulate. At the moment when a dream comes true, it can seem quite unreal. It took about three nights for me to believe it was happening.

Gus acknowledged it more quickly than I did. Any success I had was a threat to him. It must have galled him to take me out to dinner and to have the maître d' take one look at me and lead us to the best table, with him trailing behind. Women have been in this type of situation for centuries and have accepted it as normal. For a man, however, especially one who had grown up with old-world traditions, it had to be threatening. Still, I think Gus and I (and possibly many couples with dual careers) could have dealt with a changing culture if only we had been able to talk about it, and face our differences without blaming each other.

Ironically, some of the other girls in the cast used to envy me because I was married. When they came to parties at our apartment and Gus was on his best behavior, they thought I had it all. They weren't around to see what happened when the party was over.

We did manage to have some good times, in spite of Gus's growing conviction that I was going to leave him. Sometimes he and I double-dated with Chita Rivera and her boyfriend when *West Side* got a day off. We'd go to a dude ranch in upstate New York, where the beauty of nature was awesome; and we could relax, take long walks, play tennis, ride horses, go water skiing, bowling and mainly laugh in a world free of the tragic story we lived onstage.

One night at a party in our apartment where the whole cast and lots of other show people were present, Larry Kert and I sang a song from *West Side*. We were standing in front of the piano and Larry's hand was resting on it behind me. After the guests left, Gus exploded at me.

"How do you think that made me look?" he roared.

"What? How did *what* look?" I asked.

"You let him put his arm around you! You let him embrace you in front of everybody!"

"Gus, I don't even remember that. We were just singing."

"You were standing there, and he had his arm around you!"

"He probably had his hand on the piano—"

He was so enraged at me, that the next day I went back over the whole incident, wondering if I could have handled it better. Gus was getting so touchy—maybe I just had to be more understanding.

Maybe I was selfish. Maybe I was giving too much to my career and not enough to Gus. Maybe—we ought to have a child.

I talked to Gus about it.

"You're in the show. How can you have a baby?"

"I'll leave the show. I'm where I want to be. But Gus, we have to do something about us!"

"We'll be fine," he said.

"Can't we have a baby? Really, I'd love to have a baby!"

"Later. We've got time for that. Stay with the show."

I couldn't understand him. He hated what I was—yet he wanted it.

I tried being more considerate of his sensitivities, but it didn't work, and finally I had to admit that our marriage seemed beyond repair.

West Side Story had been running for more than a year when some former Northwestern classmates surprised me by coming to New York by bus to see me in the show. They came to my dressing room after the performance and we all went out for coffee. I must have been about half an hour later than usual getting home, and there was Gus out in front of our apartment building, glaring at me as I got out of the cab and said goodbye to my friends.

As soon as the cab was gone, he said, "Do you have any idea how late you are? I was about to call the police!" I was startled by his anger. I hurried inside and headed up the marble steps to our apartment, but he kept yelling at me, taunting me.

Refusing to say a word, I stumbled up the stairs. But my tears rose from deep inside me—they were the same tears I had cried for my mother.

I decided to leave Gus. I didn't want to shock my family, and I really didn't know how they would take the news, so I flew back to Chicago. For the first time I told them the truth about Gus and me.

My mother's sympathy came instantly. "You can't stay with him," she said, putting her arms around me and patting my head. My father said nothing, but I could guess what he was thinking: a man can do as he pleases in his own home. How could my father criticize my husband?

My brother Joey was right there for me. "I'll go back with you," he said. By then Joey was a prelaw student. "We'll work out a separation," he assured me.

When I called Gus and told him I wasn't coming back to live with him, he seemed shocked. "Why?" he asked. "What did I do? I'm sorry, no, we have to talk about this. When you come back, we'll talk."

Joey must have seen that I was weakening and he took the phone. He told Gus he would come back to New York with me and the three of us could meet for dinner. "Then we can talk, Gus—but I want to be there," Joey said. And Gus agreed.

When we met for dinner a few nights later, Gus listened quietly as Joey informed him that I wasn't going to live with him anymore. "It'll be a legal procedure," Joey explained, and Gus nodded. His attitude was a tremendous relief.

I was grateful that we hadn't had children together. It wouldn't have been fair to them. But having seriously thought about becoming a mother, something had happened to me for the first time. I really wanted a baby.

~ Chapter Four

*M*y two-season contract with *West Side Story* was up, and I left the show with as much sadness as leaving my family home. But the freedom allowed me to accept offers to do many of the marvelous live programs that were part of the "golden years" of television: *The Garry Moore Show*, *The Perry Como Show*, *The U.S. Steel Hour*, *Playhouse 90*, *The Bell Telephone Hour*, *Hallmark Hall of Fame*, *The Ed Sullivan Show*, *The Play of the Week* and a line of specials. I was in a television show almost every week. Because I could alternate between musicals and dramas, I was safe from an exclusivity clause in contracts that kept actors from appearing in a musical show for one week before and two weeks after a booking on another.

Rehearsals, publicity, auditions and lessons blurred the line between reality and fantasy in my life. I was working, singing, dancing and acting with stars I had grown up idolizing: Gene Kelly, Bob Hope, Bing Crosby, Maurice Chevalier, Milton Berle, Danny Kaye, Sid Caesar, Donald O'Connor and Roddy McDowall.

Having grown up on Gene Kelly musicals and mimicked

his every pose, you can imagine how *thrilled* I was to be asked to dance with him at the annual International Red Cross Gala, sponsored by Princess Grace and held at the opera house in Monte Carlo!! Just a year before (during my two-week vacation from *West Side Story*) Gene had me guest on a TV spectacular with him and Donald O'Connor. Having the honor of working with my dance idols was just one of the miracles of this business. Now we'd dance in Europe!

The musical arranger and conductor was a young un-known, to me. Michel Legrand was his name and he arrived in Monte Carlo with his beautiful wife and gorgeous sixteen-month-old son. Michel's father was a world-renowned symphony conductor who had always been on tour during Michel's childhood. Having missed out on that relationship, Michel was determined that *his* son would know his father. So at every rehearsal Michel played the piano with his baby on his lap, or sitting on his shoulders, or crawling under the piano to play with the sustain pedals, or trying to join Gene and me in a waltz or samba. I loved Michel for that patient gesture of love. And I loved Gene for his understand-ing the needs that were being met. It was a leniency I never experienced in him before or since.

Traveling with Gene Kelly in France was like being Cin-derella at the ball every day. He *is* the "American in Paris"; and since the universal success of that Gershwin extrava-ganza, the whole nation had adopted him and crowned him the heir apparent.

Since Gene was fluent in French and I spoke not a word, I clung to his side, picking up easy phrases and taking on a Maurice Chevalier laugh with a roll of the eye and shrug of the shoulder when a conversation got me in over my head. I carried a French/English dictionary in my purse and ate up the unbelievable luck of being at the choicest principality in the world, hobnobbing with princes, dukes, diplomats and Hollywood luminaries—all the while dancing in the arms of Gene Kelly!

We did a cavalcade of music and dance styles from 1900 to the current dance crazes of 1959—but the finale was a tribute to the grandeur of the Viennese waltz. Gene was in

tails and I wore the most opulent giant hoop-skirted gown
of black lace over electric blue satin, with long white gloves
and a rhinestone tiara. We were both sweating from a non-
stop effort, and as the audience rose with wild applause, all
I could think of was a quick shower, and diving into the
expensive gown I had purchased for the dinner-dance at the
hotel across from the theater. Before Gene and I could leave
the stage, the majordomo from the protocol department of
the Palace came to us at a full gallop.

"Oh you were both magnificent—so magnificent that
Her Highness wishes to see you in the royal suite behind
the royal box *at once!*" He was really winded.

"That's nice of her, but Carol and I are dripping wet
and we'll have to change first."

"Absolutely NOT!" he commanded in military tones.
"This is *unprecedented*. Princess Grace has never asked
any performers to her private suite. Have you any idea what
an insult—"

"Oh please, Gene, let's go. It'll only be a few minutes,"
I pleaded.

"Oh, all right," he gave in. And I practically popped out
of my strapless gown with excitement. We were escorted by
her palace guards to the gilded and exquisitely appointed
apartment already crowded with gorgeously resplendent ladies and ribbon-festooned men. At the center of the room
was the picture-perfect Princess in shimmering couturier
splendor, and on either side were Prince Rainier and his
father, Prince Pierre, in full-dress uniforms.

As our majordomo was presenting us like trophies to
the royal family, I tried to recall the correct behavior we were
to observe in their presence from the book I'd read. I knew
you were never to sit if she was standing, ladies were to
curtsy, men bow facing her, only shake hands if she offered
hers, address her as "Your Highness," "Princess Grace," or
"ma'am," never smoke in her presence, never wear a crown
in her presence, never wear a—Oh dear Lord, I hadn't removed my tiara, and I was in the middle of my deepest curtsy
and prayed a trap door could just swallow me up! As I rose
to full height and met her bright blue eyes, I realized every-

one's eyes were focused on the glittering, cute, but totally *offensive* fixture growing out of the top of my head. My cheeks turned red and I froze in the total silence of the room.

Like the last reel in a Disney fairy tale, the handsome young Prince reached for the butler's tray and handed Gene and me two champagne glasses.

"May I make a toast to these talented performers who captivated our hearts tonight. The music was superb, the singing magnificent, the dancing like doves on the wing, and the charm of your personalities beyond description. But best of all, Miss Lawrence, I just love your hat! Let's drink."

The first to laugh and lift his glass was Prince Pierre, who winked at me, and never took his gaze off me as he drank the vintage brew.

Princess Grace graciously laughed too, and with permission now, everyone joined in. The Prince shook my hand, and at last I could take a deep breath.

I had never experienced such gallant chivalry, and I could now understand why Grace Kelly would throw away her celluloid crown for a diamond one, as long as he was wearing one that matched. The cocktail party was over, and although we begged to be excused, Grace requested that we accompany her to the Gala so she could present us to the entire throng. Her request was definitely our command, and so on we traipsed to the grand ballroom of the Hôtel de Paris—hoop skirt, train and tiara!

Our table was near the dance floor, and as the orchestra tuned up, I heard the click of hard leather heels. Looking up from my pheasant, I saw a monocled, mustached, elegant man with a tricolored ribbon draped from his shoulder across his chest—the only thing missing was a sword! He bowed sharply from the waist and said, "Mademoiselle, voulez-vous danser avec moi?" Even I understood his body language, if not every word of his French. Now I'll tell you a secret. My costume was not mine, but property loaned to me from a number I had danced on "The Garry Moore Show." I had given my word it would come back in perfect condition, but it was designed to work alone, not on a crowded dance floor.

I stood, nodded my best "oui," and bending way over, picked up the train and draped it over my left arm to keep it from being trampled. We danced a kind of goose-stepped foxtrot, and he rattled on about the *spectacle* while I graciously accepted his kind words. Maurice Chevalier would have been proud of my guttural imitations. "Ahhh, Aaahhh, Owhhh! Monsieur, Merci," I said, blowing my whole vocabulary on the first exchange. The song over, he escorted me back to my table. But before I could even cut another morsel of food—click . . . bow . . . "Mademoiselle?" It seemed every man wanted to say he had danced with Gene Kelly's "partner," so there I was, doubled over to pick up every inch of lace, draping it over my arm, and off to the waltzes again!

Later, Gene, his wife Jeanne and I were asked to join the Prince and Princess for a nightcap at the tiny club below the gambling casino across the street. It was 5 A.M. and the predawn sky was edged with light as the Prince's orchestra led our tiny entourage down the picturesque street. They played miniature musical instruments made of silver and gold. I half skipped and danced along, thinking the one thing that would make the evening perfect was if I could dance with the Prince. When I mentioned this to Gene, he said, "Don't pin your hopes on it, kid. The rules of decorum are against you. Unless the Princess is dancing, he is not free to ask anyone to dance. Everyone's tired, and you have an early flight from Nice, remember?" He was so practical, and so right. The dimly lit nightclub held a precious few, and the musicians walked to the bandstand and played romantic French songs.

Harold Robbins and his wife joined the Kellys and me at a table, and then the Prince asked if he could sit next to me. My pulse quickened and I turned to see if Her Highness was (Oh please, fairy godmother!) dancing . . . but only two couples were swaying slowly. Then I spied Princess Grace deep in a head-to-head conversation with Yul Brynner. Their suddenly jumping up to dance was not probable. So giving up on my last Cinderella fantasy, I at least had a chance to thank Prince Rainier for coming to my rescue regarding my tiara, and he warmly put me at ease. Then I heard the familiar heel-click . . . and questioning "Mademoiselle?" I knew it . . . another diplomat wanting a waltz. Without turning, I said, "Excuse me, Your Highness," and automatically bending down to sweep my train into my arm, I rose in dance position to face a stunned and bewildered waiter with a towel over his arm. He was shaking his horrified head and hands in front of me. *"Pardon.* NON, NON, non, *Mademoiselle. Je ne peux pas danser. Seulement, quelque chose pour boire? Excusez-moi,"* and he ran from the table. There I stood mortified, like the bride left waiting at the altar . . . and that was when the final twenty-five feet of the Disney movie went into slow motion. Someone gently touched me on my shoulder. I turned . . . to face the Prince on the dance floor saying, "May I have the honor of this waltz, Miss Lawrence?"

My knees didn't buckle, but they surely scared me for a second. "Mais oui, Monsieur," I grinned, making a curtsy. He took me into his arms, and we floated across the floor . . .

Those prince types have to learn how to do everything well, and for Prince Rainier, dancing was no exception. But for me his forte will always be a quiet, compassionate talent for rescuing damsels in distress. Like the Princess, I'll bet, he could have had a career in movies too.

Not all of the stars I met were awash with the glamor and glitter of Monaco. Some were equally grand in a very different way. I often remember the day I was recording an album which Fred Astaire had financially backed on his newly formed label. Everyone knew that he spared no expense to get the perfection for which he was famous. He would have arrangements for two orchestras instead of one for that incredible richness of sound. I didn't know he had slipped in to the control booth. So while I was listening to the replays and commenting with horror on some of my mistakes, I was stunned to hear his voice quietly from the background say, "Oh Carol, I thought that was just beautiful, but please don't feel you have to take my opinion." My experience of him was that he was unassuming, shy and humble, gentle and encouraging to everyone else, and he never knew why everyone made such a fuss over him.

Rehearsal time for television variety shows was always too short, because it was expensive. So the pace of creating dance routines was extremely pressured. Yet I thrived on doing innovative lifts and steps, even though it meant more hours of practice to make them work—and on live TV there were no retakes. If you fell, you fell. If you broke a toe, you kept dancing—and you smiled more. In many ways it reminded me of the dedication and discipline I had learned in Jerry Robbins' rehearsals.

To the casual observer I must have seemed driven by ambition and stubbornness, but in my own mind I equated my personal worth with how well I performed in the dance or the play or the show. It was the only way I could feel that I was earning my right to be here, and to feel loved. The performer in me was the only part I liked or felt proud of. The rest of me made stupid mistakes and ended up selling out to stay alive. Welcome to show business!

~ Chapter Five

In 1960 Broadway musicals were still being produced with class, prestige and great expectations. One of them was *Saratoga*, adapted from Edna Ferber's novel *Saratoga Trunk* and the movie based on it. The leading female character, Clio Dulaine, was an actress's dream come true, and a part eagerly sought after. The music and lyrics were composed by Harold Arlen and Johnny Mercer, the costumes and sets designed by Sir Cecil Beaton. It was written and directed by Morton Da Costa (nicknamed 'Teek'), and Howard Keel had already been cast as the leading man. *Saratoga* was the closest thing to a surefire hit that anyone could foresee.

After a few nerve-racking auditions, the part of Clio was mine, and the magical machinery of preproduction, public relations, and rehearsals was put into gear. The cast was magnificent, about forty of us in the company, which is an enormous number compared to today's pared-down but more costly productions.

The sets were breathtaking. They included two reversible treadmills at the footlights, and a huge revolving turntable center stage. In one number the entire New Orleans French Quarter revolved before the audience as we walked in place at center stage, tricking the eye into believing we were actually walking through those famous streets.

Sir Cecil Beaton was a theatrical genius who kept creating new sets and costumes right up to the last allowable second. His eye for detail was impeccable. For example, to convey authenticity, all the draperies and costumes were made of heavy upholstery fabrics. He even insisted that I wear a real whalebone corset and lace pantaloons. I had seventeen costume changes that included color-coordinated stockings, handmade shoes, gloves, a hat, a muff, a parasol, a fan, a purse, even hairpieces. Every costume weighed a ton, and by the time we opened in New York I had little need for a corset. I weighed less than I ever had as an adult and my waist measured twenty-one inches.

I was in all but two scenes, so there was never enough time for me to leave the wings. All my changes were made there, where I was frantically assisted by two dressers, a hairdresser and often a stagehand, solicited to hold a flashlight or clear a path for me to run to my next entrance. Fortunately, *Saratoga* was my fourth show at the Winter Garden Theatre, and all the stagehands were old friends. They had made me an honorary member of their union when I was in *West Side Story* because I used to help an elderly stagehand named Mike return a heavy piece of scenery to its place. They never forgot that small gesture and they found so many ways to be helpful. I loved every gruff, softhearted one of them.

In spite of all the talent associated with it, *Saratoga* ran into trouble. It began when Edna Ferber decided she didn't want anything to do with the play because she didn't like the script. Then the show ran too long, and in order to shorten it we all were told to speak faster. There were tremendous amounts of dialogue and too many plot lines for a musical, so between that and the speed of our delivery the audience was confused, and so were we.

Morton Da Costa had directed several hits on Broadway—*No Time for Sergeants*, *Plain and Fancy* and

Auntie Mame—but he felt he had not received the writing credits he deserved for editing and doctoring all the scripts he had turned into hits. This time he was going to fulfill his dreams of being a writer/director extraordinaire. Although his tastes and talents were exceptional, on this production he was not only author and director but coproducer and publicist as well. Hats off to courage and optimism! In reality, however, no one can wear that many hats in the complex, demanding world of musical theater. The strain eventually overwhelmed him, and shortly before we were to open on Broadway, Morton Da Costa was hospitalized. Unfortunately, Harold Arlen also was hospitalized, and our company was rudderless. A million changes had to be made fast, if we were to improve on the Philadelphia critics' reviews.

To give you some idea of our difficulties, let me describe the background to the first scene in the show:

The curtain opens on a tableau of five characters dressed in 1890s period costumes. They are examining old clothes from a trunk. The setting is a Paris garret where the characters have been exiled. They are: Clio Dulaine, eighteen; her gray-haired mulatto mother who had been the mistress of a wealthy French aristocrat in New Orleans; the mother's sister (a former madam of a whorehouse in the French Quarter); a black nanny who had raised Clio from infancy; and a dwarf hired to protect the women.

Nineteen years earlier, in New Orleans, Clio's mother had been elegantly kept in her own house, but she had been careless and had gotten pregnant. She demanded that Monsieur Dulaine divorce his wife and marry her at once, and he refused. In her fury, the distraught woman pulled out a revolver and threatened to kill herself, but in the inevitable struggle that ensued, the gun went off and killed her lover, Clio's father. His death drove Clio's mother mad and she had to be cared for by her sister. To hush up the scandal, the Dulaine family sent the young woman, her sister, her maid and her bodyguard to live in Paris, where the child was born. They were paid a meager monthly allowance and were warned never to return to New Orleans.

Now, if you had read Edna Ferber's novel, you would have known all these details. But if you hadn't—poor you! The curtain went up on five characters you knew nothing about, and without a word of explanation they began to sing of their woes and frustrations:

Mama: *[who, in her fantasy world, believes she gave birth to a son instead of a daugher]* My son will someday claim his rights . . . To his rich heritage as a Dulaine/Reach to heights. . . .

Nanny: *[combing Mama's long hair]* I's here to comb your hair and smooth your brow/You're gonna find some happiness now. . . .

Aunt: *[reading the* New Orleans Gazette*]* I wonder who's the woman most beautiful in the Quarter now/Who is the Belle of New Orleans as I was once so long ago . . .

Bodyguard: I gonna take care of you now/No one can harm you nohow . . .

Clio: *[while sewing on a large petit point screen]* I'll open her house again and make my own way/I'll make them pay and then one day, I'll be respectable . . .

In opera, quintets are quite common, but not in musical comedy, and especially not in Act I, Scene 1. Nevertheless, we were using the operatic device of each character singing a short segment and establishing a melodic line, followed by all five characters singing their parts together in a quintet. One night, in the middle of our quintet, a large man sitting directly in front of me rose from his seat, grabbed his companion's hand and pulled her toward the aisle. "Come on, Maude, we're leaving: this is a piece of shit!" he proclaimed loudly.

I had just pulled my needle to the full length of its thread, directly in front of my eyes, and I froze as the man stepped over all the people in his row. In my shock, I couldn't remember my own name, let alone the lyrics and counter-point.

The out-of-town reviews were mixed. "Verbose," the critics said, but they loved the sets and costumes, and they praised the cast. With Morton and Harold in the hospital, it was extremely difficult to make changes, but something had to be done. Johnny Mercer continued to write new songs on his own, since his collaborator was incapacitated.

During the final weeks in Philly, Morton would send us notes from his hospital bed. They were typed on pieces of paper cut into strips resembling the messages in fortune cookies. The trouble was that Morton would send one of us a change in direction, such as: "When you exit in Act I, Scene 2, move to your right instead of your left." Or: "In Act II, Scene 5, when you go to the window, approach it from your right and don't turn around." Fine—except that the other actors weren't aware of these changes and we kept tripping over each other. It was chaos, but the cast was unbelievably supportive and cooperative.

When fear pervades every corner of the creative process of a Broadway show, it threatens even the bedrock of sea-soned actors. Such a catastrophe manifested itself one night when Jane Darwell (everyone's favorite mother to Henry Fonda in *The Grapes of Wrath*), joined me onstage for the critical confrontation scene that is the turning point for the whole play. She was the Elsa Maxwell of the plot and was blackmailing me (Clio Dulaine), because she had found out that I was not a French countess but indeed an illegitimate mulatto child. Either I paid up now and for the rest of my life, or she would publicly spill the beans at the costume ball where my engagement to a millionaire was about to be an-nounced.

Like every other scene, this one had also been through line changes, and Miss Darwell had all the menacing tirades aimed at shooting me down—only they *had* to be delivered like bursts from a machine gun, lethal and unrelenting.

We had celebrated her eightieth birthday during re-hearsals and she was fragile. The director had wisely placed her in an imposing chair so she could rule the scene from overpowering strength, while I was to pace and acquiesce with monosyllabic answers of "Oh?" "Well?" "No!" and "So?" while I battled the consequences of my fate. The most essential ingredient was the taut tension of a tightrope act—and she held the rope.

As the light came up, her first line came out strong and true. "So, you call yourself a countess?"

"Yes," I lied straight into her face . . . and then came a look in her eyes that is the ultimate dread of every actor, as if the light inside her brain had short-circuited. Her eyes were not only glazed but *crazed*—and frantically searching for help.

I immediately identified with her dilemma because I had tasted that terror myself, and watched others claw their way back from it countless times. If we had been shooting this scene for a film, where Miss Darwell was a brilliant veteran of so many cherished classics, the director would have said, "Cut." We would have had a cup of tea, glanced at the script again, and gone for another "take," as purely normal procedure. However, this was not a movie set, this was live theater with a live audience ten feet away. Ordinarily, the unexpected is part of the excitement and added drama of theater, both for the actor and the audience. However, in this situation, which involved such a critical personal and professional moment for one of filmdom's greats, we felt like voyeurs caught up in a "passage rite."

I had grown to love Miss Darwell not only as a masterful actress but as a generous, nurturing Mother Courage to us fledglings. Somehow, I couldn't bear her humiliation in front of her fans who were not privy to the unforeseen trials through which she was valiantly struggling. I wanted to throw my arms around her and spare her from any cruel judgment. Instead, I quickly resorted to the old stage trick of paraphrasing lines as questions to jog her memory. With that intention I said, "Yes, I am a countess. What of it?"

Long pause, her eyes blank. "Well?" she mustered.

"I suppose you're going to accuse me of fabricating my title!"

"Yes," she agreed quickly.

"And that I'm really the illegitimate child of a French aristocrat and a black mistress."

"Yes, yes!" Her eyes were aglow now.

"That would allow you to stop my engagement to Jeremy Vander Horn by revealing the truth at the ball tonight."

"Yes, it *would*," she ad-libbed, nodding approval.

"Well, I've heard enough, Madame. If you'll excuse me, I must evaluate your statements and make up my own mind. Good evening." And I strode off. The lights flicked to a "blackout" and Miss Darwell was retrieved from her throne.

Because I had to make rapid costume changes in the wings, an actor coming offstage from a new direction could keep me from getting back onstage in time—and seconds counted. In a few instances I asked some of the other actors if they could stay to one side as they exited, leaving me enough space to race back onstage without knocking anyone down. Everyone was being cooperative with each other's requests. The whole cast was making every effort to save a show that was in shambles.

So I was surprised when the assistant director, Fred, crabbily told me to stop trying to take over the direction of the play by telling everyone where to exit and enter on stage. By then we had closed in Philadelphia and were doing previews in New York.

"I don't understand, Fred," I said. "I'm not trying to take over anything. I just need some space to move." I felt betrayed. I had been in show business a long time by then, and no one had ever called me uncooperative. Driven, maybe. Hard-working and dedicated, yes. If anything, I was perhaps overly eager to please. Even when I wasn't happy with the direction I was given—and that wasn't often—I tried to make the best of it. It made no sense not to.

That night was to be our final preview, and we had been told that Morton Da Costa would be in the audience. His presence was intended to boost our spirits, but mine were too far down to be helped. There were tears in my eyes when I put on my makeup, but I held them back. I played the show with a lump in my throat. I made it as far as the curtain calls, and then I cried. My strength, control and professionalism were depleted.

I had left myself vulnerable to attack and criticism, and moments later Teek came charging into my dressing room. "No one has ever done that to me in all my years in the theater!" he bellowed. "Who do you think you are? Crying in the curtain calls!" I was still crying, but that only seemed to make him angrier.

"You've been coming between me and the cast," he went on, "and that's going to end right now! I'm the director of this show, and don't you forget it!"

I sat at my dressing room table as he screamed, bending over me, inches from my face, shaking his finger at me as if I were a naughty child. I was so hurt I couldn't utter a word in my defense. I couldn't even believe what was happening.

My mother was in the room with us. She had been with me through all the tryouts. She tried to calm Teek down, but he went on shouting until he wore himself out. When he left, I was too exhausted to remove my makeup. All I wanted to do was go home, stand under a hot shower and wash myself clean.

As soon as my mother and I got to my apartment, I headed for the bathroom. But the moment I stepped under the hot water, I fainted. My mother found me and called the doctor.

When I came to, my doctor said, "You're close to a nervous breakdown. You've got to take some time off."

"I can't," I said. I wasn't trying to be a martyr. Staying in the show was a matter of survival. I could just hear Morton Da Costa claiming that the reason *Saratoga* wasn't a hit was because Miss Lawrence wasn't strong enough to make it to opening night. If that happened, I might never get another show. So I went on opening night, and every other night for the duration of the run.

The New York reviews were like those in Philly—mixed. Nevertheless the show played for six months, which wasn't bad. I was deeply humiliated knowing I had Morton Da

Costa's scorn, but many truths were hammered into my bleeding psyche because of it.

Teek was in the hospital and hearing everything third-hand through the impressions of an overextended, over-taxed assistant forced to fulfill many roles. This meant that my side of the story had not been considered. I have since decided that direct and honest communication is the one imperative for any relationship to survive and thrive, not only for directors and actors but for bosses and employees, married couples and parents and children.

Do I think I could have saved the day and gotten the crossed wires untangled in time for our opening night? You bet your bananas I don't. But with each new production, rehearsal period and hectic dress-technical-run-through, I make sure my very best efforts reach the person nearest the control tower.

Without the approval and pride that comes with good reviews, the cast and crew of *Saratoga* presented their stiff-upper-lip grins at the theater "sign-in board" each night. Everyone knew it was doomed. That, on top of eight demanding performances a week, wore all of us down, physically and emotionally.

When the show closed, we looked haggard and really needed a rest, but we also knew that a performer is of value only on the hoof. I had heard that *West Side Story* was coming back to New York after a year on national tour—and that the current Maria was ill. The show's producers were trying something new, a limited engagement at the Winter Garden with as many of the original cast members as possible. Larry Kert was already cast as Tony, and when I was asked to join the company, I didn't hesitate. It would be like going home—for six weeks.

The public welcomed *West Side* like a prodigal son, and it became the hottest ticket in town. Every night we played to standing room only, and the producers immediately booked us into another theater the minute our lease on the Winter Garden was up. We played every empty house we could find: first, the Winter Garden, then the Broadway, the Alvin and the Hellinger.

It was during this second time around as Maria in 1960
that I auditioned for a part in *The Dybbuk* directed by Sidney Lumet for "The Play of the Week." Like several other of
these adaptations, including *Death of a Salesman* and *The
Iceman Cometh, The Dybbuk* attracted wonderful actors
who were willing to work ten to twelve hours a day at the
minimum scale of pay because the productions were so
good. When I got the part of Leah, a young woman possessed
by the spirit of her dead lover, I knew it was more than a
good role. I would be working with some of the finest talent
in the theater—Michael Tolan, Ludwig Donath, Vincent
Gardenia, Gene Saks, Theodore Bikel and Theo Goetz—and
I was hungry to learn as much as I could from them.

Unfortunately, I had more enthusiasm than energy. I
thought I was just coming down with the flu when I began
feeling exhausted all the time. I went to my doctor, expecting
him to give me some antibiotics or a shot of vitamin B-12
to keep me going in my two shows, but he informed me that
I had mononucleosis. "You've got to go to bed for at least
six weeks," he told me. "Starting *now*."

"How can I?" I said.

"You don't have any choice, Carol," he told me. "If you
don't lie down, you'll fall down."

"Can't you give me something? To keep me going for
just a little while longer? Then I promise I'll go to bed!"

Dr. Bachrach was an old friend and he knew me well.
He shook his head emphatically.

The next morning I went to the studio early and spoke
to Sidney alone. I felt it was only fair to tell him about my
illness, but I insisted that I was able to do the filming. "All
I need is a small room as close to the set as possible, with
a cot in it. That way, when you're not shooting me I can lie
down and rest up for the next scene. I promise, Sidney. I'll
get through it all right. Just tell everybody I have the flu
and not to kiss me, okay?" I held my breath, waiting for his
answer.

To a lot of people, my reasoning might have seemed
insane, but Sidney was an actor before he was a director,
and he knew that my insanity was a type known only to

hams. He agreed to let me go on. The role of Leah was very demanding physically, and in the scene where her lover's spirit was exorcised she had to be handled roughly by some of the other actors. Yet Sidney was sensitive to my need to play Leah as vigorously as we had rehearsed it. He arranged for the room and the cot, and as far as everyone else was concerned I was just nursing a cold. But as soon as the film was wrapped, I went straight home to bed—for six weeks.

Mononucleosis debilitated me so that I really couldn't do anything for myself. I had a constant high temperature that made me feel like an invalid. As always, my mother came to my rescue. She flew out to be with me, and looked after me day and night, just as she had when I was a little girl.

When I finally recovered, I was offered another role in *The Play of the Week*, again directed by Sidney Lumet. It was a two-hour television adaptation of the Japanese play *Rashomon*. I was cast as the wife, the only woman in the play. James Mitchell played my husband, Ricardo Montalban was the bandit, and Oscar Homolka was the woodsman—a marvelous cast! I couldn't wait to begin.

It turned out to be another learning experience for me, but not only about the theater.

Chapter Six

At that time there were no men in my life. As far as the public was concerned, everything I did was glamorous. I worked with some of the most attractive men in the world, and when I attended an important theatrical event I was usually escorted by one of them. That was all for show and we knew it. When you're running at top speed to get the best roles and perform them as well as you possibly can, when you're juggling auditions, interviews, photo sessions, creating new dance numbers, learning new songs and doing benefits, you have very little time for sleep, let alone romance. Unless I was working with him, I usually didn't have the time or the opportunity to meet an eligible bachelor, especially one who lived in the more stable nine-to-five world. There wasn't even time for friendships.

As hectic as my pace was, and as happy as I was with my career, I was hungry for a deep, meaningful relationship. But I didn't want the kind of affair that often happens between actors. Many of the men I worked with were married, but extramarital involvements are commonplace in the theater, especially when companies are on the road for a long time, far from spouses.

When a woman is cast as a romantic lead, she has to portray passion as realistically as possible, in spite of the fact that she may be married to someone other than her leading man. As she gets into her part, it's not unusual for her to develop a crush on her leading man, but nobody takes it seriously because it will probably end with the run of the show. At the same time, her leading man's marriage may be going through a gray period that comes along when the initial glow begins to fade. Now, what could be more stimulating than a brand-new, beautiful, witty, sexy comrade-in-the-arts being paid to make overtures to him? You can't help but wonder how *anyone* in show business stays married. Nevertheless, I wanted the real thing or nothing, and I could be quite abrupt when someone misinterpreted my hugging, kissing, Italian camaraderie as an invitation to play around.

So—on the very first day of rehearsal for *Rashomon*, when Ricardo Montalban began showering me with attention in a manner more gallant than anything outside the court of Queen Elizabeth (or Monaco!), I was suspicious. In his charming accent, he asked if he might take my coat, he complimented me on my clothes and my hair, and then he asked, "May I get you a chair?"

"Thank you."

"May I get you something? Coffee? A Danish, perhaps?"

"No, thank you."

"Some tea, perhaps? With lemon? Some honey?"

"No, thank you."

"Please—is there anything I can do to make you comfortable?"

Well, at first I thought he was just coming on strong and if I ignored him, he would give up. But no, it was the same thing every day, and it continued until we broke and went home. Finally, I realized that his beautiful, courtly manners were neither a facade nor a romantic overture. They were the normal expressions of a gentle, talented, generous man who really cares about people. Through the years that I have known him, I've watched him treat everyone with the respect and compassion with which he treated me.

Ricardo's discipline and dedication to his art were an inspiration to me as an actor. *Rashomon* is set in ancient Japan, and Ricardo played a rather primitive bandit who captured a Samurai warrior and his wife while they were traveling in a forest. When the play opens, the husband has been killed and the wife raped and left alone, but in what order and how these events occurred depend on who is telling the story—the bandit, the wife, the spirit of the dead husband, or the woodsman who observed it all. In each dramatic and violent version, the characters become totally different kinds of heroes and villains, leaving the audience to figure out what really happened and who is telling the truth.

Until I met Ricardo I'd thought men were either gentle or courageous. But he was both. After rehearsing the bandit's long and strenuous fight sequences over and over, he was obviously in a lot of pain, but never once did he complain nor allow the shooting to slow down because of him. His consideration and sympathy went to everyone—except himself.

It was most evident in an incident I'll never forget. In one scene during the bandit's version of the story, Sidney Lumet had devised an overhead shot of Ricardo and me as we lay on the ground facing each other, nose to nose. According to the bandit, the woman has seduced him into making love to her while her husband, tied to a tree, is forced to watch. In the intimate moments that follow, the woman begins to beguile the bandit into killing her cowardly husband so they can be free of him. Like a serpent, she whispers and hisses her evil plan while the camera lens makes a 350-degree revolution a few inches above the two heads that fill the frame. The photographic technique gave the illusion of being inside the minds of the two characters.

We rehearsed the scene many times so that we could end the speech and the camera's revolution at the same moment. On one take, when the camera was about three-quarters of the way around, the giant lens came crashing down and hit Ricardo on his right temple, just missing his eye. His blood was all over both of us and I was terrified. Everyone rushed over to us, not knowing exactly what had happened or who had been hurt or how badly. Ricardo remained absolutely calm. He blamed no one and assured us he would be all right as soon as the bleeding was stopped. He insisted that we go on with the filming. His only request, after a nurse stopped the bleeding and bandaged the wound, was to reverse positions with me so that his bandaged temple would face the floor instead of the camera. He was the hero of the day—and every other day, as far as I was concerned.

Ricardo and his wife Georgiana have been like family to me over the years, and we've sat down to many a dinner together. I've worked with Ricardo often since *Rashomon*, most recently in 1987 when Pope John Paul visited Los Angeles. Ricardo emceed the festivities honoring the Pope, and I was one of the performers in the program. I watched him trying to spread his arms around Georgiana and their grown children as the Pope gave them his blessing, and I saw tears in his eyes.

By the time *Rashomon* was in the can, Sidney Lumet was already casting the film adaptation of Arthur Miller's play *A View From the Bridge*, which had been a Broadway hit a few seasons earlier. It's a passionate story about a longshoreman named Eddie, a man of Italian descent, who falls in love with his wife's young niece, Katherine. But Katherine loves a young immigrant named Rudolpho who is hiding in Eddie's attic because he is in this country illegally. In his jealousy, Eddie turns Rudolpho in to the police. His guilt drives him to commit suicide and he dies in Katherine's arms. Anthony Quinn had been cast as Eddie, Maureen Stapleton as his wife Bea, and I as Katherine.

What an incredible opportunity this was for me! I didn't even have to audition for the part. Sidney requested me for it, showed Arthur Miller a kinescope of *The Dybbuk*, and Arthur gave his approval. In another way the role was an answer to a prayer, because I had just lost the part of Maria in the movie adaptation of *West Side Story*, and I was devastated. Chita Rivera and Larry Kert were also passed over, and for the same reason: none of us had an international reputation in film. We were Broadway names, well known on the East Coast and throughout much of the United States. But in Europe, where so many movies were financed and distributed, we were unknown.

Because I'd wanted to make the transition to film, that rejection was hard to take, but I understood why it had happened. Natalie Wood was a beautiful woman and a fine actress, but she couldn't sing or dance. She could, however, draw people to the theater to see the picture because they recognized her name. She could earn the backers' money back for them—with interest.

Many Broadway stars had had similar disappointments, so I knew I was in good company. Mary Martin, as great as she is, didn't make it in Hollywood, even though almost every show she was in became a movie. Mary Martin had originally played the role of Maria Von Trapp in *The Sound of Music* on Broadway, but Julie Andrews played the role in the movie adaptation because by then Julie Andrews was world-renowned for playing Mary Poppins in a blockbuster picture. But, only a few years earlier, Julie, who had played Eliza Doolittle opposite Rex Harrison's Henry Higgins in *My Fair Lady* on Broadway, lost the movie role to Audrey Hepburn.

So, yes, I needed a movie. And one that could attract a lot of attention. Then, maybe the next time I was in a hit musical I could do the film adaptation as well.

A View From the Bridge was ahead of its time, and some of its scenes were considered controversial. In one of them, Eddie accuses the young Rudolpho of being homosexual, and to prove his point he kisses Rudolpho on the lips. Now, in 1960, in America, that was dynamite, and most conservative American movie studios were afraid to touch it. A French producer loved the script and had no such qualms, but in order to qualify for French government subsidies, he had to shoot most of the movie in France—and in French. That meant we had to do each scene in English and then again in French, which I didn't speak.

I wasn't about to let a little thing like another language stand in my way, especially when there was such a school as Berlitz. With only three weeks to go before we started shooting the outdoor scenes in Brooklyn—literally in sight of the Brooklyn Bridge—I enrolled at the Berlitz School of Languages for private lessons four hours a day, six days a week.

My teacher was Monsieur Swartz, the head of the French Department, a brilliant teacher with inexhaustible patience. He came from Marseilles. At the end of three weeks I had a small but practical vocabulary, a functional ability to construct simple, grammatically correct sentences—and Monsieur Swartz's accent from the south of France. When I landed in Paris the natives thought I was neither American nor Parisian. To them I was the equivalent of Scarlett O'Hara trying to say, "Ah do declay-ah" in French. The mimic in me had simply imitated Monsieur Swartz, and that's what came out.

I was hoping *A View From the Bridge* would lead to more movie roles. I enjoyed the challenge of a part that didn't require me to sing and dance, and eventually I wanted to do more dramatic roles. When we finished shooting, the movie wasn't scheduled to open for several months. In the meantime I finished my commitments to *The Garry Moore Show*; then I turned my attention back to my first love, Broadway.

In show business, you often hear about a new opportunity from a friend in the business long before you hear it from your agent, and that was the case with *Subways Are for Sleeping*. My friend Roddy McDowall had auditioned for a part in the play, but he wasn't right for it. However, when he heard someone say they were looking for a "Carol Lawrence type" to play the lead, he called me immediately. "Have your agent call and see why you can't do it!" he said.

Roddy has been a remarkable actor from the time he was a child, and I have always admired him. He's not only an actor, but a sensitive, creative photographer with several published collections of his work. He's the kind of friend everyone ought to have, but seldom finds, and even in the backbiting world of show business I've never met anyone who could say a word against him. Back in 1959 he and I had been cast as the romantic leads in a *U.S. Steel Hour* drama, just before my separation from Gus, and he provided the shoulder I needed to cry on.

He was extremely intelligent, had a delightful sense of humor, and I felt he cared about me as a human being. I could talk to Roddy, and that's something I couldn't do with most other men. In fact, Roddy's tenderness and under-standing contributed greatly to my healing.

I did take his advice about *Subways*, and after my agent made a few calls I was offered the lead. *But*—no one would let me see the book. It was: "If *you* do it, we'll build it into a singing/dancing tour de force. We'll have treadmills whirring and trap doors opening and trumpets blaring and Michael Kidd ballets . . . and . . . and . . ."

I was so excited. I should have been alerted when I heard the word *treadmill*—one of those had nearly eaten a chorus girl's foot in *Saratoga*. But there was Jule Styne singing and playing the piano in his inimitable way that could per-suade the hardest-hearted "angels" to put up hundreds of thousands of dollars. Who was I to question anything about a show that had so much talent going for it? So I said yes, and waited for rehearsals to be scheduled for the fall.

Meanwhile, Roddy had been out of town with a musical epic called *Camelot*, and as soon as it opened on Broadway I went to see it. Later, when I went backstage to congratulate Roddy on his marvelous portrayal of Mordred, I met Robert Goulet. He was playing Lancelot, and everyone was making a big fuss over him because he was so handsome and had such a beautiful voice. His assets were obvious, but he couldn't act—at least, that's what I thought after seeing his performance. In fact, I couldn't stand him. It seemed as if he were vain and phony, as if he were trying to imitate Richard Burton, who played Arthur: talking with the same accent, drinking heavily and, according to general theater gossip, chasing every woman in sight. I noticed him hang-ing around while I was talking to Roddy and I did my best to avoid meeting him.

What I didn't know until Bobby told me much later was that he had been obsessed with me ever since he'd seen me in *West Side Story* several years earlier. "I came down from Canada just to see the show because I'd heard so much about it—and I couldn't take my eyes off you," he said. "I sat as high up in the balcony as you can get because it was all I could afford, and even up there I was hypnotized! When the curtain came down, I couldn't get out of my seat. I sat there until somebody came along and said I had to leave. But you know, I hated everybody in that audience, because they were able to get up and go home. How *could* they?"

However, that night I couldn't avoid meeting him, and for many years after that he teased me about it. I was behind Roddy as we were walking downstairs from the second-story dressing rooms, and Robert Goulet was coming up. It was a narrow staircase, and we all stopped. Bobby flashed that incredible smile of his and held out his hand as Roddy, always courteous, began the introductions: "Carol, I'd like you to meet—"

Roddy never got any further. Holding my head as high as it would go, I brushed past both Roddy and Bobby with a very formal, stuffy, "How do you do?" and Roddy had to run to catch up with me.

It took me years to figure out why I was so apprehensive about getting to know this dashing matinee idol. Why was I reluctant to acknowledge his existence? I think I was afraid of getting hurt again. I had so many doubts about myself. Onstage I could be anything I wanted to be, but privately I felt the same way I'd felt as a little girl: I just wasn't enough. So why would the handsomest man in the world be interested in me? I had eyes. I had feelings. His looks and his intense sex appeal had their effect on me, as they did on every other woman who saw him, but I wanted much more from a man. Maybe he didn't have more to give—and if he did, why would he want to give it to me? He could have *anyone*! So, no, I wasn't going to let him get to me.

He wasn't that easy to avoid, however, Shortly after we met on the staircase, we were cast as husband and wife in a lavish Christmas TV spectacular called "The Enchanted

Nutcracker" and we began working together every day. Or, I should say, we began trying to work together, because Bobby's behavior was very difficult for me to tolerate.

He would come to rehearsal late, badly hungover, and red-eyed from lack of sleep. Sometimes he was still drunk, still copying his idol, Richard Burton. But Richard was an original, a complex genius, and I felt Bobby lacked that authenticity. He came off as a poor imitation. Richard also was a brilliant, dedicated, multitalented actor—and Bobby couldn't even remember his lines. Worse than that, he didn't apologize for forgetting, or for not taking the time to learn the material. He thought he was funny, and he would giggle at his mistakes. Some people laughed with him, but I didn't. Neither did the director nor the producer. Professionalism has always been my driving force, my bottom line with which I will not compromise, and I couldn't help thinking how much this glorious-voiced, beautiful man was throwing away.

He had come out of nowhere. He was an overnight sensation. He was young and could have developed all the things he didn't yet have as a performer. He could have learned to dance and move onstage, worked with an acting teacher and learned how to put feeling and meaning into his lines. The potential was there for him to become the best that Broadway—or Hollywood—had ever seen, but only if he was willing to really work hard. I couldn't see any hint of that kind of determination, and that made me angry. Off-camera, I couldn't even be civil to him.

Instead of discouraging him, my behavior seemed to excite him. Perhaps he felt I was a challenge. "God, you've got great legs!" he'd exclaim, as I walked away from him, and sometimes when he blew his lines he'd grin and say it was my fault. "It's your eyes," he'd murmur. "I get lost in them, they're so beautiful!"

"Oh, come off it," I'd say in disgust. It wasn't even good corn.

When we finished shooting the special, I went into pre-production meetings and rehearsals for *Subways Are for Sleeping*. Usually it was fairly late when I came home at night, but my phone was constantly ringing. It was Bobby asking for a date, and I always said no.

Finally *A View From the Bridge* was due to premiere, and the previews had attracted so much attention that a gala opening was scheduled in New York. I was so hopeful about the possibilities for the film that I overlooked some minor details. My manager did not.

"Who's taking you to the premiere?" he asked.

"I don't know," I said. I wasn't dating anyone at the time. "Maybe my brother." Now that I thought of it, I really wanted Joey to be there.

"Uh-uh. No family. No friends."

"Why not?"

"Carol, you're the lead in the picture. It means a lot to your career. It's a premiere—you know, photographers and all that stuff. Now, who's going to take a picture of you if you're with your brother?"

"Oh." I was catching on. Choosing my escort was like casting a part in a play. A leading lady needed a leading man.

"What about this Robert Goulet you've been working with?"

"No. I can't stand him!"

"For a couple of hours you can't stand him? Carol, think picturewise. The guy and you—you'll look great in pictures. You'll be in every paper."

The next day I phoned Bobby and, before he had a chance to say a word that would change my mind, I said, "Would you like to take me to the premiere of *A View From the Bridge*?"

He was startled, but he recovered quickly and said, "I would be honored."

I gave him my address, he picked me up, we attended the premiere, got our pictures taken, went to a party after the premiere, and he saw me home. We said goodnight at the door to my apartment. End of scene. Oh, yes, the next day we were in all the papers, and my manager was delighted.

A View From the Bridge did very well in New York and

San Francisco where audiences were more sophisticated. But the year was 1961, and it was the first major-market movie to show a close-up of two men kissing. By the time it opened in Des Moines, Iowa, people were leaving the theater in droves, and distributors were refusing to book the film. Shortly after it opened across the country, *A View From the Bridge* was withdrawn. I was terribly disappointed, but I hoped that the good reviews I got would mean something.

Bobby was still calling me and I was still finding reasons not to go out with him. One evening he said, "What are you doing Saturday night?" and I said, "Oh, I have plans."

Then he said, "Well, how about a *week* from Saturday?"

"No, I can't. I'm busy then, too."

For a moment there was nothing but silence. Finally I heard him take a deep breath. "How about right *now*?" he asked. "What are you doing right *now*?" He sounded so hurt that I felt foolish being standoffish.

"Right now," I said, "I'm baking Irish soda bread. Would you like to come over and have some?"

He sounded relieved and happy. "The next sound you hear will be your doorbell," he said, and hung up.

He arrived within minutes, and when I let him in he looked around in surprise. "Where is everybody?" he asked.

"Who's everybody?" I said, laughing.

"Aren't you giving a party? Isn't that why you're cooking?"

"No, silly. I love to cook. That's how I relax."

"You make *bread*? Real *bread*?"

"Sure," I said, walking into my tiny kitchen. "Can't you smell it?"

He rolled his eyes toward the ceiling and inhaled dramatically. "It smells wonderful!"

He watched me take two round, fragrant loaves out of my oven and put them on the counter. "*You* made those?" he asked again, and when I nodded he said, "*You're* beautiful!"

"Let's not go into that again," I said, stiffening a little.

"But I never knew anyone who could make bread," he said, and when I looked at him I saw that he wasn't joking.

For just a moment there was an earnestness about him I had never seen. He was like a little boy seeing a Christmas tree for the first time and realizing he wasn't dreaming. I relaxed. I was actually glad I had invited him.

I reached for my bread knife. "Well, I know lots of people who are very good at *eating* bread," I said. "How about you? Want a piece?"

He took the chunk of hot bread as if it were the Holy Grail, closed his eyes for a moment and then bit into it. He finished it and held out his hand for another piece. "Take it inside," I told him. "I'll bring you some coffee." I couldn't believe it—I was actually enjoying his company.

A few minutes later when I brought a tray into the living room, I thought at first he was gone. Then I saw him stretched out on the sofa, asleep. I was annoyed and put the tray on the coffee table hard enough to rattle the cups, hoping to wake him up. He had no manners! He—oh well, he was always tired, always needing sleep. What could I expect?

I sat in a chair across from him, nibbling on Irish soda bread and drinking coffee, amazed at how different his face looked now that he wasn't able to maintain his arrogance. There was a vulnerable sweetness about him that made me forget the bravado and boorishness I found so distasteful. Why did he hide the most appealing part of himself?

He was sleeping so deeply that it was hopeless to try waking him up. He didn't even move when I lifted his head to put a pillow under it, and covered him with an old blanket I kept in the closet. Then I turned out the lights, went to my bedroom and slept very well all night.

Chapter Seven

The next morning I was in the kitchen when I heard him moving around the living room. "Want some coffee?" I called.

I heard a grunt which I couldn't interpret as either yes or no, so I looked in. He was standing in my bedroom doorway on the far side of the living room. "You're up," he said, groggily.

"Yes, I'm up. And the kitchen is this way, if you're interested."

He was getting into his Richard Burton act, his voice deep and resonant as if he were onstage, with that funny accent that didn't belong to him at all. "I—uh—woke up during the night," he said.

"Oh?"

"Yes. Actually I considered joining you in your bedroom, but I thought maybe you had a gun and might shoot me." He took the mug of coffee I offered him.

"I think you made a very wise decision," I replied. "But I don't have a gun."

His attitude became serious. "You should," he said.

"Why?"

"To protect yourself."

"From what?"

"You never know. There's always somebody out to get you." He was looking toward the living room as if he saw someone, but no one was there. Then his mood changed. "Good coffee," he said.

We both had to get to appointments and he had to go home and change, so we hurried through breakfast. When he asked me out for dinner that evening, I couldn't think of a reason to refuse. "It'll have to be late—after the preproduction meeting," I said.

"Fine with me," he said.

I kept remembering the gentle boy's face I had seen the night before and I sensed that under all the brashness was someone very lovable.

We began to see a lot of each other. Going out with Bobby was like dating a knight, because he kept playing Lancelot even when he was offstage. He opened every door, took your arm, saw you in, saw you out, adjusted your chair, hung on your every word and gazed steadily into your eyes as you spoke. His behavior was courtly—and I enjoyed it even though I didn't believe a bit of it.

But he was funny, charming, and loving—and we laughed at the same things. I was beginning to know the part of him that was warm and generous. He'd go from a smile to a hearty laugh at the showbiz imitations I'd create to amuse him. He loved classical music, and was knowledgeable about it. He would listen attentively as I shared my infatuation with Respighi or Rachmaninoff. He'd read incessantly everything from the latest novels to his main love, poetry. One of his favorite pleasures was to read such things as "The Love Song of J. Alfred Prufrock" aloud to me with an enviable enjoyment.

Like me, Bobby had been brought up in the Catholic Church, although he was getting divorced.

"But, don't worry, I provide very well for my wife and daughter. And one of these days I'll be a free man again."

"And then what?"

"Who knows?" he said. "I've never been free."

One night, as we were finishing dinner in our favorite restaurant, I was telling Bobby about my early days with Edna McCrae, and he couldn't stop laughing when I described how she used to hit us with her cane.

"I know, I know!" he said. "I had a vocal teacher who used to punch me in the chest to teach me how to breathe!"

I had been laughing, too, but I stopped. "Hey, say that again!" I asked him. He had actually spoken to me in a normal voice.

"Say *what*?"

"What you just said."

"I said, 'I had a vocal teacher who—' " Burton was back.

"No, no, not like that. Say it the way you said it before. Be you."

He shook his head and smiled self-consciously.

"Please!" I begged him.

I could have sworn there were tears in his eyes. He reached across the table and took my hand gently. "Do you realize how hard I've worked to lose myself?"

"I wish you'd stop," I said. "But why did you ever start?"

That was when he began to tell me about himself. His childhood was almost devoid of any outward expressions of love. He was born to an Irish-French Canadian family in Lawrence, Massachusetts. His parents, Joseph and Jeanette Goulet, came from Canada and worked in the Lawrence textile mills. Reminiscent of Charles Dickens's description of England in Victorian times, the taverns became the center of the social life of various mill towns, and drinking became the major diversion. I felt, from what he told me, that Bobby had had a difficult childhood. Although his handsome father dabbled in amateur acting, there seemed to be little romance in the Goulet home. But there were lots of bills. The family lived in a cramped, two-bedroom apartment on the second floor of a tiny house. Joe slept in one bedroom and Jeanette slept in the other with their daughter, Claire. Bobby was relegated to a cot in the kitchen. He said there were no Christmas or birthday presents, and no outward gestures of affection. The only time I remember Bobby telling me of an intimate moment between his parents was when he saw them talking in the living room one day. Jeanette was standing against the wall and Joe stood in front of her, bracing himself with one hand on the wall near her head. Bobby said he was so touched by their mutual warmth that he burst into tears and ran to hide.

He was eleven or twelve years old when his father died, and his mother took the family back to Calgary, where she had grown up. Like many people, he had a difficult adjustment from the city life, to which he had become accustomed, to the rural life of the farmlands of Calgary. She married again, a plodding man who had little regard for Bob's dreams of being a singer. His stepfather was stern and demanded Bob learn to be a plumber and handyman in order to be sure of his income.

In high school, classes were easy to pass and Bob prided himself on never having to study to get by. Then came a crucial algebra test in his senior year. The teacher stood him up in front of the class to congratulate him on his amazing score. "Mr. Goulet," he began grandly, "I'm giving you two points and *that's* for spelling your name right!"

The entire class was consumed with laughter and Bobby was crushed. Then he turned and walked out of the class, out of the school, never to return or graduate.

He got a job as a local radio announcer in Calgary for a while and then with no money at all left home and studied music at the academy in Toronto.

They were hard times. He had to work as a salesclerk in a stationery store and keep replacing the cardboard in his worn-out shoes from packing boxes. He'd scout out the cheapest dinner specials at the drug store and pray his mom would send him an extra ten-spot now and then. But learn to sing he did, and my heart began to melt.

The more he told me about himself, the more I could see the person he really was: vulnerable, witty, sweet-natured, sincere, thoughtful, more beautiful inside than out. He had a feeling for words that was nearly poetic. In fact, he confided to me that he occasionally wrote poetry.

"I've never told that to anyone," he said. He seemed surprised. "You do some strange things to me."

"Not strange," I said. "I just want you to be yourself."

He squeezed my hand. "With you, I can be. But not with
anyone else. Can you settle for that?"

I was so close to tears, I couldn't answer. I nodded my
head.

He stood up. "Let's get out of here," he said. "Let's get
away from all these people."

In the early days of our relationship, we seemed to be
able to give each other so much that had always been missing in our lives.

When we were falling deeply in love, we were up to our
ears in career commitments. With my full day of rehearsals
and his nightly performances, the only time we had to be
together was after midnight. But I had learned well from my
mom how delectable a late supper could be, and I cooked
the most enticing feasts I could muster. Almost every night
Bobby would dash from his curtain calls to my tiny apartment, where garlic-garland aromas greeted him at the ele-
vator door. Clio, my Yorkshire terrier, hysterically wagged
her whole body at the sight of her favorite playmate. As a
boy, Bobby had never been allowed a dog, and he spoiled
Clio royally.

I knew that when he was growing up his overworked
mother had little time and no inclination to cook. He told
me that he always believed beef was supposed to be the color
and consistency of thick cardboard. There were few spices
or variety, and no treats. Meals were necessities, except for
the times when Bobby's childless Aunt Laura would slip him
a nickel so he could run down the block for a candy bar.
That's where his taste-bud adventures ended.

Well, I had a perfect audience for my culinary creations!
I introduced him to food touched by the genius of my mother's recipes: pastas he'd never heard of, artichokes, avocados
and endless Italian delicacies. Each meal always included a
delightful surprise, and his appreciation and joy were something to behold. Cooking is much akin to producing a show:

it's a theatrical, sensuous experience of candle-lit ambience, music and graciousness that, if done well, evokes a standing ovation. Bobby's version of an ovation was to whisk me in his arms and carry me into the bedroom.

I lived for those beautiful, intimate moments. Being with Bobby was my only happiness, and oh! how I clung to him, physically and emotionally. How warm and safe I felt when we were together.

Naturally I didn't tell my parents that we were living together. But one evening—in fact, it was my birthday— my mother surprised me by coming to New York without telling me. There she was, standing in my doorway, and Bobby was in my bedroom with the door closed. I knew I had to get around to explaining things, but I didn't know how to begin. Then my mother went to hang up her coat in the hall closet, and there were Bobby's clothes. She turned to me in horror. "What? What—" was all she could say, and the scene was so slapstick I couldn't help but laugh.

"Bobby, you'd better come out," I called to him. My mother had already met him once when she was in New York before, and she adored him. But this was something entirely different. "Oh!" was all she could say when she saw him in his robe.

Bobby was very considerate. He got dressed and said he had to go out for something, leaving me alone with my mother. The moment he was gone, my mother's hand went to her throat and her eyes rolled upward.

"No, Mom, don't have a heart attack!" I said. "It won't do any good!"

She dropped her hand, and looked at me. "It won't?" she said.

"No. I'm not a little girl, Mom. I've been married and divorced, and I've got my own life."

"Do you love him?" she asked me.

I put my arms around her. "Yes," I said. "Very much."

"You gonna marry him?"

"We don't talk about that. But we're very happy, Mom."

She held onto me and began to cry softly. "I'm just afraid you're gonna get hurt," she murmured.

I had spoken the truth to my mother—but not quite all of it. Bobby and I were happy. The things that used to bother me didn't matter anymore, because I could see through them to the depth, beauty and potential beyond. I excused his drinking. I knew he was trying to keep up with Richard, but I thought that once he was out of *Camelot* he would be different. I saw the way he was with women but I believed him when he said that with me he could be different. Whatever he did, however he behaved, *I* knew the real man. And when he was with me, he could be that person. Eventually, with my love and support, I thought he could be himself all the time with everyone.

I just wanted to make him happy. I wanted to show him what love was, because he had never known any. I really believed that if I loved him enough, I could heal all the hurt he had known. He was certainly healing me and making me feel more alive and happy than I'd ever been. If we could be surrounded by a home full of real love, he would feel safe, and everything would be perfect! . . . Was that Cinderella, or an old Betty Grable movie?

It was also true that we never talked about marriage. But I thought about it. Everyone in the theater knew about us. I'm sure they expected us to get married, but no one ever said anything about it. Maybe they felt, as I did, that Bobby wasn't quite ready.

I was. It was different from the way I felt about marrying Gus. Then I wanted to make everyone else happy and stay in New York. But now *I* wanted to be happy, and I didn't care where I lived as long as I could be with Bobby.

I was twenty-eight years old. I had done so many of the things I wanted to do in the theater, and although I didn't want to give up my career, I knew there was more to life than I had. I wanted a real home and a real husband and children, and I didn't have much time left to get started. In those days, twenty-eight was a little late to start having babies. As close as Bobby and I were, I never shared those feelings with him. Something always told me it wasn't the right time. We were too busy laughing and going to parties and being successful.

I had always realized how desperately Bobby needed to lift himself out of that tiny cot in the corner of a kitchen where he'd weave his dreams. When we first started dating, he used to ask me what would make me happy. I said, "First of all, a home and happy children—preferably in the quiet seclusion of the country, with lots of lawn and trees and peace and love."

Bobby was doing very well in those days. He was earning good money on Broadway, he had a recording contract with Columbia Records, he was doing television specials and people were falling down every time he appeared. Without saying a word to me, he bought a house that fit my fantasy perfectly, and one afternoon he drove me all the way to Purchase, New York, to surprise me. There I saw a tree-lined driveway curving precariously up a steep hillside for more than half a mile, which burst upon a huge stone, three-story house on seventeen acres of woods—one and a half hours from Broadway! There were rolling lawns, thirty-seven dogwood trees, a forsaken, weed-infested tennis court, a sunken Olympic-sized pool, a giant playroom with a pool table, and sixteen fabulous rooms to explore.

I was delightedly overwhelmed. Even for an experienced homeowner, making that mansion livable would have been an enormous undertaking. Neither of us had ever owned anything! But we were sure going to have fun redoing it together. And we did.

We planned our first weekend stay as soon as the sale was closed, before electricity, telephones or even water were turned on. We left immediately after our respective second shows on Saturday night. Armed with flashlights, a kerosene lamp, a large sleeping bag, pillows, towels, matches, bottled water and picnic coolers full of wine, Scotch and a host of our favorite foods, we set out on our first camping trip. Our dog, Clio, as always, came with us and sniffed out every corner and bush.

Bobby had brought a hatchet and while I was setting our "table," he cut some wood. We needed a fire to keep us warm in the early winter chill—and also to complete the setting. It was 4 A.M. when we finished our candle-lit feast.

We placed the sleeping bag in front of the fireplace where the embers were still glowing from the fire, and settled down at last.

Clio was under the covers beside me, and suddenly she began to growl menacingly. She fought her way to freedom. "What is it, Clio?" I asked, hoping she merely wanted some fresh air.

She bolted from me and, barking furiously, ran to the door leading to the sun porch and the dark outdoors. In between her barks it was eerily quiet.

Bobby got up instantly. Since there was no armor or sword at hand, he grabbed the only weapon we had—the hatchet.

"Where are you going?" I whispered.

"To find out what's the matter," he said.

"Not without me, you're not!" I grabbed his free hand.

Out we went, naked as two jaybirds, stalking shadows, following a three-pound shaggy ball of fur with a ton of courage. It was freezing cold and terrifyingly dark, but Bobby held my hand and challenged whatever it was out there. At that moment I believed we could conquer anything together.

We never discovered what provoked Clio, but we finally came running back to our warm covers to thaw out. Laughing hysterically over the imaginary dragons we had just slain, we fell asleep holding each other very tight.

When we walked through silent woods, which we both loved to do, we were often like two children holding hands. We were passionately sexual, and after the exhausting bliss, we could relish the quiet contentment of an embrace or a gentle touch.

Once, when we spent a few days in the country and had an especially wonderful time, I said to him, "Wouldn't it be nice if this could go on forever?" I wasn't exactly referring to a vacation, and he knew it.

Immediately he stopped smiling. "No," he said abruptly, And when I looked at him in surprise, he said, "I haven't been single long enough."

It would have been less painful if he had slapped me in

the face. I had no reply and resigned myself to being rejected again. I turned, as usual, to the only safe arena I knew: my career.

Professionally I still had a lot to learn. After *West Side Story*, I seldom had to audition for a show. Scripts were shoved under my nose and all kinds of promises were made. Ever since I saw my name up in lights that first time, I promised myself that I wouldn't allow fame to go to my head, but it got to me in a way I didn't expect: I stopped trusting my own judgment.

Everything about *West Side* had been so perfect that all the cast had to do was show up for each performance and we were terrific. I had yet to learn how rarely that happens in the theater, and especially in musical theater—a most treacherous medium. In a musical, every single part has to be absolutely perfect in itself and able to stand on its own. The audience should be able to enjoy the dancing, the story, the music and the lyrics by themselves, or the whole thing won't work when all those parts come together. And, in spite of the superb creative energy that went into *Subways Are for Sleeping*, it simply didn't work.

"Please," I begged David Merrick, "let me out of this. You don't have to make good on my contract. I'll leave quietly. You can get so many other actresses to play this part, but I *can't*. I just don't believe in it."

But I couldn't get out of my contract, so I did the best I could with the part. Everyone else in the show did too. I don't think I have ever seen that many people work so hard to make something come together—and get absolutely nowhere. Sometimes that happens, and no one knows why. Even the critics praised everyone for trying to save "a drowning whale." But drown it did, although David Merrick deserves credit for keeping it running for six months with all kinds of inventive promotions. We closed in the summer of '62.

That fall, Bobby left *Camelot*. I was in *Night Life*, a new play by Sidney Kingsley. It was a fascinating drama about characters who not only interacted with each other, but also spoke their innermost thoughts aloud in soliloquies. I played a cocktail lounge pianist, a complex role that gave me a chance to prove myself as an actress, and Neville Brand had the lead role of a union organizer/gangster. Unhappily, Neville sprained his foot just before we opened in Philadelphia and had to play his role with the aid of a cane, which destroyed the menacing strength of his character. Once again, we were struggling to keep going.

Bobby's manager, Norman Rosemont, had big plans for him. He booked him into the Persian Room at the Plaza Hotel and his shows were sold out well in advance. I knew he would be a hit, and he was. Everybody, including the critics, loved his show. He was stunning. He was singing at the top of his form, and he was lean and strong. He had worked very hard on his act and had learned how to move on a stage. When he left the floor and walked out into the audience, every woman thought he was singing only for her and applauded wildly. Then, a few nights after he opened, something extraordinary happened. One woman threw her room key at his feet as he finished his act. He looked startled, but he smiled as if to say, "Who, me?" After he sang an encore, a few more keys landed at his feet.

When I teased him about the keys after the show, he laughed and said, "That was Norman's idea."

"What do you mean, his idea?"

"He paid them a few bucks and gave them the keys," he said. "It'll be good publicity."

"You don't need that kind of trickery," I told him. "You're better than that."

"Norman knows what he's doing," Bobby snapped.

The keys were only the beginning. Women began throwing their underwear onto the floor, and did that ever make the newspapers!

Norman was pleased. He was booking Bobby into the best clubs all over the country, and taking the credit for his success. Bobby believed him. Funny, Bobby could be so arrogant and such a braggart, but he never actually realized how good he was, or could be.

While he was at the Persian Room, he had a birthday. It was November 26. He didn't think I knew about it, but I planned a surprise party for him. I had a huge cake made and hid it backstage, ready to wheel out as he ended his act. I couldn't wait to see his eyes light up.

That same night, a beautiful actress sat at a ringside table with her current boyfriend. As usual, the Persian Room was packed and as Bobby finished each song, the audience responded not only with applause but with cheers. He gave everyone goosebumps—that is, everyone except the actress, who looked the other way, waved to a friend across the room, giggled at something her boyfriend may or may not have said, and whispered in his ear. She ignored Bobby.

Now I have to tell you something about performers. We can't see everybody in a theater or a nightclub. Maybe we can see the first few rows or the ringside tables, but not much more, because of the spotlights in our eyes. But we do see. And we're always watching the way people respond to our performances. We don't want to, but we can't help it. The response is why we're there. Performing is a two-way street. We give—you give back. Or you don't. And if one person doesn't respond, that's the one who gets our attention. If someone in the first row falls asleep, a performer doesn't see all the other people giving him a standing ovation. He comes offstage thinking, "I didn't do anything right tonight because that guy fell asleep." Maybe that guy hadn't slept for the past six nights and finally passed out because he was sitting down and enjoying himself—but you can't tell that to an actor.

I saw what was happening and I thought, "Oh, well, it's his birthday, and I'll make him forget all about it." When he finished his encore, the band went into a flourish and on I came, wheeling the cake on a huge cart. Everybody got into the act, singing and congratulating Bobby. But the actress and her boyfriend were gone.

Later, in his dressing room, Bobby said, "Did you see how she yawned?"

I knew whom he meant. "Oh, she was just trying to get your attention—don't let it bother you," I said. "Take it as a compliment." He did.

A few days later we were going to eat Thanksgiving

dinner together between my matinee in *Night Life* and his show at the Plaza. He was late arriving at our restaurant, and he had a strange sort of smile on his face. He kissed me lightly on the cheek and sat down, but when the waiter offered him a menu he waved it away. "I've already eaten," he said, "but I'll sit with you while you eat."

I thought he was joking, so I began to laugh.

"I had my Thanksgiving dinner," he said, watching me carefully, "with that actress."

I was stunned. He didn't have to tell me about it. He could have said something like "I don't feel like eating right now"—unless he *wanted* to hurt me.

"How could you do that?" I asked him.

"It was easy. I called her up."

"When?"

"Last week," he said, "after she came to the show. You were right—she *was* trying to get my attention. So, she got it."

I felt ice-cold. "Obviously," I said, "while I was doing my matinee, you were doing yours—of a different sort."

He was amused by that. "You have to understand something, Carol," he said, motioning the waiter to bring him a drink. "I'm not married to you."

"No," I said, standing up and reaching for my coat, "and you never will be."

He tried to take my hand, but I pulled away from him. I was not going to cry! "I don't want marriage," he said. "You know that. I've finally got my divorce, and I like being free."

"Congratulations!" I said. "Enjoy!" I left him there and went back to my dressing room.

For a long time I didn't feel anything. I went to the theater. I performed and I came home. I did a lot of work on television specials: *The Ed Sullivan Show, The Dean Martin Show, The Perry Como Show, Studio One, Philco Playhouse,* all of them wonderful, exciting productions. As an actress I was growing, but as a woman, I had stopped living.

Bobby wrote to me once. It was an odd letter in which he said he was sorry we had to end the way we did. He also said he was worried about me because I was working so hard. He always did think I was driven, and compared to the way he approached his career, I was. I had been lucky, but I worked very hard to make that luck count. I was always trying to become a better actress, a better dancer, a better singer, because I think that's the way an artist must live. Bobby had superstar success because he was phenomenally gifted, so he never saw the value or need of spending his few free hours with teachers and coaches.

I was glad he was on tour because that meant we weren't likely to run into each other. But early one evening, several weeks later, I was having dinner with some friends in a small Italian restaurant down the street from *Night Life*, when I felt as if someone were staring at me. I turned around and there was Bobby. He looked tired and lost, and all I know is that when I saw him, the part of me that had stopped living came to life again. As soon as he saw me smile, he came over to our table.

"I hoped you'd be here," he said, ignoring the others. He knew that I ate there whenever I did two shows a day. He sounded desperate, as if he needed something urgently.

I held out my hand and he took it. "Sit down, sit down!" I said, and someone pulled a chair up next to me. "How *are* you?"

"Okay, I suppose," he said. "No, that's a rotten lie!"

"Have you eaten anything today?" I asked him.

"No."

"Here," I said, pushing my plate in front of him. "Get some food into you."

He picked up a fork and began twisting some strands of spaghetti around it, but with his left hand he reached for mine. "I really have to talk to you," he said in a very low voice.

"Eat."

"Can I see you after the show?"

"*Eat!*"

My poor friends. We absolutely forgot they were there. After my show we went back to my apartment. He told me about his tour and said his manager had more bookings than he could handle.

"How wonderful! You must be very happy," I said.

"No, I'm not, damnit!" he said, punching his fist into the arm of the sofa.

"Why not?"

"Because I miss you so much," he said. "Carol, you win. I guess I really do love you."

"Okay," I said. "I want to be with you, too—but not the way we were. I'm not going to be here for you while you're out sleeping with every woman you see!"

"All right!" he said. He stood up and walked back and forth. Then he stopped and looked down at me defiantly. "We'll get engaged," he said.

That's when I cried. I was so happy. I thought of all the wonderful things we could share and do together. He was everything I ever wanted and more. My emotions were exploding, and I'll tell you only that every romantic cliché in existence was filling that moment and I bought them all. I didn't think anyone had ever loved this much before.

A few nights later he came to my apartment while I was in the bathroom putting on my makeup. The telephone rang and he called out, "Can you get that?" When I ran to the nightstand I saw something glittering next to the phone. It was a ring. No box, just a ring—a beautiful pear-shaped diamond ring. I never found out who was calling because I couldn't even pick up the phone. I sat on the bed and all I could say was, "O-o-oh!"

I was ecstatically happy. Although we hadn't set a date for the wedding, I knew Bobby loved me.

As for my career security—that depended on how fast my footwork was. Unfortunately, *Night Life* was another short-lived production. It was time for me to prove to Broadway that I could do more than play the tragic Maria everyone associated with me. Since I could sing and dance, and also loved to play the clown, the best place for me to spotlight those talents was on a nightclub floor. In the early sixties, nightclubs were very important in the entertainment business, and if your act was well reviewed, you could take it to clubs all over the country.

Putting my own act together was a new adventure for me. It was like producing a mini-musical, and it could cost as much as $100,000 to do it right. If you tried to cut even one corner, you would eventually pay dearly for it.

It helped if you could dance, but even if you could, your steps had to be brilliantly choreographed. (After all, I had worked with Jerome Robbins!) You had to sing the latest hits, with lush, versatile accompaniments. You needed innovative arrangements, a dance-sensitive conductor, a personal drummer and a lead trumpet player. You needed dancers or singers, or both, to back you up and customize your performances. Your costumes had to be designed to change like magic right before the audience's eyes to match the many moods you'd portray. And why all this expense and effort? Because the competition was keen and careers were fragile and needed constant refurbishing.

I got Tony Charmoli to choreograph my act, and he came up with something no one had ever done—and no wonder! He took the concept of an electrician's ladder and redesigned it. So, at one point in the show I came on singing and holding on to the top of this whirling, ten-foot-high ladder. It was fitted with revolving casters and was pushed at a furious pace by two young men the audience could barely see, because the spotlight was on me and they were in the dark. I said to Tony, "You must have planned this act for Sonny Liston!" It was an exhausting hour-and-a-quarter marathon that kept me singing and dancing every minute. I loved it!

We broke in the act in a little club in Columbus, Ohio. From there we went directly to my opening at the Persian Room. It was the most prestigious pinnacle in the nightclub world. And it was a tough place to introduce a new show because the audiences were sophisticated, knowledgeable and demanding. They expected and usually got the best. I guess it went pretty well, because from that performance, Ed Sullivan called my act "the greatest nightclub act I've ever seen!" in his column and on his TV show. Every other reviewer gave it raves. The Persian Room was sold out.

From there I went on a short tour, which wasn't a simple matter. I took with me a secretary, two male dancers, a trumpet player, a drummer, a conductor and the ladder—which came apart in three sections that fitted into three enormous black fiberglass cases especially made for them. I was glad for every minute we had spent in preparation and rehearsal, because when we opened at the Coconut Grove in Los Angeles and the curtain went up, I froze. It was right after Ed Sullivan had told the country about my act. I was paralyzed by the glittering gallery before me—every famous face I'd revered since I was a little girl in Melrose Park singing and dancing for passersby from an open garage door.

I was most struck by what we called the Hollywood Royalty—George Burns, Gracie Allen, Jack Benny and Mary Livingstone in the center ringside table, like soloists surrounded by a massive choir.

Before I could utter my first greeting, my top lip froze, cemented firmly to my front teeth. George Burns, being the old pro that he is, quickly recognized the expression on my face. He rose, slowly put down his cigar, waved at the crowd, and winking at me said, "Go get 'em, kid," and began the applause that kicked off the show with a standing ovation.

Backstage afterward, I got a chance to thank him for the compassion that allowed me to recapture my breath—and my power of speech. Many years later I got to publicly thank him for that gallant gesture when we played Caesars Palace in Las Vegas together.

That winsome foursome returned over and over with influential friends at ringside, laughing and cheering at all the right places as if they'd never seen it before!

I saw very little of Bobby during those months because each of us was on a nightclub tour and going in different directions. So when one of us was appearing somewhere, and the other had a few days off, we would grab the occasion to get together. One such time was when he was playing in San Juan, Puerto Rico, and I hopped a plane to be with him.

Harry Belafonte was appearing in another hotel nearby, so we arranged to get together. Because of Harry's involvement with the Peace Corps, he invited me to their base camp the following day. Bobby would join us as soon as his schedule permitted.

Now I don't know if you really know Harry Belafonte or not, but he is one of the most outspoken and committed people involved in many worthwhile movements going on in the world. He gave tremendous time and energy to help President John Kennedy start the Peace Corps, just as he supported Martin Luther King in his civil rights programs. Magnetic, charismatic, and blessed with a vibrant and contagiously joyous energy, Harry was universally attractive, unparalleled in his ability to communicate, and passionate in his zeal to make this a better world. He could set audiences moving and tapping like no one I've ever seen, and he carried this ability to inspire into important places to help heal the planet. With his wit and enthusiasm he painted visions of a future world we could build together.

It was Harry who provided me with my greatest accomplishment by talking me through the official Peace Corps "Confidence Course." Based on the "Outward Bound" program, it required me to do such things as traverse a tight-rope bridge sixty feet high, scale walls thirty feet high and swing Tarzan-style with ropes over streams to drop on the opposite shore. And then there was the famous "pamper pole" . . . you can imagine where that got its name!

Experiencing Harry's ability to be a coach, confidant, comforter and taskmaster was a gift all by itself. Without him, I not only would never have finished pulling myself through that eye of a needle—I would never have started!

Dirty, grungy, sweaty, sunburned and ecstatic, we gave an a cappella concert to the Peace Corps kids at the training base, at the request of Harry's dear friend, the Camp Commander. Exhaustion was balanced by exhilaration, and we all loved it.

Ultimate showman that he was, Harry had already choreographed the finale of our day together. He wouldn't tell me where we were going. We just arrived at this lovely, unassuming, typically Spanish home overlooking the water. And out front to greet us was the great master himself— Pablo Casals. Like a gift from heaven, I spent one of the most memorable, but relaxed afternoons of my life. We had delightful and lively conversation, and Harry asked Pablo to play for us. As if it were no big deal—no more important than if we had asked for a glass of water—he picked up his cello and nourished our spirits with what the Bible must mean by "the sounds of men and of angels."

He said later, "Carol, I loved the music of *West Side Story*, and I know you must sing contemporary songs to survive, but promise me you'll never stop singing the sublime music like this." Then he walked not to his cello but to his piano, and played the loveliest Schubert art song— and sang it. I cried all the way through. It was sheer beauty.

How very blessed we were to be with people who were improving the world with their art and wisdom. The only way I felt I could continue to warrant my place in their company was to constantly create more innovative and compelling truths in my own media. I was feeling the inspiration from Casals combined with my usual sense of inadequacy.

I asked him about his day. He said, "Of courrrse, I prrracteece severrrral hourrs in the morrrning, and morrre in the eeebening, but my favorrite time is when I watch the cowboy Westerrrn movies on telebeesion, because when I was young, I met the rrreal cowboys in my tourrrs, and gambled with them. They are good gamblerrs. But the best gamblerrrs arre the Chinese." Everything about him had a rare joy and vibrance that I experienced only one other time—when I met President John Kennedy.

He picked up his cello again, and as the sun was setting behind him across the water, it felt like everything in his being—the curve of his bald head, his arched back, the circle of his arms—all seemed to meld into oneness with his instrument. There was a glowing aura that was visual, audible and sensual as if it were enveloping all our senses— as though we all were part of the instrument being played. It was all so simple—yet more grand than the most jewel-bedecked ballroom I've been in.

Please, if you haven't already, read the autobiography of Pablo Casals, *Joy and Sorrows*. In it he says, "Each second we live is a new and unique moment of the universe, a moment that never was before, and never will be again. And what do we teach our children? $2+2=4$ . . . We should say . . . you are a marvel. You are unique. In all the world there is no other child exactly like you . . . You may become a Shakespeare, a Michelangelo, a Beethoven. You have the capacity for anything." You too will be inspired and encouraged by his life, I'm sure.

To move from the sublime to the ridiculous. Harry called the next morning, and invited us waterskiing. Bobby wouldn't risk getting water up his nose and endangering his voice. I admitted I didn't know how to ski and Harry dismissed that with "I'll get you an instructor, okay?"

"Sure," I said.

"Meet me in my lobby, and you'll be a pro by noon."

We drove to a dock in the shelter of a small lagoon and soon I was being towed behind a speedboat manned by sweet Puerto Ricans who couldn't *believe* that Maria of *West Side Story* spoke no Spanish! My feet were secured to the huge skies with tips up and out of the water. I was crouched into a pretzel shape with my knees smacking against my chest and my nose (sometimes) just above the water. I held on to the bar fiercely, bobbing wildly and squeezing my lips together as half the lagoon rushed into my sinuses. Spitting, sputtering and struggling to breathe, I tried hard to smile and even harder to understand the instructor's commands as he yelled from the stern in broken English. "Putta yo hanz? No . . . No . . . Yo"—then he'd turn to Harry for the proper word—"Yo ellbowz outa." I could see Harry shaking his head sadly and trying to be patient as Carlos continued. "Pushha yo feet, I meana you nose? . . . No, I meana yo knees . . ."

That was enough. I heard Harry say, "Excuse me, Carlos." Then he leaned over the back of the boat and shouted, "Parallel your feet, tips up, push down on your heels, lock your elbows and lift up your ass!!"

In a split second I sprang out of the turbulent water, erect and secure on the crest of success at last.

"Look Harry," I yelled. "I'm really skiing." And with that first clear breath of air, POP went the clasp on my bikini top. It flew off my body—followed closely by the two rubber falsies it had imprisoned. The unbelieving shock on the men's faces was hilarious, but I was too humiliated to laugh. I instantly released the line and plopped into the cover of the water. Harry dove right in, chasing my delinquent top—I grabbed one falsie and he retrieved the other along with my bathing top. He gallantly stuffed them into his trunks, took off his T-shirt and helped me put it on while I was treading water. We laughed hysterically and to this day, it remains an inside one-liner. "Carol, how are you? Been waterskiing lately?" Such shared experiences are what Gary Smalley in his *Hidden Keys to Successful Relationships* seminars and tapes calls the "cement of emergencies and solutions in teamwork that harden into bonds for life."

I began to wonder if my wedding would ever take place. Bobby's manager, Norman, certainly didn't want it to happen because he thought marriage would hurt Bobby's image as every woman's dream man. By that time Norman was managing my career, too, because my former manager had died and a second choice had not worked out. Ideally, a relationship with a personal manager should feel like that of a concerned and loving member of your family. Although Norman said he had always wanted to manage me, he and I didn't get along.

It seemed to me that Norman was doing his best to keep Bobby and me apart. He would book Bobby in Miami and me in Chicago, or Bobby in San Francisco and me in New York. "Why can't you book us into the same city?" I asked him. I already knew that Norman and Bobby were fifty-fifty business partners, unlike the usual manager's fifteen-percent arrangement such as he had with me.

"Tell you what—let me put you in his show."

"I'd love it!" I said. I couldn't believe he was on my side. He wasn't.

"You'd have to take second billing."

"Okay." After all, we were engaged, so what did it matter? It was the show that counted.

"And he gets the big piece of the money pie," Norman went on.

"I guess that's all right," I said, "as long as it stays in the family."

"Good!" Norman said.

As Norman planned, the fact that I appeared with Bobby helped his image and show enormously, because most people enjoyed watching two people in love sing songs to each other. Our act broke records wherever we played. But I still wasn't comfortable with Norman. Sometimes he didn't publicize my name at all, so that even when we played in Chicago, my hometown, some of the people who knew me didn't realize I was on the bill with Bobby. The tour was titled *Robert Goulet in Concert*, although the cast included the Step Brothers, the Weir Brothers . . . and me! But when I mentioned anything like that to Bobby, he got very upset. "You just dislike Norman because you're jealous of him!" he'd say. "You know how much he loves me." I felt that perhaps Norman was trying to cause friction between Bobby and me so that one of us would call off the wedding. I began to keep my objections and my anger to myself. Given time, Bobby and I would solve all our problems—I was certain of that.

When I met Bobby, I had already built a shell around myself. We were both equally pressured by the demands of show business. We handled them differently, but felt the same way about them. Of course, it's a given that privacy is forfeited to the public and press, who scrutinize every action no matter how hard you try to live up to your press kit bio. Besides, you're already exhausted by the demands of your normal day: learning lines; keeping all the directions in your head; press conferences; picture calls; looking after hair, skin, makeup and body; doing all the exercises; learning dance routines; never catching cold; getting sleep; and always being witty, charming, adorable and entertaining. There's never a moment when you can relax and enjoy yourself.

So when you finally meet someone who is in the same boat, someone who understands the pressures you're under, you plan to run away together. You dream of going to some sequestered place where you can be yourself and feel safe. Bobby's fantasy was to retire to a lighthouse. That's what I kept thinking Bobby and I would be able to do one day.

At last, we were married on August 12, 1963, at the Plaza Hotel in New York City. We didn't have time for a honeymoon because the next day we had to continue working. But, as someone said at our wedding reception, we looked just like the two little figures on top of the wedding cake—perfect together.

Not everyone agreed. My secretary asked, "Do you think it's a good idea for you to marry someone in the same business?" And a dancer I had worked with wondered how I was going to feel, walking into a room with a husband who was prettier than I was.

As different as the comments were, they were telling me more about my future than I wanted to know.

Chapter Eight

Bobby and I shared so many pleasures in life. We both were active, almost "hyper" people who loved taking long walks, playing golf and swimming. We read a lot and I loved listening to him read aloud. He laughed at my jokes and appreciated the clown in me. We both liked the country, and the big old mansion in Purchase, New York, was a perfect retreat.

Bobby was the best audience a cook ever had. He ate everything I put on the table and raved about it. He was also the kind of friend who was right there when you needed help. Nothing was too trivial or silly to consume his interest if it was something you wanted to discuss. Sometimes I thought maybe my stories weren't really that funny, or my cooking wasn't all that terrific, and maybe Bobby laughed so hard and ate so lustily just to please me. No matter—I enjoyed that sweetness in him.

But sometimes his mood changes were so extreme that I felt cut off from him. Having been raised in an emotionally charged family atmosphere, I knew that even the heartiest singing, dancing and laughing could change in a moment to

111

bitterness that could last a lifetime. But usually there was a reason; someone said something, or said it in a way that gave offense, someone criticized, or someone didn't praise extravagantly, someone wasn't there when he should have been, or someone was butting in all the time. In Bobby's case it was a dense gloom that settled on him for no apparent reason. A sunny day could depress him—because tomorrow might bring rain. Good news wasn't a reason to smile—because sooner or later your luck would change. I was learning something about the Irish: they don't always laugh. There is a dark side to their gaiety, a relish of things melancholy.

But so many good things were happening in our lives that I could easily gloss over Bobby's mood swings. One special highlight—and an honor I will always cherish—was an invitation from President John F. Kennedy to join him, along with some of my colleagues from the entertainment community, for a press conference in the Oval Office. The occasion was to announce a show at Madison Square Garden, in which we'd be performing, that would kick off the President's re-election campaign. Although I'd always been an avid supporter and admirer of President Kennedy, I was nonetheless unprepared for the magnitude of his charm, intelligence, humor and personal grace.

I flew in from California on November 19, 1963, and was briefed the following day, along with the other guests and rows of cameramen and reporters, for the meeting with the President. We all waited anxiously to be admitted to the inner sanctum of the White House, and finally the time came. I went to the door, expecting a staff member to open it and let us in, and was totally overwhelmed when the President himself swung open the door and extended a warm handshake in greeting. His famous grin, sparkling eyes and robust manliness radiated electricity.

"Miss Lawrence, won't you come in? Lyndon Johnson tells me that your act at the Persian Room is phenomenal. I can't wait to see some of it in the show at Madison Square Garden."

I didn't even know that the Vice President had seen my act—let alone discussed it—and that the President would be gracious enough to mention it! My knees began to wobble, but I managed a "Thank you, Mr. President," smiling from ear to ear.

The President had a personal greeting for all of us. Then we were asked to stand in a formal pose for the official photos. Miracle of miracles, I ended up at President Kennedy's right side.

A week earlier, *Life* magazine had run the precious shots of little John Kennedy under the President's desk. In the awkwardness of dozens of flashbulbs bursting and clicking noisily, I said, "Mr. President, having seen the photos in *Life* magazine, I wanted to ask you—is it true that John, Jr. *really* runs this office?"

"Yes, it is," he responded, "and if you tell anyone else you'll find yourself in deep trouble!" He laughed, looking straight into my eyes.

At that very second, one of the cameramen took our picture, and it was that particular photograph that was picked up by the Associated Press and reproduced in papers all over the country and the world. My father was so proud that he used that picture on his insurance calendars.

Worried that I would be alone that evening in a city that wasn't home, President Kennedy had asked his sister-in-law, Ethel, to invite me to Bobby Kennedy's private birthday party that night. She caught up with me by telephone at a television studio in the area, and extended the invitation. I was deeply touched by the President's thoughtful concern, but I was a newlywed and had promised my husband I'd return home that evening.

As it turned out, that was to be the last family gathering of the Kennedy clan—for John F. Kennedy, the shining hope of our country, was assassinated two days later in Dallas. I could never understand how his family and friends survived losing him. My life was only touched by him for one day, yet when I learned of his death, I was stricken with a grief I've felt only for my own parents.

It was a terrible time of tragedy. The whole world seemed to be careening out of control, and changing too fast to fathom.

For Bobby and me, life was changing personally and professionally. Musicals used to open one after another on Broadway. New talent kept coming forward. And if Broadway wasn't as well known in Podunk as it was around New York, it was a powerful launching pad to television and Hollywood. But in the early 1960s tastes were changing.

Young people were doing odd-looking dances with or without a partner, and sometimes with hoops sliding up and down their bodies while they spun and wiggled and weaved. Something called rock 'n' roll was captivating them, but those of us who thought we knew a lot about music said, "Don't worry, it'll pass." It did. It passed us by completely. New performers with their new music gave concerts instead of starring in a musical or doing a nightclub act. They could give a concert in a stadium or a field, and either way the audience was many times the number of people who could squeeze into a Broadway theater. The cost of admission was much less, too.

The first sign of change that we noticed was television's move to the West Coast. When Bobby and I started working in TV, the studios and executives were based, and their decisions made, in New York. Then suddenly they were in Los Angeles. Every time we were on a TV show we had to fly out to California for a few days. I wondered how many jobs we didn't get because we weren't right there when casting was done.

Although neither of us wanted to leave New York, we agreed that it made sense to live where TV and films were made. We rented a home in Los Angeles while Bobby was making his first movie, *Honeymoon Hotel*. The picture would turn out to be a disaster, but Bobby didn't know that at the time. He was fresh from Broadway and nightclub triumphs and was ready to make it in films. During the day, while Bobby was on the movie set, I made the rounds of houses with real estate agents. Usually I'd return to our rented house just as Bobby finished work, and I'd prepare his dinner.

As soon as I saw the right house, I couldn't wait to tell Bobby. He came home late from shooting that night, and I had already put on my nightgown and negligee. I was curled up on the sofa, waiting for him. I tried to describe what I thought was wonderful about the house, but then I had a better idea. "C'mon, let's go look at it."

Bobby didn't want to come. He was dead tired from shooting all day and the last thing he wanted was to house-hunt. "Buy whatever you like," he said every time I tried to draw him out about his own preferences. I knew enough about him by then to recognize things that were important to him. I thought he would love this house, but I needed to be sure.

After convincing Bobby to go with me, I threw a cape over my nightgown, and we were out the door. I didn't expect to see anyone because I thought the owner of the house was away. But when we got there, she was home, and in spite of the late hour she was only too happy to let us in.

This house was on almost four acres, which in Beverly Hills is a large piece of property, and Bobby liked plenty of space. He also liked to be high up where people couldn't get to him, which I could understand, because in our profession privacy is both a luxury and a necessity. Bobby had more than the usual number of intrusions on his privacy because everywhere he went, women mobbed him. It was part of his attraction as a performer and something he and his manager orchestrated with great care. I had seen it. I had been there when women of all ages pushed past me to get to him, some of them even handing me a camera to take a picture of them wrapped around my husband.

As I led him through the house that evening, I could see he was excited. "This is beautiful!" he said, and his face had that unguarded boyish look of wonder he rarely let anyone see. "It's a castle." We were standing in the living room, which is the size of a house itself. It was designed for magnificent parties where clever, talented people could come together.

"Well, not quite a castle," I said. "It needs a little work to make it a home."

"I don't care," he said, taking my hand and leading me into the dining room. "This is where we belong." He stopped in the center of the room, which was mirrored from floor to ceiling on all sides. Delicate vines of ivy were painted along the borders of the mirrors and around the windows and doors. "Imagine the feasts we can have here!" Bobby loved parties.

We were told that the dining room had been designed by Don Loper with the express command never to put electric lighting in the room.

"That's perfect—we'll have candles. Hundreds of them. Thousands of them. We'll hire somebody just to light them and blow them out!" I loved the way the Irish in him could turn reality into a fairy tale.

"It's absolutely perfect," he said and pulled me close to him. I couldn't believe that any two people could be as happy as we were going to be.

I was hoping we could settle down somewhere because I wanted to have a baby as soon as possible—although I didn't think travel would be a problem, because we could take a baby anywhere with us. We were making very good money, so we could afford a nanny. I made an appointment with my gynecologist and began keeping temperature charts. When I got pregnant, which didn't take long, I started attending Lamaze classes. This baby was going to get the right start!

I knew that Bobby didn't want a baby as much as I did. But he didn't object. He also didn't want to get involved with anything connected with my pregnancy—that was women's work. I understood. Growing up in such a strange family, he didn't know what it was like to feel that the child would be a part of him. I was sure that would change once our baby was born.

During the summer, when I was about five months pregnant, we spent as much time as we could at our home in Purchase. It was our last summer there, because we were now living in our wonderful house in Beverly Hills, and had put our beloved home in Purchase on the market. It was a sad time, because there were the usual disappointments in Bobby's career after the *Honeymoon Hotel* flop. We hated to give up that house, especially since we had moved to California only for practical reasons—not because we loved it.

One weekend, when some friends were staying with us,

we were all out by the pool. Bobby was in the water wearing his face mask to avoid getting water in his nose, and I was lying on a floating lounge chair. We were going out to dinner that evening, so I had set my hair in rollers and tied a scarf around my head. I had closed my eyes and was enjoying the warmth of the sun when I felt a tug. Bobby was holding onto the lounge chair, squinting up at me and grinning.

"Hi!" he said, rocking the lounge a little.

"Hi," I said, smiling back at him. I knew how much it meant to both of us to do absolutely nothing but enjoy ourselves.

Then he rocked the lounge a little harder and I sat up.

"Please, darling, don't do that!" I said.

"Why not?" His smile was devilish.

"Because I don't want my hair to get wet. I want it to look nice tonight." I didn't think he would understand how unattractive a woman can feel when she's pregnant, and how important a thing like hair can be at such a time.

"Oh-h-h?" he said teasingly, and with one quick motion he flipped the lounge out from under me and I went into the water.

When I came up, coughing, sputtering and livid, he was laughing. He splashed at me with the palm of his hand. Since I was already wet and my hair a mess, I said "Okay, if that's the way you want to play," and in one motion pulled off his face mask and splashed him back. I knew he would hate that.

It all happened so fast. "Goddamn you," he yelled, as he grabbed my arm and pulled me out of the pool. I screamed because the sudden violence terrified me. All I could think about was the baby in my womb getting hurt. Our friends came tearing over to us and pulled Bobby off of me. They drove me to a doctor immediately. "The baby seems to be all right," the doctor said after he examined me. "But you aren't—has this ever happened before?"

"No."

"Do you really want to go home?"

"No."

Then I wondered, where would I go? I didn't want to be alone. I couldn't work. I didn't want to go back to Melrose

Park and live with my parents until my child was born. And the child—I wanted our child to have both its parents. I couldn't deprive our baby of a home and a family because of one outburst. I imagined how Bobby must be feeling, and the sympathy I felt for him began to work on me. We had been married only a few months when I became pregnant —maybe I was in too much of a hurry. He hadn't even had time to get used to being a husband. I knew he loved me. I knew he never meant to hurt me. He just lost control of himself and so did I. It would never happen again.

When I told the doctor that I had changed my mind and wanted to go home, he said, "I think I'd better call your husband first."

He got Bobby on the phone and I heard him explain how fortunate we were because the baby wasn't harmed. "But your wife has more than physical damage, Mr. Goulet. When she came in, she was in shock."

I heard him say, "Yes, yes, she's going to be all right. Yes, she wants to come home and your friend will drive her. Now—would you like to talk to her?" I saw the surprise on his face as he put the phone down.

"What did he say?" I asked him.

"He said, 'I have nothing to say to her.' "

That remark was one I was to hear many times in the years ahead. And when I got home, Bobby was watching TV with a glass of vodka in his hand. He didn't even look up.

I went upstairs and lay on the bed. I pulled my knees up as close as they would fit until I could feel some warmth in my body. This was also the one way I could feel my baby, vital and alive, inside of me. This got my mind going again. Instead of feeling anger toward Bobby, I began to see the ways in which I had been responsible for escalating his rage toward me—and ways in which I could improve the situation between us. (The wonderful thing about taking responsibility, I have discovered, is that only then is change and progress possible. Since I am the only person I'm in charge of and can change, if I take no responsibility, I have no power in a situation, and despair and hopelessness are all that's left.) Convinced there was much I could do to bring happiness back to our marriage, I fell asleep, hopeful again.

Our son Christopher was born on November 17, 1964, in New York, where Bobby was performing at the Plaza. The birth was relatively easy, and I proudly brought him into the world without the aid of anesthesia. I was the hospital's first Lamaze patient and nurses kept saying, "Are you crazy? Why are you putting yourself through this?" When they saw me doing my breathing exercises, they thought I was in agony, and even though I tried to explain why I was panting, they were skeptical. Bobby hadn't gone to the Lamaze courses with me, so I had the help of a Lamaze-trained coach, but the doctor wouldn't allow her into the predelivery room with me. When, at the right moment, I gave two good, hard pushes and Christopher was born, the nurses were amazed. "Did you see that?" they kept saying to each other.

When my doctor rested our baby on my breast, I was grateful that I wasn't groggy with some kind of medication. I didn't want to miss a second of that absolutely beautiful experience. He was so alert and, even though he was too young to see, he looked directly at me. He was such a healthy baby, and I had wanted him so much! That moment became the happiest, most vivid memory of my life.

It was a few minutes before midnight, and I wanted to share the event with Bobby before his second show.

"May I call my husband?" I asked my doctor. He looked a little perplexed. Then one of the nurses told him there was a phone in a room next to the operating room.

"I suppose so," the doctor said.

Still on the delivery room table, I was wheeled to the next room. Someone dialed the number for Bobby's suite at the Plaza. "I just want you to know that you have a son," I said when I heard him answer.

He didn't say a word. "What's the matter?" I asked him.

"Nothing," he said, but his voice sounded strange.

"You're not saying anything," I said.

"I can't," he said. "I'm crying."

The next night Bobby walked in on Johnny Carson's

show, even though he wasn't scheduled to appear, and passed out cigars. I didn't know he was going to do that, but I was watching the show in my hospital room. Bobby looked so proud and happy! Especially for his sake, I was thrilled that our first child was a son. Eventually I hoped to have a daughter, but not right away. Maybe in a few years, I thought as I drifted off into sleep. At that moment I thought I had everything a woman could possibly want, and I thanked God fervently for my blessings.

Even as an infant, Christopher was a happy baby with the most incredible basso profundo laugh. Hearing him in the next room, I could have sworn he was at least a few years old. The only time he showed any displeasure was when his pacifier was taken away from him—and our nanny, Petey, took it away often to wash it thoroughly. Petey was the most scrupulously clean woman I have ever known, and a gem of a caregiver. Only later, when she left, did I discover that not all nannies were like her.

Christopher was baptized in the Catholic Church, in St. Patrick's Cathedral. I remember how excited I was holding him, standing next to Bobby in a long line of parents and infants awaiting their turn to approach the priest. Ours was quite a group; my mother and father were there, plus my brother Joey and his wife Mary Lou, Christopher's godparents. Christopher was sucking on his pacifier and it fell to the floor. Well! Petey snatched it up and put it in her purse. Nothing on earth could make her give such a germ-ridden object to the child in her charge. I knew what was going to happen and I whispered to Petey, "Please, just this once, couldn't you give it back to him?"

Petey shook her head fiercely. "Absolutely not, ma'am!" and from that moment on, it was hard to hear anything but the deep, deafening wail of an infuriated baby boy. I looked at Bobby in desperation, but he threw his head back and laughed. It was contagious. The unfortunate priest standing ahead of us looked up and down the line to locate the din and scowled, but there was nothing we could do. Christopher howled throughout the ceremony—he and all the other

My father and mother
on their wedding day,
June 8, 1930.

My brother Joe and I.
I was 9; he was 5 going
on 6.
(*Maurice Seymour*)

My tap solo in a dance recital.
(*Maurice Seymour*)

Mr. and Mrs. Cosmo (Gus) Allegretti, January 7, 1956.

With Larry Kert in the balcony scene from *West Side Story*, 1957. (*Fred Fehl*)

The wedding scene. (*Graphic House Inc.*)

We took *West Side Story* outdoors to shoot this scene for the album cover. (*Friedman–Abeles*)

With my parents, Mike and Rose Laraia, at the New York opening of
A View From the Bridge, 1961.
(*Friedman–Abeles*)

Robert Goulet visits me in
my dressing room at the
Schubert Theatre. He was
appearing across the street
at the Majestic in *Camelot*.
(*James Demetropoulos*)

Robert Goulet and I were
married on August 12, 1963,
at the Plaza Hotel.

(*Roy De Carava*)

Our fans thought Bobby
and I were the "perfect
couple."

Proud parents with our son Christopher, 4 months old.
(*Globe Photos*)

The day of Christopher's christening. Notice the pacifier in Bobby's hand—when it popped out of Chris's mouth and onto the floor, he howled!

Our son Michael was 10 days old and just home from the hospital. Big brother Chris (15 months) checks him out.

Halloween was always a big event in our family. We'd work for weeks on costumes and props. Here are Michael and Christopher as Wilbur and Orville Wright. I made the plane with the help of my secretary, Vince Naso.
(*Associated Press*)

Teeing off—well, almost.

Bobby and I in a scene from *Carousel*, spring 1965.
(*H. Ray Middleton*)

The Goulets on tour, 1966.

Bobby and I in a television production of *Kiss Me Kate*, 1968.

Doing a TV show with Johnny Carson.

In a television special with Donald O'Connor and Gene Kelly.

The *Dean Martin Show*.

With Johnny Mercer and Rosemary Clooney on Bing Crosby's TV show.

On the *Ed Sullivan Show*, with Bob Lone and Steve Harmon, two wonderful dancers from my nightclub act.

At the White House with President John F. Kennedy on November 20, 1963, just two days before his assassination.
(*Cecil W. Stoughton*)

The strain of our marriage was starting to show.

My sons were growing up. Mike was 14; Chris, 15 in this picture.
(*John Engstead*)

Here I am with some wonderful backup dancers from the audience.
They had never been on a stage in their lives!

In Africa with the World Vision documentary team, 1980.
(*Eric Mooneyham*)

babies ahead of him—and the priest found it necessary to shout at the top of his lungs to be heard.

Now that we were a family, I wanted to work with Bobby as much as possible because that was the only way we could be together. And with Petey to help, I began looking forward to performing again. I had taken time off during my pregnancy, because I didn't want to risk doing anything to endanger our child, but I missed the stage. As soon as my doctor said I was in excellent health, Bobby and I made plans to do *Carousel* in San Francisco.

Carousel had been a hit on Broadway some years earlier. The score by Rodgers and Hammerstein is hauntingly beautiful, and the story is dramatic, even tragic at times. But when I began to study the characterization of Julie, the role I was playing, Bobby lost patience with me.

"You don't have to be Sarah Bernhardt," he said, when I tried to analyze a scene with him. "Let's just go over the lines!"

"But we've already done that so many times!" I said.

"Oh, I suppose you already know your lines," he sneered. "And mine, too, probably."

"No," I said, trying to soothe him. "I don't. But I'm trying to figure out how my character feels about your character."

"She thinks she's too damned good for him, that's what," he said, throwing the script across the room. "She thinks he's a bum!"

"But she doesn't!" I insisted. "She loves him! She sees what's underneath that big bully facade—and she loves the little boy he doesn't dare to be!" Only then did I realize that our roles were pretty close to home.

He shook his head and laughed. "Good God, Carol, this is a musical!" He was at the bar reaching into the cupboard for a glass. It was ten o'clock in the morning.

"Bobby, wouldn't you rather have some coffee? I could make some."

"No," he said, smiling and shaking his head. "I don't want coffee. I want a drink."

Christopher and Petey came with us to San Francisco

and slept in a bedroom adjoining ours. The hotel management made quite a fuss over Christopher and provided him with a brand-new stainless steel crib, which Petey insisted on scrubbing thoroughly before she would put him in it. Christopher says he still remembers that crib—"it was like being in a jail," he says—but I don't know how that can be possible, since he was only five months old.

Bobby was drinking more than usual and he was very short-tempered. Whenever I brought Christopher near him, he waved us away. I knew why. It wasn't Christopher and it wasn't me. He was worried about his career. His first two movies had failed at the box office, so there was no hope for another. He was still in demand on TV, but he really wanted to do another Broadway show or a nightclub tour. A lot depended on what he did in *Carousel*. Yet instead of working hard to make the show a success, he was embarrassingly casual about it.

The worst possible thing happened. The reviews were split right down the middle. Critics praised me and panned Bobby.

After the show, we went up to our suite, being careful to whisper and walk lightly so we wouldn't wake Petey and Christopher in the next room. It seemed like a good idea not to mention the reviews, but I watched Bobby carefully in the mirror while I sat at my dressing table taking off my makeup. He had had a lot to drink downstairs, but at least he wasn't drinking more.

Ordinarily a good review makes me happy because it means someone recognized what I was trying to do with a role. But I got no pleasure from the *Carousel* reviews. They felt like eerie omens of trouble to come. I truly wanted Bobby to be successful. I wanted the world to know that he was more than a gorgeous face and a thrilling voice. And competitive as I can be, I would have given anything to reverse the critics' reviews.

In retrospect, I can see how difficult it must have been for Bobby to work with me. I have more of my father's stubborn, prodding pursuit of perfection than I care to admit. I have always attempted to communicate my passion for creative work to anyone who would listen—and Bobby had no choice. Since we worked and lived together, there was no way for him to escape. My unbridled high level of energy was the antithesis of his laid-back, underplaying style, and we were both impatient with our differences.

These insights came later. None of them occurred to me that night in San Francisco. I was lost in my thoughts when Bobby put his hands on my shoulders. The smile on his face was enigmatic.

We'd gone to bed and as I turned out the lights, he asked, "How'd you like the reviews?"

"Oh, you know how critics are," I said, trying to be calm. "I never pay much attention to them."

"I do," he said, "and I don't like you competing with me. I think it's time to get you off my stage."

I tried to squirm free of his hands, but he said, "Sh-h-h!" reminding me that Petey and Christopher were next door. The more I resisted him, the stronger he got. We struggled silently and I felt tears spilling down my face, "No! No! Not this way, please," I mouthed. But this way was exactly what he wanted.

I kept hoping I wasn't pregnant. I wanted our children about three years apart so that each one would have a chance to become a separate individual with a distinct identity. Besides that, the timing would be disastrous. A pregnancy was an obstacle to the resumption of my career. Broadway has a very short memory, and before *Carousel* I hadn't worked for almost a year. If I took another year off, producers would forget who I was and I might have to begin all over again. They might also say, "Who? Carol Lawrence? Oh, she's too busy having children! Let's get someone else." Producers want things to be simple.

I hadn't given up on my marriage. I knew we had problems, but who didn't? I also held on to my dream that we could become an outstanding theatrical couple. I thought of Eli Wallach and Anne Jackson, Jessica Tandy and Hume Cronyn. Why couldn't we follow in their footsteps? Did they have all these behind-the-scenes problems too? Were they keeping their public stage talents separated from their private debacles like we were? Was I being selfish and naive to think we ought to have everything we had and constant happiness, too? I didn't want to talk openly about our relationship, but I sure wished other people would talk about theirs, so I could have some frame of reference, some sense of "norm."

The hardest part of my life for the next few weeks was pretending to the world that we were still the two little figures on top of the wedding cake—because that sold tickets—and pretending to Petey and Christopher that everything was all right.

Then I thought I recognized the early signs of pregnancy but I kept hoping I was mistaken. Finally a doctor confirmed my suspicions.

My feelings were so tangled, so ambivalent. While I was furious with Bobby on the one hand, I felt like the luckiest woman I knew on the other. And while I wanted to throw myself into resuming my career, I felt an extraordinary tenderness toward the child I was carrying. Its very existence began to heal my memory of the vindictive act that had given it life. It was the child that enabled me to feel again. I wanted it to know it was loved from the moment it was born. Given that, perhaps this child could be the person his father was afraid to be.

Our son Michael was born on March 27, 1966. I had had a difficult pregnancy. Thank God, Bobby was able to be there for me. Gowned and masked in his green surgical outfit, he was in the operating room keeping everyone in hysterics with all of his bawdy jokes, while I tried conscientiously to do my Lamaze breathing effectively enough for the purpose. No luck. After ten hours of constant labor, the contractions became unbearable, and my doctor said, "The baby is too large to deliver normally—you've got to have a cesarean or you're not going to have a baby." We consented, and I was given a spinal injection in preparation for the saddle block.

Later that evening, Bobby and his buddies came by the hospital after they had been out celebrating. They were drunk and boisterous as they came down the hall toward my room. Bobby pushed his way into the nursery and picked up Michael, waving his lighted cigar in the air as the nurses tried to stop him from bringing our son to my room. I was lying flat, under strict orders not to turn over or sit up for twenty-four hours, until the effect of the spinal tap wore off, but I turned my head to see what was going on.

Bobby was too euphoric to know what he was doing or to listen to anyone's warning. Passing our baby to one of the nurses, he reached down and pulled me up into a sitting position. "What do you think of this guy?" he said proudly.

He didn't know about my spinal injection, so he didn't mean to hurt me. I would have liked to take part in his joy and their fun, but the pain started shooting through me and making me nauseous.

By then the supervisor and several nurses swept into my room, ordering everyone to leave immediately, and helped me to lie back down again.

I had migraine headaches for months. My doctor said that was a normal result of disregarding the seriousness of a spinal tap.

For days I fought to get my strength back. I had never experienced any surgery, and along with the normal depression after delivering, and migraine headaches, I was miserable. My only happy moments were feeding my son, when Bobby came to visit, and Sister Mary Margaret. St. Vincent's Hospital had a regular staff of nurses peppered with sparkling nuns in crisp white habits. Sister Mary Margaret was a lean sprite with gold-rimmed spectacles and twinkling blue eyes that validated every line of "When Irish Eyes Are Smiling." She picked up my spirits every time I heard her lilting soprano near my door. It was her delight to bring baby and bottle to each proud mom at feeding time, but her trademark was to sing a different theme song for each infant.

"For it was Mary, Mary, proud as any name can be" she'd warble to a wee baby girl, or "Liza, Liza, skies are gray."

I had figured that she'd probably carry in Michael to the strains of the rousing gospel song: "Michael, row the boat ashore, Hallelujah." I even anticipated joining her for a chorus, but no. In she came to the strains of "Hello Michael, well, hello Michael, it's so good to have you back where you belong! You're lookin' swell, Michael . . ." She seemed brimming with joy, and charmed everyone.

On the third day, she was quite late on her rounds to my room and I got worried. Then she bounded in, a bit out of breath, but singing: "Hello, Michael" and not missing a beat. She handed Mike and his formula over and said in her rhythmic brogue, "Sure and that's a big boy you have there in Michael and I'm not wantin' to be tellin' tales out o' school, you know, but . . ."

"What is it, Sister?"

"Well it's him that made me late this mornin'. He's the biggest bruiser in the whole nursery you know, and so he gets hungry long before the others. And lets us know about it too! So, I'm always runnin' to feed him a little early. Then I collect any milk that the wee ones can't finish and give him an extra bonus as it were. Well as I was changin' him I held him straight in front of me and he began to laugh at me in such a darlin' fashion that I couldn't help joinin' in. Well, to my surprise and with perfect aim, he proceeded to pee all over me brand-new white habit from top to bottom . . . still laughin' all the while. Of course, I had to go back and change my whole outfit and *that's* why we're late."

I had to hold back my laughter because of my stitches, but I'd hear others down the hall laugh freely as she recounted her adventures with Michael to them.

A couple of days later I was to be released. I began to put on a soft pink dress I knew would hide the cumbersome, stiff, mummy-wrapped corset that started at the top of my thighs and ended at my waist. It acted as a support to keep the new stitches of the C-section mending properly. I was thrilled to be out of a hospital gown and on my way home. The nurses and nuns were supporting and tender as they eased me into the wheelchair and placed the blue-bundled Michael in my arms. Sister Mary Margaret had scraped every spare ounce into his bottle and he slept like an angel. Gorgeous from birth, Michael looked like the cherub-cheeked ad for Gerber's baby food, and that unique ecstasy reserved for new mothers swelled my spirit to overflowing.

Bobby arrived at the maternity ward surrounded by buzzing nurses, ambulatory patients and their visitors eager for autographs. He had signed me out and wheeled me to a waiting swarm of reporters and flashing photographers. The usual expected questions were flung at us, and we tried to liven the answers with wit and quickly turned puns and phrases. We were used to this routine. Finally, we were in Bobby's Stutz, homeward bound. I hadn't seen Chris for five days and ached to hold him in my arms, I was forbidden to carry him or even lift him for fear of rupturing the stitches in my incision. What confusion for his sixteen-month-old psyche.

I couldn't run to him, swoop him up over my head, whirl him around or hug him to my heart with gleeful squeals of "How's my Chrissy . . . Oh how I've missed you!" Neither could there be the half a million kisses and tickles and a romping roll on the floor. Instead, Chris had to wait for me to be seated in a straight-backed chair and then be placed haltingly on my lap and told he could hug Mommy but "gently . . . no, *gently* Chris!" The crowning blow came when Dad brought in a squirming puppy—or *something*—in a blanket, which every familiar face immediately focused on and began cheering, cooing and exclaiming over. Just yesterday all this tomfoolery had belonged to Chris alone, and as I kissed him and felt his little arms tighten around my neck, I longed to reassure him that there was more than enough love and attention and approval to share with his brother. But he was only an infant, and sibling rivalry was a painful reality we would have to deal with for years to come.

My incredibly wise and sensitive nanny, Petey, sensed my fatigue and picked Chris up from my lap and helped me climb the stairs to the bedroom. I went straight to bed and fell into the best sleep I'd had in a long time.

When I awakened, it was sometime during the night, and a dim light from a lamp helped me to remember that I was home. Bobby was lying in bed next to me, and I snuggled against him. I felt him stiffen.

"Something wrong?" I asked.

"Maybe," he said.

"Can I help?"

"Yes, as a matter of fact, you can."

"How?"

"By giving me a divorce."

I sat up and looked at him, sure this was his idea of a joke. "Are you being funny?" I asked. "We just brought our son home from the hospital today."

He didn't even blink. "I love someone else."

Whether it was the exhaustion from the week, the continuing migraines, the postpartum depression, the relief of being safe and secure in my own home—whatever, they all began to collide. My coping mechanisms were paralyzed or nonexistent, and my body began to scream NOOOOOOO. I had no control over myself. The sound didn't belong to me, it seemed to be coming from someone else, some entirely irrational place, until all of a sudden, the wracking sobs were pierced by a pain that felt as if either my heart or my stitches were bursting.

"Ooh God, help me!"

"Carol, I . . ."

"No . . . no." I tried to stop crying, for I couldn't stand to make the pain, physical or emotional, worse—my life was more than I could cope with as it was.

From then on, I had only vague, dreamlike memories of the gentle touches of Bobby and Petey soothing me and redressing my bandages. Several days later, I was up and around.

In his book *The Road Less Traveled*, M. Scott Peck discusses our propensity to bury a problem for which we have no solutions. I did exactly that, and Bobby didn't bring up the subject of divorce again. But as Murphy's Law would have it, there was always one more thing that could go wrong. It had to do with Bobby's television series, *Blue Light*, in which he played an undercover agent. It wasn't renewed.

Then his manager, Norman Rosemont, convinced him to return to the Plaza Hotel's Persian Room, where he had been such a success a few years earlier. Bobby liked the idea. It didn't bother him that the Persian Room needed him as much as he needed a change of scene. Clubs weren't doing well anymore, and some of the best ones had closed. Getting Robert Goulet to appear was a coup for Norman, because he had just been appointed booking agent for the Plaza.

By then, nightclub acts had changed. They had become extravaganzas with backup singers, sets, innovative lighting, contemporary hits, special material, patter and humor customized for each performer. Nothing had been created for Bobby's return to the scene of his nightclub debut.

"At least put a new act together!" I said when it became obvious to me that he was going to do the same old show.

"Why?" he said. "They loved me before."

"Of course, they did! But this is now! People remember what kind of songs you sang the first time, so you have to do something different. You have to surprise them—that's what audiences want."

"Norman knows what he's doing—and he wouldn't let me do anything wrong. So shut up, damn it!"

His return to the Plaza was widely publicized and I could feel the anticipation in the audience the night he opened. It was a sellout crowd, with every critic sitting at ringside. Bobby opened his act with "If Ever I Should Leave You" from *Camelot*, just as he had before—and I could see from the look on his face that he realized almost immediately that he was making a terrible mistake. The audience was disappointed, even indignant, and they let him know it. There was no electricity between him and them, and the applause at the end of each song was barely polite. When Bobby left the floor and walked among the tables, singing to the women, they stared back at him, unimpressed.

The hotel management had arranged a party after the show for reviewers and special guests, and they asked me to act as hostess. I forced myself to smile as I stood near the door, greeting the guests as they came in. Most of them were not smiling, and one of the critics whispered to me, "Your husband has one helluva nerve coming back here with a warmed-over act! How could you let him do that?"

Later, when we went upstairs to our room, Bobby was very quiet. I went into the bathroom to take a hot bath, and

I heard something over the noise of the running water. I looked into the bedroom and saw Bobby sitting on the bed with his head in his hands. He was crying.

I put my arms around him. "Darling, please! It'll be all right," I said.

"No, it won't!" he groaned. "I'm washed up! I'm a has-been!"

"That's not true!" I said. "You have so much talent!"

"Who's going to believe that now?" he said.

"I do. A lot of people do! You'll never be washed up. You just had a setback. We all have those."

He turned to me and shook his head. Then he put his arms around me and held on as if he were a child afraid of the dark. I knew the next day, when the reviews came out, would be even worse for him, and I was glad I had decided to come with him to New York. I was just sorry his hopes had backfired so badly.

He was afraid, and I knew why. His own success was so extraordinary, and it had come so swiftly that he was afraid it would disappear in the same way. And if it did, he didn't know how to get it back. He had no confidence in his own talent. I understood how he felt because I had dealt with the same fears myself. I had made some bad decisions too, and had had to suffer the consequences. I had done things under pressure that I didn't like to remember.

Bobby didn't know how to reach out for help. When he was frightened, he wanted to hit something. Or someone. But maybe now he could begin to realize that I was on his side, and that the only thing I wanted was to love him.

I was back to Square One: whatever was wrong, I could fix it.

Chapter Nine

For a while after the Persian Room disaster, Bobby thought his career was over. So did his manager. Norman told Bobby he had no future in the United States and suggested he tour Australia, where he had a glowing reputation, but had never appeared. During the next several years he went on tours all over the world, and he found that he could still draw an audience back home. As often as possible, the boys and I went with him when he traveled.

Whenever I see a young mother with toddlers squirming in and out of her grasp, juggling a plastic-coated diaper bag and tote full of playthings, I know exactly how she feels. I'm not complaining about squirming children or the games a mother has to invent to keep them attentive—that was the fun part for me. Having a nanny made it possible for me to have my sons with me while I kept my career going, but I'm a hands-on kind of mother and I enjoyed my children enormously.

Bobby's tours often took him overseas, so he was away for long periods of time, but I took the boys with me when I went on the road. I wanted them to see what I did when I was away from home. We traveled like pioneers, except that our covered wagon was a U-Haul. It was chock-full of all the necessities for two toddlers: a refrigerator, hot plates, two cribs, two highchairs, a playpen, inflatable toys, regular toys, a portable turntable, records and tons of their favorite books. Whenever possible I'd cook our meals wherever we happened to be staying. Maybe it wasn't typical of the way most performers traveled, but having the boys along made it fun for me. While I was performing, they would stay with their nanny, but the rest of our time was spent together. We saw every museum, every historical site along the way, plus sights that some people might have thought ordinary, but which were very special to us. For instance, smokestacks.

Michael loved factories with smokestacks. When he was about eighteen months old, he couldn't connect the letter "s" with anything that came after it, so when we passed a factory he'd get all excited and say, "Mommy, Mommy, look! A 'moke 'tack!"

Christopher, being fifteen months older and proud of his command of English, would turn and say, "Michael, how many times do I have to tell you? It's s-s-mokes-s-tack." to which Michael would respond, "Good Chrissy, you see the 'moke 'tack too?"

When I was on tour with *Funny Girl*, I decided it was time for the boys to see me from the audience. Before a matinee, they were in my dressing room and saw me in my opening scene costume, a beautiful beaded, "Roaring Twenties" type of coat, with a cloche on my head. I was Fanny Brice, the star, very glamorous. I kissed Chris and Mike, sent them out front with their nanny and got ready to go on. What I didn't consider was that in the course of the first scene I underwent a complete transformation in appearance. In a flashback, Fanny Brice the star had to turn into Fanny Brice the aspiring child, right before the audience's eyes. It happened in seconds. Off came the cloche and down came the pigtails; off came the beaded coat, leaving me in knickers and a middy blouse. In one quick turn I was wearing horn-rimmed glasses. And when I opened my mouth I was the raucous, brash, young Fanny Brice who wanted only one thing—to be on the stage—and she was gruff with anyone who doubted her ability to make it.

As young Fanny, I was confronting a character named Mrs. Strakosh. "I'll show you, Mrs. Strakosh!" I said, and with that I heard the most wonderful, outrageously loud child's voice screaming in the audience, "Where's my *Mommy*?"

"Sh-h-h!" I heard his nanny say. "That's your Mommy, with the glasses."

"No!" Christopher insisted. "That's not my Mommy! Who took my Mommy? Where did she *go*?"

We were performing in a theater-in-the-round and everyone in the audience could see him. By then they realized whose child he was and they chuckled appreciatively, knowing there was nothing I could do. Poor Christopher would not be consoled and had to be carried screaming out of the theater.

I needed a moment to get back into character. I was so touched that I was crying and laughing at the same time.

Sometimes we drove as much as five hundred miles on our day off when the show moved to another city, but that was a pleasure. We took our time and enjoyed the view. Once we were driving at night and the moon was especially bright. Christopher was up front with me and Michael was in the back enjoying his favorite pastime—eating. In fact, Michael was becoming rather chubby.

"Mom, why is there a moon?" Christopher suddenly asked me. He was at that inquisitive age.

"Well, Christopher," I said, wondering just how much science he could handle, "you know how the sun lights up the daytime sky, don't you?"

"Sure," he said, as if that was kid stuff. Then I began to wonder how much science I could handle. Anyway, I decided to simplify.

"It's the moon's job to light up the nighttime sky—the same as it's the sun's job to light up the daytime sky."

Christopher nodded and seemed satisfied. But from the back seat came the crackling sound of a pretzel bag as Michael, his mouth full, seriously intoned, "And it's *my* job to eat!"

How fast those years went! And all the time I realized that once the boys went to school I could no longer take them with me. I began to plan for ways I could work closer to home.

Running three households—we now had homes in Las Vegas and Wyoming, as well as in California—and managing all the people required to take care of them took a lot of my time. Bobby wanted no part of management. His job was acquiring property and my job was looking after it. If someone had to be hired, that was my job. If someone had to be fired, that was my job, too, because Bobby never wanted to be the bad guy. Neither did I, but somebody had to do it.

It would be easy for me to blame my exhausting schedule on the demands Bobby made on me, except, you see, he didn't make demands. We both simply expected that a wife would do certain things. Like most ex-wives, I look back now and think he wanted a woman who did nothing but see to his needs and his comfort, a woman who never complained, never asked for anything in return, never criticized or found fault, a woman who absolutely worshipped him. But then many women want that in a husband.

I didn't know what a wife ought to be. I assumed that a woman found that out when she married the man she loved and tried to make him happy. Whatever he wanted her to be, that's what she became. And if she wanted something else, something for herself, she had to put in overtime to get it. I was trying to be the woman Bobby wanted, but she was very much at odds with the person I really was— and with the mother I was, and with the performer I was trying to become. So, of course, I fell short of all my goals because they conflicted with each other.

I have not been active in the feminist movement, but I have great respect and appreciation for the help both men and women, husbands and wives, have derived from the attention the feminists have focused on relationships. I like the idea of seeking a healthy relationship by encouraging the partners to be fully accomplished individuals, able to pursue their own goals and yet to mutually negotiate the support and expressions of love they each need from the other. From this basis of strength and understanding, happy homes and confident children can be produced, to heal and end the cycles of dysfunction that author John Bradshaw so brilliantly describes in *The Family.*

Helpful as all this is to me now, it was not available information to me at the time, so I continued to blunder through my best efforts, trying to juggle everything perfectly, which was enough to drive anyone nuts.

Looking after Bobby took a great deal of my time. I bought all his clothes, with the exception of his suits. I showered him with presents to make him smile, and to prove how much I loved him. I went on tour with him as often as I could, even when we weren't performing together, so that he and the boys and I could be a family. Bobby was losing that wonderful ability to laugh and to enjoy life, so I kept trying to think of new ways to amuse him and keep his mind off his career. I'd tell him funny anecdotes about something Mike or Chris said, or I'd act out the scenario of a play I'd seen. With all the required time apart I tried every way I knew to make our time together happy, since we knew another separation would be coming up.

His first Australian tour had been a tremendous success. I could hear it in his voice the night he called me near the end of it. "Instead of going straight home," he said, "I thought we might take a vacation."

"Great!" I said. "Where to?"

He made up the tour on the spot. "Let's see—we'll go to Hong Kong, Tokyo and Venice, and Paris, then New York, and home."

It seemed like a wonderful idea—an opportunity for a second honeymoon, I thought. Unfortunately, we should have checked it out with a travel agent before we started, because it was winter, and for good reason few vacation in these places in winter. Australia and California were warm at that time of year, so we didn't think in terms of heavy coats.

"I'll meet you in Hong Kong," Bobby said.

The minute I arrived, my teeth began to chatter because it was freezing. At the hotel, I found out Bobby hadn't checked in yet, so to surprise him, I went to a gift shop and came back with my arms filled with ceremonial candles and incense. I set them all around the room and lit them, then I settled in to enjoy their flickering, fragrant beauty.

It was late afternoon when Bobby landed. I was as excited as I used to be in the old days, anticipating our time together. But the moment I heard his key in the lock I knew he was drunk. Maybe he wasn't terribly drunk, I thought. Maybe just a little wobbly, but still able to enjoy being together in a strange country, in a room filled with exotic scents.

"Hi," he said when he saw me. It was a feeble greeting and he was unsteady on his feet. He was wearing his dark glasses, a sure sign of a hangover.

The only thing I could do was help him into bed. The next day he didn't remember the incense or the candles, or even how I came to be there.

We went on to Tokyo, which also was bitterly cold, but we had a wonderful time with a Japanese guide named Hari M. Hata who kept us moving. We went to the No Theater, to the Kabuki Theater, to operas and concerts, and then on to Kyoto and Nico. We took long train rides through the beautiful Japanese countryside too. One late afternoon, when we left an ancient temple, we both were so cold and hungry that we begged Hari to take us to someplace warm. To our horror, he took us to dinner in what looked like a paper house. There was no heat in it and the doors were wide open, but Hari told us to sit down on the floor as a gracious woman brought out a small cooking utensil and knelt down to prepare our meal. In a very short time the room took on heat from the sukiyaki being cooked—and, helped quite a bit by the spicy ingredients, we began to peel off the layers of clothing we wore. By the end of our first course we were cozy and comfortable.

We got to know Hari a little better that evening. He told us he was recently married. His wife had been chosen by his father and she didn't cook. His mother-in-law lived with them, he said. "Mother-in-law cook," he explained. "Wife no cook." He said no more about either of them, but he was intrigued when Bobby told him that he and I had married because we loved each other. I was deeply touched by the way Bobby said that.

We moved so quickly on our vacation that I never got around to buying more appropriate clothing. I hadn't brought any boots with me, and Europe was damp as well as cold. In Venice, it caught up with me. I got deathly ill and spent three days in bed, unable to break a 104° temperature. It was a terrible strain of European flu and I felt like I was going to die. The honeymoon turned into a disaster. I went home, still sick, and Bobby went on to Paris where we had arranged to meet his daughter from his previous marriage.

During my recuperation I had a lot of time to think about my career. Although I enjoyed working with Bobby, I felt I was losing my professinal identity. I wasn't "Miss Carol Lawrence" anymore; I was " . . . and Carol Lawrence." I needed to remind producers that I could do more than play the happy wife of Robert Goulet. Summer stock was the best way to do it, so I took on some roles that gave me an opportunity to demonstrate my versatility. I did *The Unsinkable Molly Brown* and *Funny Girl*. These productions got me back to Broadway, where I replaced Mary Martin in *I Do! I Do!*, with Gordon McRae replacing Robert Preston. But I did these shows over a period of years, and I didn't develop my career as intensely as I did when I was younger and single. I had other compelling interests—and a few concerns.

The rigors of being a gypsy on tour again took its toll physically, but with them came funny moments that thankfully distracted me from dwelling on the painful truth that my home was torn in two.

To illustrate, in a summer stock tour of *Molly Brown*, we arrived at the enormous civic auditorium in Atlanta for rehearsals and were following a company of *Hello Dolly*. The horseshoe ramp on which Dolly sings the title song framed the orchestra pit and was still up. So I asked if we could use it for Molly's opening song, "I Ain't Down Yet." The ramp was very narrow but had the power to bring the hopeful little dynamo within inches of the audience—and that's my favorite theatrical device.

Perhaps the mightiest anthem for any youngster striving to lift himself out of the muck and mire of his circumstances is Molly's first song. The event that kicks off the song is a beating she unfairly gets from her three older brothers, who never stop teasing her about her unattainable dreams of rising from the squalor in which they live. They ask:

"Who do you think you *are*?"

"Why I can be anybody . . . even a queen ifin' I wanted to!"

In mock tribute, they give her a broom as her scepter, an old quilt as her royal cape and a tin bucket inverted over her head as her crown. She then leads her three "courtiers" onto the ramp in a triumphant last marching chorus. It certainly worked opening night, for it nearly stopped the show. But the boy who put the bucket on my head was an understudy and was too gentle—so it almost fell off several times. Since both my hands were occupied I couldn't adjust it. Before the second night's performance, I asked my new "brother" to be really firm and push the bucket onto my head so it would stay on. My oh my, did *he* take direction well! The bucket was shoved onto my head with such force that it completely covered my eyes and rested on the bridge of my nose.

I wasn't sure we'd ever get it off—but *more* importantly, it left me with the tiny space between the rim of the bucket over my nose and my cheeks as my only peephole. If I tipped my head all the way back I could just barely see ahead of me, and by bobbing my head up and down I kept the floor in sight. With such handicaps, you'd think I wouldn't even consider going out on the precariously narrow ramp fifteen feet above the concrete floor of the orchestra pit. Right? But . . . NO!! Out I strode for three mighty steps, and then disaster struck! My left foot missed the ramp and I teetered into the pit. My sense of time went into a warped mode and it was like a dream in triple slow motion. I could see my body as if I weren't in it, turning head over broom over tin bucket . . . bouncing off the wall and crashing into shiny gold instruments, music stands, brown chairs and a tornado of flying pages of music—not to mention tuxedoed musicians. Heaven broke my fall with soft, though unwilling, bodies, and when my senses returned to reality I was bombarded with a barrage of four-letter words strung so tightly together that even Lenny Bruce would have blushed.

I had completely wiped out the entire saxophone section, and the priceless tools of their trade were paramount in their minds, way above personal injury—theirs *or* mine. The rest of the orchestra was racing through the number, and all I could think of was getting back up on the ramp. I grabbed a chair, put it against the wall, stood on it, jumped high enough to get a good grip of the ramp's edge and, grunting, chinned myself up.

When I had fallen in, the whole audience gasped with a disappointed falling inflection, "OHHHHHhhhh." Like when a football misses the space between the goal posts.

Now, as if rising like a Phoenix, my head, shoulders, torso and knee surfaced from nowhere and as if on cue, the audience reversed their tune in amazement. "Ohhh-HHHHH???!?" On my feet and motioning to my dumbstruck brothers, I yelled, "Come on, follow me!" We jumped into the middle of the song and returned to the center of the stage for a rousing finish pose. DaDA!!!

Needless to say, *this* time we stopped the show cold! When the applause had finally waned, I walked, in character, to the edge of the stage and peering down at the saxophone section called, "Are ye al'right down there?" And not waiting for an answer, with thumbs up, I yelled to the audience, "He's *fine!*" Well, that stopped the show AGAIN. My brain raced gleefully, "It's only seven minutes into the show and we stopped it twice! Why couldn't we just put a mattress down there and keep the bit in?" It sounded like a great idea while my adrenaline was at its height—only when I got into the wings did I see how many places I was cut and scraped and how many bruises I'd sustained. It was a few days later, when I was at the pool with Chris and Mike, that Michael said, "You know, Mom, you look like a little Dalmation puppy." And he was right.

I loved being a mother, watching two infant boys grow into distinctly different personalities. Once, when I was working at Top of the World in Orlando, Florida, I saw an artist demonstrating oil painting on a TV program, and on impulse, I called the studio and asked for the woman's telephone number. I got in touch with her and asked if she could possibly come to our hotel and give us a few basic lessons in painting, something I'd always wanted to learn but had never had time for. She said she would be delighted. Between shows for the next few days, Chris and Mike and I worked on our oil paintings side by side at a round table with three small easels where we could compare each adventurous stroke. We still treasure those paintings as well as the experience of doing them together. They're quite simple as far as technique goes, but they say a lot about us as a family.

At times Bobby would take the boys hiking and exploring the rustic hillsides around our home. The natural brush was thick and thorny with outcroppings of rock, and the incline was very steep. Sliding down was fun, but the long trek back up to the house was exhausting. Once when they were four and five years old, the boys started climbing up, Bobby pushing Chris up to a safe ledge and then shoving Michael up behind him. This went on for some time until Bobby turned to help Michael but found he was lagging way behind. When Bobby asked him what he was waiting for, Michael called back, "A bus, I think."

As you might suspect, Bobby and I were not entirely in accord on child-rearing techniques. I was inconsistent, volatile and no doubt overprotective. I considered him to be distant and harsh. He said he didn't want his sons to grow up with any doubts about their masculinity. But I felt he went too far in that direction. When Chris or Mike fell down, Bobby would be furious with me if I rushed to comfort him. "Don't pick them up!" he would shout at me. "You're turning them into faggots!" He absolutely forbade them to cry, no matter how much they hurt.

And there were the guns. Bobby loved guns and owned many of them. At night, at home, he slept with a loaded, cocked rifle and a .45 magnum both lying on the floor beside the bed. I never dared go to the bathroom in the night for fear of being taken for a burglar, but worse than that, I feared Chris and Mike might have a nightmare and come into the bedroom unannounced.

"Why the guns?" I used to ask him.

"This is a rotten, dangerous world," he would tell me, "and you never know who's going to come over that hill to get us."

This deeply disturbed me. Regardless of how many members of the National Rifle Association should side with Bobby against me, I've never understood how we can be more peaceful by bearing arms against each other.

Bobby liked to play golf, and one day when he came home from the course he said, "Guess who I played with?"

"I can't," I said, "Who?"

"Pat Boone."

"Oh?"

He dug in his pocket for a wrinkled piece of paper and handed it to me. There, in his handwriting, were the words, "Bel Air Pres."

"What does it mean?" I asked him.

"It's the name of a church, Bel Air Presbyterian Church," he said. "You told me you wanted Chris and Mike to go to Sunday school."

For several years I had drifted away from the Catholic Church because I felt wrapped in rigid rules, taboos and guilt. Nowhere could I find a sense of forgiveness and relief. I had not yet heard of priests like Matthew Fox, who teach wonder, celebration and gratitude as the basis of our experience of God and the world, rather than sin and guilt. His book *Original Blessing* tells us that we are miracles of God's creation and creativity—truly blessings—and that God's spirit, divinity and love are within each of us. How

different my life, home and marriage would have been—and
the world for that matter—if those had been the precepts
on which we all were raised. I would never have needed
another church.

As it was, I had been longing and searching for a different kind of faith, one that would comfort me, that would fo-
cus my attention on creation, beauty, wonder and miracles
instead of on my weaknesses and chastising me for them.
That was the reason I hadn't had Michael baptized early in
his infancy. I didn't want him to be brought up as a Catholic,
but I didn't see any alternative, so when my mother and father later demanded that he be baptized at the age of one, I
said, "Okay, if it means that much to you, then do it. I'm
sorry—I can't participate." But the boys were older now and
going to school, and I wanted them to have some religious
instruction, so I had been asking people about Sunday
schools. It didn't matter what the church denomination
was, because I didn't know much about those things.

I was grateful for Bobby's interest. "I think I'll go to a
service there this Sunday," I said. "Want to go with me?"

"Not on your life," he said.

So I went to the Bel Air Presbyterian Church, which
wasn't far from where we lived. I had never attended a worship service in anything but a Catholic church, which is
ritualistic and formal. I was unprepared for the warmth and
spontaneity I found in this new congregation. The music
was so different from what I had known! The choir and the
congregation sang gospel songs in ordinary words that described ordinary human feelings and problems while the
rhythm drew us all together. When I walked in, I didn't know
anyone there, but by the time I left I felt as if I were in my
mother's arms. And the minister, instead of warning us of
God's displeasure, talked about God's love! Not only that—
he spoke about Jesus Christ as if he really was a friend. I
had never known about this kind of religion, and I wanted
to learn more. On my way out, I enrolled Christopher and
Michael in Sunday school and myself in a Bible study course.
My appetite for this totally new approach to God was rav-
enous. After so many years of restlessness and discontent,

I was finally getting what I needed from my faith: a sense of God's presence. It was to change my life completely, although not immediately.

It was satisfying to realize that God loved me, but it was very difficult to hold on to that conviction when things weren't going well. Have you noticed that in your life? I kept thinking that if I didn't do everything right, God would stop loving me. I hadn't come far enough to believe, beyond any doubt, that God loved me no matter what I did or didn't do. So when Bobby and I had problems I was under twice as much pressure to solve them, because now I wasn't trying to please only my mother, my father and my husband, but God as well. It was much later when I began to understand that I could neither earn God's love nor lose it. He simply gave it to me—for keeps.

I respected Bobby's right not to want to go to church. For years I had felt the same way. But I wanted him to share in this wholly new joy somehow, so I asked if he'd enjoy having Pat and Shirley Boone and the minister and his wife, Donn and Carol Moomaw, over for dinner. He jumped on this idea with unexpected enthusiasm.

Dinner was as usual: a feast with candlelight and warm hospitality. We sat in the soft glow: the conversation was scintillating and fun. Then Shirley laughed, "Oh, if that isn't the perfect illustration of John 3:16." Then she turned to Donn, who said, "Exactly, and it brings to mind II Corinthians 9:15." Bobby looked at me and crossed his eyes quizzically, as though I should be able to explain it. I hadn't the foggiest, so I shrugged my shoulders and went to the kitchen for more garlic bread. It sounded as simple and flowing as the beautiful French phrases that Bobby sprinkled into his conversations, but in our ignorance, this Biblical shorthand could have come from Mars for all we knew. After our guests left, Bobby and I were hysterical over this brand-new language with which we were totally unfamiliar.

However, aside from making me laugh, the obvious comfort it provided the four of them set in me a longing to know what they knew, and experience the relevance to my life that the Bible obviously held to theirs. If I live to be a thousand I will never forget the evenings Pat and Shirley spent surrounding Bobby and me with their friendship, counsel and prayer. They put their love in action, and we both felt it.

I wanted Bobby to go to church with me, and every now and then he did. He enjoyed the service and the music and especially Donn Moomaw's sermons. He shook hands with everyone on the way out, but as far as I knew, that was the end of it. Once, however, he went to a different church without me, and when he came home he mentioned, rather casually, that he had gone up to the altar when the minister asked new converts to come forward.

"You *did*?" I said. "Oh, Bobby, how wonderful!"

"Well, I wanted to help him out," he said.

"What do you mean?" I asked. "Help him *how*?"

"I thought if I went up, probably a lot of other people would, too. It's like priming the pump."

Several times after that I heard stories about Bobby showing up in different churches, and going up to the altar when a minister gave the call to come forward. Once he even took Christopher and Michael with him, and the woman who told me about it was so happy that he had "brought not only himself but his sons to the Lord."

When I questioned him about it, Bobby said, "No, of course I wasn't serious, but the priest—or whatever you call him—"

"The minister."

"Right, the minister. Anyway, all through his sermon he kept looking at me as if he really wanted me to do something. So, when he gave all that talk about coming forward, I thought I'd back him up. I wanted to encourage him."

I've always wondered if he was *really* moved in some of these services and just needed to cover up with me by sounding cavalier, afraid to seem vulnerable. I mean, why would he even have gone in the first place, if he wasn't looking for something? But today, I can only wish him well in his life, and get back to working on my own.

My own exploration into faith was quite different. I had joined a women's prayer group in Bel Air Presbyterian

Church. I was getting the kind of support I needed to face up to Bobby's and my deteriorating relationship. For the first time in my marriage I was able to talk about our problems in complete confidence and without fear of judgment. We were just a group of women asking God to help us deal with situations that were more than we could handle by ourselves. For me, that wasn't always easy because I was so eager to jump in and do everything by myself, and that often created more problems than it solved. But gradually I was learning to be more open to sorrow, and to God, and to loving gestures from friends.

As Colleen Townsend Evans says in her book *A New Joy*, "Happy is the woman who honestly faces her loss and opens herself up to sorrow in her life and in her world. Because she trusts God to come to her and heal her wounded spirit, she finds a new and deeper meaning in His presence . . . He is there in the loving gestures of the friends who walk close beside her . . ."

In the meantime, another actor, himself a recovering alcoholic, recognized Bobby's symptoms for what they were. "Your husband is an alcoholic, my dear," he told me, after watching Bobby's behavior during rehearsal for a show we were in. "There is nothing you can do to help him, and the sooner you realize that, the better it will be for both of you."

"You're not serious, are you?" I said, stunned. Somehow, the word "alcoholic" couldn't apply to *my* husband.

"I am," he said. "But don't take my word for it. Why don't you come to an Alcoholics Anonymous meeting with me and hear it from others?"

A few nights later I sat with him and listened to the members—all alcoholics. In testimonies, they talked openly of their anguished experiences: their inability to stop drinking once they started, the blackouts, the violent changes in their moods, their desperate insistence that someone else was the cause of all their problems, the manipulation and the dependence, the distortion of reality, the beguiling charm they could turn on to get their way, and the rage that followed when they didn't.

"It's a disease," they told me. "You don't cause it, you

can't control it, and you can't cure it." I didn't have to say a word—they told me what was going on in Bobby's and my life. I left that night with more information and more questions than I'd ever had.

"But what *can* I do?" I asked my actor friend when he saw me to my car.

"Go to an Al-Anon meeting," he said. "That's for relatives and friends of alcoholics—because they need help too. Chances are you're aiding his alcoholism without knowing it."

During that time I was doing eight shows a week, so I didn't take his advice right away. And I was stuck in my old patterns of behavior, thinking I could *do* something. Going to a meeting didn't seem like enough. So I made an appointment with a Los Angeles psychiatrist who specialized in treating alcoholics and their families. After listening to me through several visits, he concluded that Bobby was possibly in the advanced stages of alcoholism. When I told him about the guns, and being with Bobby when he drove down the road on the wrong side at high speeds, he said, "One way or another, he could kill you and your children." He asked me if I thought Bobby would agree to come in and talk to him.

"It won't be easy," I said, "but I'll try."

When I wanted to discuss anything serious with Bobby, I used to write him letters, some as long as eighteen pages. It was the only way I could finish what I was trying to say without his walking out on me. I took a lot of time writing the letter about the psychiatrist's request, and I tried to make it clear that we were not going to talk about *his* problem but *ours*—which was true. If anything, I was still searching for the key to making Bobby happy, because I was convinced that if he were happy, all our troubles would go away. To my surprise, Bobby was cooperative. He agreed to see the psychiatrist with me.

Knowing Bobby's drinking schedule, I made the appointment for the morning. But as we were leaving, Bobby went to the bar and pulled out a large mug with "Camelot" stamped on it and filled it to the brim with vodka. He brought it with him out to the car and climbed in the driver's seat. By the time we arrived at the doctor's office twenty-five minutes later, the mug was empty.

Bobby was at his cordial best meeting the doctor, but after a few minutes of polite conversation he said, "May I have a drink?"

"Of course," the doctor said. "What would you like? Coffee? Tea? Ginger ale? A diet soda . . .?"

Bobby smiled, "No, no," he said, shaking his head. "I mean a *drink*. Vodka, scotch—something like that."

"I'm sorry," the doctor said. "I can't give you anything alcoholic."

"Then I can't stay," Bobby said. The smile was still in place as he stood up, offered his hand to the doctor and walked out. Once again my hopes had gone up—and then plummeted. Alcoholics are expert manipulators, but I didn't know that then. I kept asking myself what I had done wrong.

Finally, I went to an Al-Anon meeting. What I desperately needed was to be included; to be held, understood and counseled by someone who really knew what I was going through, including (or maybe especially) the things I was still denying.

My first experience there was a composite of emotions. I was terrified that I would be recognized, with the resulting whispers that accompany celebrity status. On the other hand, I was anxious—as all performers are—that perhaps I wouldn't be recognized. I also felt nervous about the implied admission I was making to the world just by being there. All of this was combined, oddly enough, with some of the most uncontrollable belly laughs I'd had in years.

That night we all sat in a small classroom, grown-ups cramped into those silly one-armed chairs that made teeth-jarring noises when we tried unsuccessfully to adjust our oversized frames. You could easily spot the "regulars" who hugged and cheered each other for making it through the week. They stood in clusters. My friend and I sat apprehensively waiting for the school bell to signal class time, but instead a middle-aged woman wearing an old sweater, blue jeans and a wry crooked smile, twinkled her eyes at me and opened the meeting.

"Hi everybody, my name's Patsy." Everyone but us rookies, chimed, "Hi, Patsy."

"Since I saw you last week, lots has happened! Sam, as you know, is my recovering alcoholic husband who's been in the program for two years. Well, we got a call while watching TV that our son George had been in an auto accident and that our signatures were necessary before they could do surgery on him.

"We got to the hospital as they were wheeling George into the operating room. Don't you know, Sam runs over to the gurney, grabs George and starts shaking him while screaming, 'You son of a bitch! You should know better than to drink and drive! You dirty son of a bitch!'

"Now I'm pounding on Sam's back, yelling 'Stop that, you damn fool—he's unconscious. You'll really kill him. Stop Sam, please!'

"It took a team of interns to pull me off Sam and Sam off George. Then Sam ran out of the place crying his eyes out.

"I signed the papers and waited in the hall for hours until the doctors said everything possible had been done and that George was holding his own. Thank God!

"Just before dawn, I drove into the garage and went inside. As I passed the big window in the living room, something in the yard caught my eye. There was Sam, spread-eagle on his face in the middle of the lawn—dead drunk. And there I stood in the middle of July, in Burbank California, praying for a blizzard!"

The whole room laughed, and Patsy laughed loudest of all. Her humor gave us the encouragement and strength to try to emulate her honesty in our fledgling efforts to face our own experiences.

Today, I look back on the front lawn of my own life and see it strewn with countless bodies—relationships I have mishandled, trusts turned into betrayals, mistakes realized too late, violence to body and soul I didn't think I could survive, and crumbled goals that used to be childhood dreams. Like Patsy, I could pray for a blizzard, or I could face and examine the events and choices that led to all that debris, and pray for "the courage to change what can be changed, the serenity to accept what can't, and the wisdom to know the difference."

The warmth with which I was welcomed at that first Al-Anon meeting and the counsel the heads of AA and famous stars gave me was overwhelming. I was so grateful, that when they asked if I would be willing to entertain at their annual convention in Palm Springs, I jumped at the chance as a way to say thank-you. It was the year that Betty Ford was the guest of honor of the gala. I walked out on stage, and the first thing I said was, "My name is Carol, and unless I were a member of Al-Anon I wouldn't be able to stand up here and sing and dance." The cheers and stomping were thunderous. Their approval was close to the sound of the opening night of *West Side*.

Right after the show a very illustrious and respected actor (in my opinion one of the finest alive today) called me and said, "If ever I can be of any help, please don't hesitate to call anytime, at any hour. I want to be there for you. Here are my home, office and private phone numbers." I did call him to ask him to talk to Bobby on New Year's Day, when I had to narrate the Rose Bowl Parade on TV. He arrived very early in the morning, cooked Bobby breakfast, and walked and talked with him for hours. As I drove up the driveway in the early afternoon, he was getting in his car to leave. I was hopeful about their time together until he said, "He's not ready, Carol, not by a long shot."

I needed more encouragement and insight into my situation, and I got it from others at the Al-Anon meetings. As I heard wives and daughters, sons and husbands, describe the same nightmares and pretenses that I was living through, I began to understand what Al-Anon means by calling someone like me an "enabler." By compensating and covering up for Bobby, I was enabling him to go on drinking without paying the consequences. I got him off the hook.

Detach yourself, I was told. Let him fall on his face—and let him lie there until *he* picks himself up. If he starts to beat you up, get out of the house. Don't come back until he's sober.

It was good advice, but very difficult to follow. In my case, I felt, impossible. My career was too closely entwined with Bobby's to let the world see how far he had deteriorated. I would go down with him. And even if I were willing to let that happen, I couldn't allow our children to suffer the consequences. I *had* to keep up a front, not only for Bobby, but for all of us.

As for getting out of the house when he was in an ugly mood, where would I go? I didn't want to leave Chris and Mike alone with Bobby. If I took the boys with me, where would *we* go? I couldn't take them to my parents' house because I had work to do.

Something in me said I was making excuses. I knew the Al-Anon approach was the right one, but I wasn't ready for it.

I needed a friend, someone to confide in, whom I could trust. For the first time in my life I realized that I didn't know how to make a friend or be one. I had spent so much of my time learning how to sing and dance, audition and perform, I had never invested my time or dedication in those far-reaching values of friendship, loyalty, being there for someone in need. And I had never made myself vulnerable enough for someone else to know I needed a friend. I had always prided myself on not airing my problems in public, but now I realized no one really knew me. I could see that Al-Anon was going to have an impact on many areas of my life!

Why didn't I go to my family for help? I did. Not at first, but later in my marriage I told my mother and father how things really were with Bobby and me. My mother was furious and begged me to leave him. My father said nothing, but I knew how he felt. My pain may have caused him sorrow, but he would not interfere in the affairs of a man and his wife. Later, when he and my mother were visiting us one summer, I saw how irrevocably imprisoned he was in the old-world culture.

Bobby and I were discussing a few songs I wanted to add to our act. They were contemporary songs, and Bobby objected vehemently to some of the lyrics. "I can't sing that garbage!" he screamed at me. "Do you really expect me to call you 'Baby'? I *never* call you 'Baby'!"

"Then substitute something that's comfortable for you," I pleaded. "Sing 'Honey' or 'Darling'—or 'Doodlebug'!"

He was at the bar getting ready to pour himself a drink, and the bottle was empty. "I don't sell out!" he said, reaching in the cupboard for another bottle and glaring at me.

My mother and father were sitting in the den, and they could see as well as hear what was going on. I lowered my voice. "I don't sell out, either," I said defensively. "But this is a pretty love song—and what it says is that you and I are in this century. We can't go on singing the same old songs!"

Instantly, the argument became physical. When my mother tried to defend me, she was brought into the fray. Then just as quickly, it was over. Bobby opened the new bottle and finished pouring his drink. My father, sitting a few feet away from us, hadn't stopped watching television.

My brother Joey was the only one who could offer me help. "When you are ready to get out of this, you call me," he said. "Anytime. *Anytime.* Do you understand?" I knew what he was saying—and I knew he was right.

Why didn't I leave? Looking back, there is no way I can answer this even to my own satisfaction. At the time I clearly wasn't ready. Psychologically—according to the Myers–Briggs test—I test out as a person who hangs on to visions and relationships longer than most would, because I keep seeing possibilities of improvement. Also, I loved Bobby more than I ever had expected to love anyone, and my dependence centered entirely around him. I could see that the boys loved him with all their little hearts, and that he loved them. Did I dare tamper with their capacity to trust? Or risk damaging their capacity to love? Somehow my pain and hardships seemed comparatively shallow and insignificant. Maybe Bobby was healthier than I by trying to get out of the marriage so much earlier—I can conjecture endlessly, but it doesn't matter. At the time, it felt like there was a definite answer somewhere—in neon lights—if only I could find it.

So I kept putting up with the disappointments and seeking new sources of help. I'd say, "Next week I'm going to see Dr. So-and-So, and he'll tell me what to do." But Dr. So-and-So couldn't tell me a thing I hadn't already heard. Then I'd think, "Well, I can't leave Bobby now, because next month we're opening in a new show, and if I drop out of it, that would be unprofessional. So I'd go through with the show, but then it would be Chris's birthday, or Michael's, and I couldn't leave my son's father right before his birthday. Next it would be Christmas. And after that it would be a trip we had to take. I'd think, *maybe that's what we need, to be alone, away from all the hangers-on. Maybe that will change him . . .*

NO! NOTHING CHANGES!

The terrible truth about living with an alcoholic is that your bottom line, the alcohol, is always there. Or whatever made the alcohol have to be there is still not being dealt with.

The hardest thing in the world is to get the alcoholic to face *why* he drinks. Maybe it's genetic, maybe it's a chemical imbalance, maybe it's anesthetizing childhood pains, maybe it's hiding from reality, but until the alcoholic starts *wanting* to face those reasons, *your* wanting makes no difference at all. It had taken a very long time, but finally those truths were beginning to get through to me.

Chapter Ten

$\mathscr{E}$arly in 1973 I learned that I was pregnant. It was an accident, perhaps some contraceptive fallibility. And I reacted with panic.

We had a busy summer scheduled. For a long time I had tried to get booked into Las Vegas as a single act—I suppose I had seen what was coming and realized I had to reestablish myself as a solo performer. Before Bobby and I were married, and for some time after, I had headlined in several clubs. But ever since we'd put our acts together for a double billing at the Frontier and had broken every record for attendance, that was the only way the bookers could see us. The casino managers really didn't want to take me alone, but they agreed to give me a chance and I was grateful. I accepted second billing to Shecky Greene, a magnificent comic. He was a wonderful talent and we got along well, both offstage and during our performance together as the finale to the evening.

After Las Vegas I was to join Bobby for six weeks of concerts and six weeks of a new production of *I Do! I Do!* with Bobby and me playing the leads. We would be on the road for a long time. I also had landed a Bob Hope TV special to promote my new nightclub act. I couldn't do any of those things if I were pregnant. Yet I had put my career aside before, so why was this time any different?

Abortion had been legalized in America, and many feminists were saying that it was better than giving birth to an unwanted child. That isn't what swayed me. My decision to have an abortion was an attempt to save myself, the first I had ever made in my life and a mistake that haunts me today. But had I been forced to have the baby at the time, I would have had to be taken away in a straitjacket.

When I tried to discuss it with Bobby, he became enraged. "Absolutely not!" he screamed at me. "You're a monster, a killer! You're a whore!" Then his eyes narrowed. "Wait a minute—it's not my baby, is it? It's somebody else's baby and that's why you want to get rid of it. Who've you been screwing?"

"It could never be any child but yours," I sobbed, "and you know that. If we can just get through this summer, I promise you that in the fall I'll get pregnant again." It was a senseless thing to say, but that was the way my mind was working and it terrified me.

"You can't murder my child!" he said.

"It's not murder!" I protested. "I'm trying to survive!"

"Is this what your crazy new religion tells you to do?" he demanded. I couldn't answer.

My "crazy new religion" couldn't help me at that point in my life because I didn't know enough about it. I had only begun to study the Bible. I knew that a person *could* get close to God, and that Jesus Christ *could* help human beings solve their most difficult problems, but I hadn't been there yet. I still thought God wouldn't have anything to do with me if I wasn't perfect. I had been a mother. I knew what it was to bring forth new life, so I certainly wasn't going to ask God to understand why, this time, I couldn't do it. I knew I was wrong. I just didn't know what else I could do.

In spite of Bobby's protests, I consulted a gynecologist.

"You can check into the hospital as early as tomorrow," he said.

"All right. Tomorrow will be fine."

I felt like a criminal as I counted the money and got ready for the hospital. I began to cry and I knelt down on the floor to pray, but the words wouldn't come. I had the same feeling about God as I did about the women in my prayer group. They had been so sympathetic, so understanding, when I talked about my troubled marriage. They wanted so much to help me keep it together. But when I told them about this problem, they became distant, and soon the group broke up. I felt completely alone, convicted and guilty, yet cornered.

The initial G was on all my luggage, and I checked in as "Mrs. Gold." I was foolish to think I could conceal my identity. Everyone knew who I was and they let me know that they knew. Granted, I was sensitive and only too ready to assume guilt for what I was doing, but I have never known such coldness from a hospital staff.

I had the support of my mother and my brother, whom I had told about my decision. I knew how difficult it was for them, sincere and devoted Catholics, to approve of what I was doing, so I asked them not to be with me. But I knew they still loved me.

The following morning I went into surgery and gratefully went under the anesthetic. I was groggy for the rest of the day. I awoke the next morning, early, and looked out my window at a sunny spring day. And I wept. I hated what I had done, but I remembered all the reasons for it and I knew I would do it all over again, given the same circumstances.

On the third day after I entered the hospital our nanny picked me up and I went home. Bobby wasn't there. I went upstairs and began to pack. I was due in Las Vegas one day later. I went to bed alone and fell into an exhausted sleep.

When I left for my opening in Las Vegas the following morning, Bobby refused to speak to me. He was doing a show in Lake Tahoe. Every day I was in Las Vegas, I called him several times, but he wouldn't accept or return my calls. I wrote to him and he didn't answer my letters. Once again my work became my refuge and I threw myself into my new act. It was a success.

Shecky Greene, who had known me for a long time, could see that I wasn't myself. Onstage I was full of energy, but once I was off I was exhausted both physically and emotionally. For the entire three weeks I never went anywhere; I just stayed in my room. Shecky used to come by and say "Hey, what's the matter with you? Why don't you have a little fun?"

And I'd say, "Oh, I'm waiting for Bobby to call."

"So—he can leave a message."

"No," I told him. "You see, he's very angry with me and I want to be right here when he calls."

Soon Bobby and I were scheduled to open in a concert and I knew I had to get through to him or we would never be able to work together. As soon as I finished working in Las Vegas, I went to Tahoe to see him. "I will never work onstage with you again," he said the moment he saw me.

"Bobby, if you go through with that threat, then we can't do the summer tour, can we?" I said. I was determined not to raise my voice, not to get excited. I had to make him hear me. "We can't be in *I Do!* and not be onstage together. We can't do a concert and not be on the stage at the same time. It would be like doing *Gone With the Wind* and not burning Atlanta. People come to see us together."

I stayed there for two days, talking to him whether he was drunk or sober. I begged him to be realistic. "I know you are beyond anger with me. But we still have a family and we still have work that means something. We can't do it alone—we need each other."

"All right," he said, "we'll do the tour and all the other things. But I won't say anything nice about you onstage—and I mean that."

He was referring to a little dialogue we used to do in our act, when he would tell me what a great cook I was, and I would tell him that I loved his singing and he would tell

me that I was a good dancer. It was only husband-wife banter, but his refusal to do it anymore hurt me.

That summer was agony. I tried to spend time with him
before he drank, looking for ways to make him laugh, but
he wouldn't give me that satisfaction. If we were watching
TV and a program made reference to the abortion issue, he
would turn to me accusingly and say, "See—that's you."
Once we were having dinner with some friends who had
come to see our show, and one of the men said that any
woman who underwent an abortion should never be forgiven because that was the worst kind of sin. Bobby quickly
glanced at me with a strange half-smile on his face and I
was afraid he was going to say something, but the man's
wife got there first.

"You know," she said to her husband in a gentle but
firm tone, "I don't think you'd feel that way if you were a
woman."

Abortion is not the simple matter its opponents or pro-
ponents make it out to be. It is not only a choice between
ending or not ending the life of an unborn child. A woman
has an abortion not because a pregnancy is inconvenient
or because she doesn't want to be bothered bringing up a
child, but because she's trying to survive. And before we
can solve all the complications of the abortion issue, I think
we have to acknowledge why women do it, and have some
understanding of the pain they suffer in its aftermath.

Before this decision, I was basically comfortable with
my choices, with my direction in life. But after the abortion,
which at the time was the best of the available alternatives
as I saw them, my confidence and clarity were gone. I have
since been comforted by the Life Spring Seminar, which
gives as an example a person in a burning building. He can
only save himself by jumping into one of three piles of dung:
one two feet deep, one five feet deep and one ten feet deep.
End of choices. Some of the problems we face in our own
lives may be as desperate, and the solutions as unattractive.
From outside it is all very easy to self-righteously judge, and
to wonder why anyone would want to do such a disgusting
thing as jump in a pile of dung. But never from outside can

we see into another's mind. That's why the Native American maxim "Never judge another until you have first walked seven miles in his moccasins" is so wise.

I decided that the best, the only thing I could do to end my pain and Bobby's bitterness toward me was to have a child—as soon as possible. I didn't say anything to Bobby, but I started keeping track of my temperature.

The following spring after school was out, Bobby, Chris, Mike and I took a Mediterranean cruise aboard a yacht we'd leased. Bobby always liked to be on water, and I hoped the cruise would improve his spirits, but he was gloomy and reclusive. Our itinerary was to take us from the Greek islands and then circle the lower boot of Italy and fly from Rome to Moscow and Leningrad.

Usually I enjoyed sailing, but I was suffering from hemorrhoids, an ailment that frequently afflicts dancers, and I was uncomfortable most of the time. Then I missed my period, and from that day on I began to cherish the child I was certain I was carrying. The pain of the hemorrhoids got worse, and when we arrived in Rome I asked Bobby to help me find a doctor. "An American doctor," I said, "so I can understand what he says."

At my request, the doctor took a blood sample to determine whether I was pregnant. The test was positive. I wasn't worried about the hemorrhoids; I had recovered from them before. I was ecstatic about the baby.

Michael always said that he didn't like being the baby of the family. He wanted to be the first to know if I became pregnant again. So when I left the hospital and went to our car, I said to Bobby, "Please, I have something to tell Michael." Bobby was puzzled by that until I leaned over to Michael and said, "Michael, I want you to be the very first to know that I'm going to have a baby." He was thrilled. Bobby was not.

"Oh, my God!" he said, slamming his hands against the car. "What are we going to do about that!" I didn't take him seriously.

Throughout the rest of our trip I was still in a lot of pain, but I tried not to let it interfere with the fun I had with the boys. We saw many magnificent treasures and land-marks. When we came home we still had another month off, and we went straight to our house in Wyoming.

As beautiful as it was there, it was not my favorite place to be because there was too much for me to do. It was an enormous house on top of a hill and the view was incredible, but the wind was constant and every time we opened a door or a window the house was filled with silt. It was impossible to keep clean, but I tried.

One day I was down on my knees scrubbing a flagstone floor, because you can't clean a flagstone floor any other way, when I felt a different kind of pain. I was hemorrhaging!

"Bobby!" I screamed. He was in the den. When he saw me he seemed to sober up immediately. He knelt down be-side me, trying to pick me up.

"I need a doctor," I told him. "Bobby, I'm scared!"

I was bleeding profusely and he helped me into the bathroom. Then he called the hospital. I didn't know what else to do but sit on the toilet because, even at such a ter-rifying time, I didn't want Bobby, and especially the boys, to see the amount of blood I was losing. When Bobby came in he put his arms around me and kept whispering, "It's all right, you're going to be okay." He told me he had to take me to the hospital as soon as I thought I could move.

I felt the baby coming out of me and I screamed. Bobby held me tighter. "I've lost it! I've lost it!" I sobbed as he held my head against his chest. "Hold on to me," he told me, lifting me up. When I was standing, he reached over and flushed the toilet.

I remember arriving at the hospital. Someone helped me onto an operating table and someone else called for an anesthesiologist. I was moved very quickly down long, nar-row corridors and through several doors. Someone bent over me and said, "Oh, now, what are you crying about?"

I said, "I lost my baby."

I felt the needle go in. "Well, now, you just stop crying, okay?" the same voice droned.

No, I thought, *I never will.*

By the time I came to, the next day was nearly over. I

felt very weak. Worse than that, however, was my awareness that I had lost the new life I had hoped would rectify the cardinal sin of my abortion. A dark depression came over me, and sleep seemed my only comfort.

On the following day the nurses were overly kind as they helped me prepare to leave the hospital. Bob played the concerned husband until we reached our car. Then as he opened the door for me, he said, "I'm really glad this happened, Carol. And relieved, too. I didn't think we could make it work."

I felt as if he were twisting a knife in an old wound, especially after our torment about the abortion. Hot tears welled up in me, but I held them back. At home, alone in our bedroom, I let them spill over as I collapsed onto the bed and cried myself to sleep.

I was told to stay in bed for several days, and not to lift anything for a long time. The doctors said I would feel weak for a while because I had lost so much blood, but the weakness was more than physical. I had lost the ability to hope. I felt I was being punished.

Michael and Christopher spent a lot of time with me, trying to cheer me up with their games and laughter, but I knew they were watching me closely. For their sakes I wanted to get well, so I forced myself to eat when I really had no appetite.

I allowed myself to think I could talk to Bobby as a friend. I tried. I began to tell him how I felt and how much the loss of the child meant to me. I told him how I still grieved over the child I had aborted.

He wouldn't let me finish. "You *are* being punished," he said, coldly. "God is trying to show you that you can't decide when a child can or cannot be born." He stood up and looked down at me as if he were some kind of judge. "You deserve exactly what you got."

Chapter Eleven

I used to believe that no matter what was wrong with a family, the holidays could fix it. I stopped believing that on New Year's Day, 1976.

Bobby and I had been married for thirteen years. Our sons Chris, eleven, and Michael, nine, were bright, talented and loving. We still lived high up in Beverly Hills in our magnificent house that epitomized "Old Hollywood" before the age of income taxes, when movie stars could afford to indulge their taste for beautiful things. We were so secluded that we couldn't see any of our neighbors. Looking west over the canyons, we could see beyond the city of Los Angeles to the Pacific Ocean, and, toward the northeast, the San Fernando Valley stretched out to the horizon. Who could ask for anything more?

As much as Bobby and I loved that house, we didn't spend much time in it because we were on the road performing most of the year. However, we did make an effort to be there for the holidays. Every year the holidays worked their magic until I just knew that everything was going to be all right. But like most things magical, the illusion never lasted very long.

We were spending the holidays quietly. Bobby had had eye surgery a few days earlier, and had come home groggy from sedatives. I was giving him antibiotics every two hours around the clock, so I hadn't slept much. His doctor had told him to avoid alcohol while he was on medication, but Bobby paid no attention and began drinking as soon as he came home.

On December 30, we were in bed before midnight. Sometime around dawn, I felt Bobby getting up. I had almost fallen back to sleep after having given him his latest dose of medicine. "Do you want something?" I asked, though I wasn't fully awake.

"Don't get up," he said. "I'm just going down to make some coffee."

He sounded all right. "I'll come down when the alarm goes off," I answered sleepily.

The next thing I heard was the telephone on the night-stand next to the bed. I was up instantly when I saw that the intercom light was on. Bobby was calling me from the kitchen.

"Get down here! I'm bleeding to death!" he shouted. I could hear pain in his voice.

I ran downstairs and pushed against the heavy swinging door to the kitchen. The light was on and Bobby was at the sink holding his hand under the faucet. There was blood all over him and the sink. He was sweating; his face was gray-white. As I ran to him, I almost slipped on the water that was all over the floor.

Later he told me that he'd spilled the water when he was trying to make coffee, which infuriated him. He took his anger out on the swinging door. Somehow, when he pulled it back toward him, he caught his right hand between the door and the frame as they came together. The nails on two fingers had been ripped from their beds and stood perpendicular at the cuticles. His fingertips were crushed and bloody.

Our doctor was out of town for the holidays, but the

doctor covering for him said he would see Bobby in the hospital emergency room. I raced upstairs and threw on some clothes. While I was changing, Bobby poured himself some vodka and drank it down fast. It hit him hard, and when I came downstairs a few minutes later he was slumped in his big leather chair, unconscious.

Somehow, when you need it, you find the kind of strength you didn't know you had. I couldn't get Bobby on his feet, so I dragged him out to the car and pulled him up into the front passenger seat. By the time we arrived at the hospital, he was coming to, but he was mumbling drunkenly and wasn't able to walk.

An orderly helped me put him in a wheelchair. I was torn by conflicting emotions: fear that Bobby was going to lose his fingers, embarrassment because so many people saw how drunk he was, and anger over his disregard for himself and for everyone who cared about him. Would he *ever* stop trying to destroy himself? It was a question I asked every time he sought relief in the numbness of alcohol.

"What did you give him?" the doctor asked me when he saw Bobby's condition. He said it as if it were my fault that Bobby was drunk. When I explained that Bobby drank vodka after taking sedatives and antibiotics, the doctor said, "Well, he sure doesn't need any anesthesia for surgery."

"Will he lose his fingers?" I asked.

"Can't tell yet," he said as he watched Bobby being wheeled into the operating room.

Fortunately, the doctor was able to save the fingers. "But he's not out of danger," he told me. "There's a risk of infection, so he's got to follow orders. If he gets gangrene, it's all over." He wanted Bobby to stay in the hospital for a few days, but Bobby refused. He didn't want any more people to see the stitches around his eyes. Reluctantly, the doctor gave him more sedatives and more antibiotics, and we went home.

We were supposed to leave for Acapulco in a few days so Bobby could recuperate from his first surgery, but the doctor who treated his hand said absolutely not—he couldn't go anywhere because his fingers might become infected. "I won't be responsible for what happens if you take off for Mexico," the doctor said. But even on the way home Bobby insisted on going.

"Why?" I said, trying to reason with him. "Your eyes can't take the sun yet, and with your hand in bandages, you can't do anything."

His jaw muscles tightened. *"We're going!"*

"But you heard the doctor—"

"What the hell does he know? That goes for you, too! You think you know everything, don't you?"

"I'm sorry, darling. I know you're in a lot of pain. We'll be home soon." I tried to placate him because his tone was frightening me.

I drove fast, knowing well every sharp turn in the steep winding road to our house. It was mid-morning when I pulled in between the white brick walls flanking our driveway. I felt, as I often did when I reached that point, that we were leaving the world behind. In my hurry to get Bobby to the doctor, I hadn't closed the big iron gates at the top of the driveway, so I was able to pull right into the garage. Before I could turn off the engine, Bobby got out of the car without a word. He went into the house through the laundry-room door.

I rummaged through my bag for the antibiotics the doctor had given me. I took one out of the envelope and put the rest in the refrigerator next to the others. Then I ran upstairs to check on Chris and Mike. They were just getting up, unaware of what had happened.

When I went downstairs I found Bobby standing at the bar in the narrow corridor between the kitchen and the den. He was pouring vodka into a glass filled with ice cubes. "Bobby, no!" I yelled, grabbing for the glass. "You know what the doctor said. This could kill you!"

He pushed me away and went into the den. "I don't want to hear any of that!" he shouted. "I *need* this!" He turned on the TV and with his drink settled into his big hooded black leather chair for the rest of the day. I knew better than to interfere with him in this mood, so I went about preparing dinner for the next day's festivities.

Finally, I persuaded him to go to bed, and helped him upstairs. I gave him the antibiotic, and by then the sedatives were taking effect. I looked for something I could use to tie his hand in an upright position as the doctor had advised, so that the blood wouldn't accumulate in the tips of his fingers while he was sleeping. I took the belt from his robe and began winding it around his wrist, but even in his stupor he fought me, swinging at me with his free hand. After a few attempts I managed to loop the belt around the bedpost and make a clumsy knot. I stood at the foot of the bed watching him until he stopped squirming and began breathing regularly.

I felt as if I had been holding my breath for hours, and only then did I feel I could let it go. My mind hurled accusations at me: *If only I hadn't let him go downstairs by himself . . . If only I hadn't gone back to sleep after he got up . . .* It was a familiar experience. I had always felt as if everything that happened were my fault. The usual gnawing, nebulous sense of guilt washed over me.

I set the alarm for two hours later, when Bobby's next dose of medicine was due, and lay down next to him, too exhausted to sleep. Oh, well, tomorrow was another day— no, that wasn't true. It was already tomorrow, New Year's Day. I had forgotten about that, and about what the first day of a new year always meant to me. It was a chance to start over, to try to avoid repeating the same mistakes of the past.

Lying there in the darkness, I remembered how much Bobby meant to me. He was the center of my life. I knew the man behind the matinee idol. I held on to my belief that we still loved each other somehow. As the sun began to rise, pressing through the closed draperies of our bedroom, I told myself that we could be happy. Once again the holidays were working their magic, or so it seemed.

By the time I went downstairs later that morning, our housekeepers had already left. We had given them the holiday off, which was fine with me because I enjoyed cooking and doing things around the house. We had arranged to have my mother and father fly in from Chicago on New Year's

Day to stay with Chris and Mike while Bobby and I went to Acapulco, and I knew that the moment my mother set foot in the house she would begin preparing wonderful Italian feasts. "Food is how Italians say 'I love you,' " my mother always said.

Outside it was a January day in California, with temperatures in the sixties and a coolish sun trying to make its way through the morning smog. But inside it was Melrose Park. I had draped evergreen garlands everywhere—around doorways, along mantelpieces and winding up the wide staircase from the entrance hall to the second floor. In the living room was an enormous Christmas tree decorated with as many ornaments as it could hold. Holly, mistletoe, candles and bowls of Christmas tree balls were everywhere. The only thing missing was snow.

I made some coffee and ate a little cereal. I decided to wait until Bobby woke up before making his breakfast. If he was hung over, he wouldn't even want me to mention food. He'd just want coffee. And then some vodka—he said it cleared his head. By dinnertime he'd likely have consumed quite a bit of vodka, but he'd be ready to eat by then.

I was surprised to see him standing in the doorway, looking at his bandaged hand as if it belonged to someone else. He looked so pale and wounded that I felt sick for him. I wanted to be part of his healing.

Early in the afternoon on New Year's Day, I brought my mother and father back from the Los Angeles airport, and the first thing my mother said when she walked into the house was "Oh, not another puppy! Why do you need that?" She was referring to Bobby's new dog, a seven-month-old Shih Tzu, which came running to meet her. Bobby had seen the dog in the pet shop and felt sorry for it because it had been there for six months and no one had purchased it. The poor thing had been in a cage all that time, with no love or attention, and it reminded Bobby of his childhood. The dog wasn't housebroken yet, and as I went for some paper towels to clean up an accident, I said, "Please, Ma, don't start with the puppy. Bobby's in no mood to hear that you disapprove. He's aching all over."

"But you've already got two dogs," my mother said. "Why do you need this one? You can't take care of it, you're gone too much."

"Rosie, you've always got an opinion about everything," my father said. "We don't need that, either."

My mother was about to argue the point with him, and I knew that the last thing I needed was the two of them going at each other. "Ma—please!" I begged. She sighed and shrugged her shoulders. I knew how hard it was for her to hold her tongue, and I hugged her for trying. She put her arms around me and I felt steadied by the warm, immediate affection I always got from her.

My father went to get some of their bags from the car and I called for Chris and Mike to come and help. I don't think they even knew we were home because they were in the den with Bobby watching a football game on TV and the volume was up. They came racing out, shouting their welcome, almost knocking my mother down with squeezes which she pretended were crushing her.

"You boys are so big," she said. "You gotta stop growing or you'll go through the roof."

Chris and Mike dashed outside to see my father, and my mother pressed her hair in place. "Now," she said, bringing her hands together and looking around the kitchen, "where's an apron?"

I laughed. "Mom, you just got here."

"That's all right—we still have to eat, don't we?" she said, taking charge, because the kitchen was indisputably her domain. It was, in fact, the only place in the entire world where she felt she mattered. "You can't throw the food together—you have to do a few things with it first."

But this time there was very little for my mother to do because I had already prepared dinner. And, in a way, our roles were reversed as my mother followed me around the kitchen, trying to be helpful. "Is it cooked enough?" she asked me, holding out a ribbon of fettuccine on a large spoon for me to test. I bit into it slowly and nodded approval.

"Let's ask Bobby," she decided suddenly, and headed toward the den where Bobby, the boys and my father were watching another football game. Her deference to the man of the house was typically Italian.

"No, Ma," I said, and the sharpness of my voice stopped her short.

"Why not?" she asked. I had hurt her feelings.

"I'm sorry, I didn't mean to say it that way," I apologized. "But you know how he gets. Just let him be. He'll be all right in a while." I knew that my father and the boys were trying to do the same thing, because they too recognized what a dark mood Bobby was in. Nobody in the den made a sound until he did, and only when he whooped out loud over a play did they join in.

"Don't do this, don't do that," my mother muttered. "I can't do anything right."

I was familiar with that feeling and I sympathized with her. For years I had been trying to find out what Bobby needed to make him responsive and happy again.

It was after five o'clock when my mother and I set the table in the breakfast room. We ate most of our meals there, because it was cozier than the mirrored dining room. Then we went into the den to announce that dinner was ready. My mother was ahead of me, and as she entered the room the puppy came waddling over to her.

Realizing that her earlier comments about the dog had been a mistake, my mother was eager to make up for it. So she reached down to pat the dog, saying, "Oh, what a nice little puppy you are." I didn't think anyone even heard her because the television was so loud, but all of a sudden Bobby lurched forward in his chair and shouted to all of us in general, "Do you see that? I'm not putting up with that in my house!"

We all looked at each other guiltily, and I said, "What do you mean by that?"

He pointed at my mother. "She's talking while I'm watching my football game!"

My father, who could be quite diplomatic, tried to appease him. "Look, Bobby, don't take it personally," he said. "Rosie doesn't understand football. She didn't mean anything by it."

"No, Bobby," my mother pleaded. "I was just telling you that I like your little dog. In fact, I like him better than football." She was trying to make him smile.

"That's it!" he exploded. He slammed his empty glass down and stood up. "I'm leaving!"

Everyone in the room remained silent, not wanting to provoke a further outburst. I had seen and heard this before, yet I still hoped he might be kidding. When he left the room and I heard him go up the stairs, I decided to follow. I had to see if this was really happening—New Year's Day, a family dinner waiting, and my husband was "leaving"?

I found him in his dressing room, stuffing things into a small bag. "You can't be serious!" I said, trying to get in front of him so he would have to look at me. "It was such a little thing."

He pushed me away and glared at me. "You see," he said, raising his voice, "how you always take their part? You never stick up for me!"

"That's not true!" I shouted back at him. He was pulling underwear and pajamas from drawers and putting them in the bag.

We had been through this many times before, and even though I knew the answer, I asked him where he was going.

"To my boat—to find some peace!"

His yacht was his cocoon, and sometimes I wondered whether he started these arguments so he would have an excuse to get away from people. But this time he was not able to look after himself.

"For God's sake, Bobby, you've had a serious injury," I said. "And your eyes are still healing. You need antibiotics every two hours—at least take them with you if you're going to your boat!"

He turned toward me and with an angry warning in his eyes and a deliberate separation of each word said:

"Leave-me-alone-and-stop-telling-me-what-to-do!"

I knew that look and tone of voice. It meant that any more words might be dangerous.

I ran out of the room to get the antibiotics and almost

collided with Michael on the stairs. He must have heard us shouting at each other, because he was crying as he scurried past me into his room. I wanted to go after him to try to comfort him, but I knew Bobby would leave within seconds. I went down to the kitchen, where I found Christopher standing very still, his eyes large and filled with fear and confusion. I wanted to put my arms around him, and I knew that was what he needed, but I couldn't stop. I pulled the refrigerator door open and took out both the antibiotics and the sedatives. I heard Bobby run down the back staircase and go out the laundry-room door that led to the garage. I knew it would take him a few seconds to get to the second garage, a separate building where he kept his beloved Stutz Bearcat, so I ran out the kitchen door into the driveway.

"Please, Bobby, wait! Take your medicine with you! Please!"

Maybe he didn't see me in the rearview mirror of his car. Maybe he hadn't been looking. All I remember is that the engine raced with a deafening noise and the car lunged in reverse. I jumped to my right just far enough for the car to pass without hitting me. Bobby swung the car around in the arc, backing it toward the front of our house and, without looking at me, screeched down the driveway. Whether he even knew it or not, he had almost run me down, and the shock of it paralyzed me. I stood there, clenching the two bottles of capsules, and the most important thing in my mind was how to get them to him.

I turned back toward the house and I saw Christopher standing in the open kitchen doorway. I'll never forget the expression on my child's face. His eyes were dark with anger, and a deep red flush was high on his cheeks. Then I saw something in his right hand. It was a pocketknife, and it was open.

I was no longer in shock; I was suddenly aware of everything about that moment. "Chris, is that a knife?" I said gently.

He looked at me and his mouth opened, but no sound came out of it. Then his eyes closed tightly and he began to sob. I put my arms around him and rocked him from side to side as if he were a baby. I cried, too.

"It's Michael's knife," he said. "It was his Cub Scout knife."

"What are you doing with it, Chris?" I asked him.

"We didn't want him to hurt you," he said. He was trying so hard to stop crying and he couldn't.

"Michael went upstairs and got his knife and gave it to me," he said. "He couldn't do it, but I could."

"Do what?"

"If he hits you one more time, I'll kill him."

"Christopher! Don't say that! He's your father."

"I don't care! If he ever hurts you again, I'll get one of his guns and kill him!"

My God! Nothing Bobby had ever said or done had cut as deeply as these words coming out of my son's mouth. I knew how powerful Chris's feelings for his father were and how desperately he wanted his approval. So I blamed myself for placing him in this situation that tragically made him stand up against the man he loved most in the world.

Bobby had walked out on us many times before, and he always went to his boat. Getting him to come back was a familiar ritual; I would wait until I thought he was sober and I would call. I would minimize whatever had happened and suggest meeting on the boat so we could talk. There, I would tell him what had preceded his going to his boat. He was usually aghast, apologetic, remorseful. He would want to send letters saying he was sorry. Every remnant of the thoughtfulness for which I loved him poured into his anguish at the thought he might have hurt someone. Out of habit, and still somewhat in shock, I began to estimate how long I should wait before calling him.

Chris's agonized revelation brought that truth home to me. I thought of Michael, somewhere inside the house. He was only a little more than a year younger than Chris, but he always looked to Chris as his "big" brother. It was just like him to run for a weapon and then hand it to Chris. It happened all the time when they were playing games. But this was no game. By refusing to admit that my marriage to Bobby was a failure, I had set up my sons to conceive of a terrible crime—and even though the crime was only hypothetical, they may still be paying a price for it. And so am I.

I wanted to take the knife from Chris, but he wouldn't give it up. I started to walk him back to the house, speaking very softly. "Let's go back and eat some dinner, Chris. Everything's on the table, and Nana and Grandpa are here. Maybe later, when your father calms down, he'll come back."

"We're not going to let him hurt you," he said, wiping his arm across his face. And even after we sat down at the table, Christopher kept the knife next to his plate all during dinner.

As I got ready for bed that night, I knew that I wasn't going to call Bobby. Nor was I going to the boat the next day. I didn't want to talk to him because I really didn't have anything to say. I had lived with my decision to seek a divorce for only a few hours, but already I was feeling some relief. I was tired of pretending to be happy. I was tired of trying to figure out where our marriage had gone wrong and why—and what I could do to make it better. And I was tired of denying that I was tired. Somehow I had to let go.

Late that night I got up and looked out at the millions of lights glittering below me in Los Angeles. I had never thought about it before, but I wondered why so many people were up at that hour, and how many of them were alone.

Chapter Twelve

$\mathscr{W}$aking up on January 2, 1976, I knew I had a lot of things to do, but I wasn't quite sure where to begin. When your husband walks out on you, your sense of identity changes. You feel as if you have to make some kind of declaration that you and he are no longer together. Some people have to be told. Some can wait. But then there are questions. What do you say when someone asks you why? It's not the same as sending out an announcement that the two of you ran off and got married. People never ask why when that happens, although perhaps they should. People just slap you on the back or give you a hug and say, "Wonderful!" If they have any questions, they keep them to themselves. When you separate, *everybody* wants an explanation, even if they could see it coming from a mile away. There's something about a marriage breaking up that makes everybody feel entitled to the inside story.

I could just imagine what would happen if someone asked me why I didn't want to live with Robert Goulet anymore. It would be easy to tell my sad tale and elicit their sympathy, and then possible amazement. Everyone has at least as bad if not worse pain in his own life and commiserating is a popular indoor sport. The only drawback is that the nodding affirmations freely given face-to-face too often turn to stilettos of "I told you so," "Who does she think she's fooling?" and "I'd like to hear his side" once you've left the room. I couldn't stand that, but it looked as if I would have to.

My second decision was to get up and make my sons some breakfast. They would have questions, too. Maybe they wouldn't put them into words, but I would see them in their eyes. *Is Daddy coming home? Did I do something wrong? Do you still love me? Does Daddy? Do you and Daddy still love each other?* I would have to answer those questions as well as I could, little by little. I didn't even know some of the answers, and Mike and Chris weren't old enough to understand some of the others.

The next thing I had to do was get on the phone. There were important calls to make. The first was to Kurt Kaiser, head of the recording division of Word, Inc., a conservative Christian book publisher and music company. After the success of our first album, *New Friends*, I had signed a contract to record another album of gospel music with them. I had chosen the songs and my conductor had made the arrangements, but I hadn't done the recordings. I thought it was only fair to let Word know that their wonderful new Christian recording artist had done what many consider to be an unchristian thing: separate from her husband.

"I have to be honest with you, Kurt," I said, trying to keep the emotion out of my voice. "We'll probably get divorced." I told him that if Word wanted to pull out of the contract, I would understand.

He didn't pause for a second: "Carol, this must be a very painful time for you. We want to support you in any way we can." He said the contract would stand and wanted to know when I thought I might begin recording.

I was amazed. The people at Word certainly had to be concerned with their standing in the conservative Christian community, but they weren't threatened by the prospect of a divorce. I was deeply moved that their Christian commitment was more directed toward the anguish of a human being than their public image. This and their confidence in me gave me a lift.

My next call was to the account executive at Young and Rubicam who handled my contract with General Foods for the International Coffee commercials I had been doing for the past two years. I was nervous. I had no idea how the news of a divorce would affect the people at General Foods, who, until then, had been happy with the way the public identified me with their product. If anything, the commercials gave me better exposure than any show I could have done, because they were run during "The Tonight Show," "The Today Show," the six o'clock news and so many other programs. It was almost as valuable as having a series. The money was very good and, best of all, I was able to earn a living without traveling. It was especially important for me to stay close to my sons while they went through the trauma of divorcing parents, so I was a bit shaky as I dialed the agency's number.

The account executive didn't think we had a problem.

"Well, in some of the commercials I mention Bobby," I reminded him.

"So—we just won't mention him anymore."

I was glad he couldn't see me because I had tears in my eyes. I couldn't live on the coffee commercials alone, but at least I had money coming in.

My next call was to the psychiatrist I had consulted about Bobby. I asked him if he would see Chris, Mike and me, together or separately, as soon as possible. I thought we might need professional help in getting through the emotional turmoil ahead of us. At his suggestion, I made appointments for the boys to see him privately and then for all of us to consult with him together.

My immediate concern was to consolidate my finances so we could go on living in our Beverly Hills house because it was the only home my boys had known. I didn't want them to change schools, leave their friends or do without the lifestyle they took for granted because I didn't want them to blame me for any sacrifices they had to make. I wanted to prove to them, to Bobby and to myself that I could give them everything they needed.

It was a foolish effort, because even though Bobby had ups and downs in his career, and was ill-advised at times regarding his money, he made a great deal of it, and I couldn't hope to match him on that level. But since I already felt so guilty about depriving my sons of a father, I couldn't bring myself to take anything else from them. I would hold on to our home even if I had to scrub floors to do it! I told my manager I wanted work and I wasn't fussy. That was another mistake, but it's hard to sit still and make long-range plans when you're scared. And I was scared.

Our divorce took four years, several lawyers and a fortune in legal fees, and ended in the worst kind of bitterness between Bobby and me. At first Bobby seemed stunned when he learned that I was serious about the separation. I was stunned too and would never have had the strength to go through with it had I not had cemented in my memory the fierce expression of a loving, little eleven-year-old ready to kill his own father because of the debacle we had made of our marriage.

When Bobby was served with the papers establishing our separation, he was furious. "I never want to hear your voice again!" he said when he called me. And he did his best to make that possible. For many years, even after our divorce, he wouldn't speak to me directly. I always had to go through a series of go-betweens: his valet, his secretary, his lawyer, and later, his new wife.

Bobby wanted everything to be simple. "Carol can have the house," he told our lawyers, referring to the house in Beverly Hills. "I'll keep the rest."

"*Wait* a minute!" I said when I heard that. "We've got two other houses—plus a lot of other holdings!" So the disposition of our property became a court battle, but not the only one. Our disagreement over Bobby's treatment of the boys when they visited him on weekends became the other.

From the very beginning of our separation, I wanted Bobby to spend as much time with Chris and Mike as he could, because they needed his reassurance, as well as mine, that they had done nothing to cause the breakup. They were already showing signs our psychiatrist told me were typical of children whose parents separated, and I wanted to spare them as much as possible. Bobby used to get infuriated when he caught them with their elbows on the table, and one day Chris said to me, "Do you think Dad left because I didn't keep my elbows off the table?"

"Oh, darling, of course not!" I said, putting my arms around him. "It has nothing to do with you. Or with Michael."

He didn't look convinced. "Well, I just wondered," he said.

Michael, who had been exceptionally bright and outgoing, was becoming reticent. He had always excelled academically, not only because of his natural intelligence but because he was very disciplined. Whatever study goal he set for himself, or whatever instrument he wanted to learn, he would hole up and pursue with a commitment and intensity most Ph.D. candidates would kill for. But now his grades were going down too, and I asked him if his school friends wondered why his mother and father weren't living together. He said, "No—most of the kids at school, their parents are divorced too. It's cool."

Through Bobby's various intermediaries I told him he could see the boys whenever he wished. I asked only that he give me forty-eight hours' notice so that I could be sure that they weren't planning to do something else when he was available. I should have known better. Bobby never was one to make plans. When he wanted to see his sons, he wanted to see them, period. He would have someone call and announce that a limousine would pick them up in twenty minutes. Sometimes, even though Chris and Mike were eager to see their father, his short notice meant they had to give up a Cub Scout meeting or a get-together with their friends. Sometimes they weren't even home and would be devastated to learn that they had missed Bobby's invitation.

It made me mad to have to go through so many people

to get to Bobby, and his responses through them were always harsh and uncooperative. Finally, I had to seek a court order stipulating that he had to give me the forty-eight hours notice. I did it reluctantly, not only because I wanted to be the "good guy" but because it cost me a fortune in legal fees. The anger it aroused in Bobby made it that much harder for Mike and Chris.

From the beginning, our separation had aroused the interest of the press, and I couldn't blame them because we had done such a good job of convincing them that we were the perfect couple. But I decided to keep the details private because, even though part of me wanted people to understand what I did, I knew I would only hurt the children if I told the truth about our marriage. I turned down all requests for interviews, and whenever I was promoting a show my press agent stipulated that I was not to be asked any questions about the divorce. Once, when I was on a morning TV show to talk about a telethon I was hosting, the interviewer suddenly changed the subject.

"Tell me, Carol," she said as if we were the best of friends, "what made you walk out on Robert Goulet?"

I was furious, but managed to keep my temper under control. "You know, you agreed not to ask me that question," I reminded her as politely as I could.

"Yes," she said, "but your fans really want to know why."

"No," I told her, "my fans are more understanding."

Meanwhile Bobby was projecting his own version of the breakup and doing it in public. He went on the talk shows, and wept when he was asked what had happened. He insisted that he still loved me and had no idea why I left him. "I guess it was the competition," he said, implying that I didn't like playing second fiddle to him. He painted me as the ardent feminist, more interested in my career than my marriage. He claimed he was starting to drink heavily because he was lost without me. Once, on a talk show, he said I refused to allow him to see his children—and that accusation gave Mike and Chris a lot of trouble at school. Sure, their friends knew all about the divorce, but they couldn't understand why I wouldn't allow my sons to see their father. And when they told the boys what a bitch I was, my boys fought back. They came home very upset. That was when I found it very hard to keep silent. I wanted to sue the producers for encouraging Bobby to wash his version of our dirty linen in public. I wanted to go up to the highest point in Los Angeles, wherever that is, and shout, "Hey, everybody, let me tell you how things really were!" I wanted to let my Italian temper have its way—but I knew better. *Don't do anything more to hurt your kids*, I kept telling myself. I was on the phone often to Joey, who kept reminding me that if I wanted the furor to die down, I had to bite my lip until it bled.

Even in divorce, children have the right to expect parents to be there for them and to help them deal with their problems. Maybe they can't voice their needs, but they have them. And even if the parents aren't getting along, they should at least be able to take them out to dinner and behave like civilized human beings instead of bitter enemies. I wish now that both Bobby and I had been able to see beyond our differences to the uncertainties of our sons, whose lives and loyalties were torn in two.

The last thing I wanted to do was take Bobby to court for some of the things that happened when Chris and Mike were with him. But it was the only way I could deal with him because he refused to talk to me or to listen to any of the requests I made through other people. To spare the boys the ordeal of testifying against their father, I let a lot of things go by. But there were two I had to stop, because they were endangering the boys' lives.

Whenever Mike and Chris came back in the limousine after visiting their father, they said very little, and I didn't want to make them uncomfortable by questioning them. But when they began to express reluctance to go to Las Vegas, where Bobby was living, I knew there had to be a good reason. There was. Apparently, Bobby used to put them in the trunk of the Stutz Bearcat whenever they went anywhere.

"Why?" I asked the boys. It no longer mattered to me

that they didn't want to tell me what was going on. I had to get at the truth.

"Mom, you know how the car is," they said. "There's only enough space for two up front." How well I remembered that car and Bobby's pride in it. It had gold-plated knobs and chinchilla rugs, and Bobby had paid a fortune for it. "I want people to turn around and stare at me when I drive this by them," he had said.

"But where will the boys sit?" I'd asked him.

"It's got two back seats," he said, pointing to the narrow slot behind the driver's seat. Maybe two dolls could have squeezed in there, but not two long-legged boys. Obviously Bobby had to reckon with that fact when the boys visited him, and if he had someone with him up front, the only place to put the boys was in the trunk.

"You mean he closed the trunk?" I asked them. They nodded solemnly. "While he drove you around Las Vegas? In the desert heat?"

Yes, they moaned miserably. What a painful dilemma for children to face: afraid to be locked in the trunk of a car, but not wanting to betray their father by telling anyone about it.

I called Bobby immediately and, through the usual screening, asked him not to put the boys in the trunk anymore. His reply was: "I'll do what I damned well please! They are my sons!"

I was furious and called my lawyer, knowing very well it would mean another appearance in court, more media curiosity and a legal fee that would take another huge bite out of my dwindling financial resources. But I had no choice.

I also didn't like Bobby's favorite pastime on his yacht of shooting at sharks with a high-powered gun from the deck. What he did on his own was his business, but I was sickened by the fear in my sons' eyes when they came home from boating with Bobby off Catalina. Bobby didn't deny what happened. He was proud of it. He and his captain would chum the waters with chunks of raw meat to attract sharks and then shoot them. Chris and Mike had nightmares about the bloody frenzies that went on as the sharks attacked not only the meat, but each other—and the boys were afraid one of the shots would go awry and tear a hole in the boat, causing it to sink. I also worried that the boys could get a ricocheted shot by mistake. The boys' night-mares indicated they shared that fear.

Again, I asked Bobby to stop what he was doing. Again he refused. And again I sought protection from the court.

My requests for restraining actions were always granted by the court because Bobby was my best witness. He usually showed up hungover, treating the matter as if it were a farce. To explain why he thought it was perfectly all right to lock the boys in the trunk of his car, he produced snapshots of Chris and Mike sitting in the trunk and smiling at the camera.

"You see, your honor," he said to the judge, grinning and waving the photographs, "they were perfectly happy to be there!"

"May I have the photographs, Mr. Goulet?" the judge asked.

"Oh, I can't do that, your honor," Bobby giggled. "They're the only copies I have."

How sad it was for Mike and Chris to go through the embarrassment and discomfort of giving their testimony in the judge's chambers. Bobby agreed that the proceedings should be conducted in private, but even so, the press had ways of finding out what was going on. Or, worse than that, of speculating. It was humiliating to see our pictures and names on the front pages of those tabloids you can't help reading when you're standing in the supermarket checkout line.

I was going for a no-fault divorce, which should have been a short, simple procedure. I had no intention of in-terfering with Bobby's future career by specifying all the problems of our life together. But I wanted financial provi-sion for our sons and a fair share of our accumulated hold-ings, and that's where Bobby fought me. "She can support herself," he said of me, and I agreed with him. But support for our children and provision for their education were imperative to me. We were at an impasse that looked as if it could last forever.

Michael and Christopher were at the age when children seem to change from minute to minute, right before your eyes, and I was concerned about the lack of a strong male authority figure or role model in their lives. I was taking courses and reading books furiously to learn how to guide them through their teens. I encouraged them to join young people's groups in our church, and I will always be grateful to the young youth leader at Bel Air Presbyterian, who would take the boys to baseball games and keep an eye on them when I was away and they were in the care of housekeepers.

My own attempts at being a father were pathetic. As a child, I was too busy dancing to learn how to play ball, so when I tried to pitch to Mike and Chris I usually got belted in the face with the ball because I didn't know how to catch or duck fast enough. I took them to Little League games, but I didn't know how to coach them the way the other boys' fathers did.

When I had to be away from home for more than a few days, I asked my mother and father to come live in our house, because I thought it would be good for the boys to spend more time with their grandparents. Nothing is Utopia. My mother was a bundle of indulgent love and the boys adored her, but my father was as strict as he had been when I was a child, and the boys, being another generation removed, resented his unflinching authority. He would stand over them while they did their homework, ready to scold them the moment they lifted their gaze or pencils from the paper. Whenever I came home, I found my children at war with my father, and of course I ended up in the middle.

During my marriage I was so busy looking after Bobby, and so preoccupied with his unpredictability, I'd never taken a good look at my parents. With Bobby gone, I was suddenly aware that my mother and father weren't well. Even my father's judicial bearing couldn't conceal the amount of weight he had lost and the drawn look of pain that deepened the lines of his face. My mother's eyesight was poor—from diabetes. She still wasn't sticking to her diet, and when her hand went to her chest I knew that she was no longer acting. Both refused to let me take them to a doctor. They always said they had enough of that back home.

As I always had in times of confusion and pain, I threw myself into my career. I was busier than ever with shows, nightclub acts, concerts and performances. It's funny how some small thing you've taken for granted becomes an entirely unexpected source of comfort and relief. My own nightclub act taught me to start laughing again, at least for the moment.

One of the biggest hits in my act was "Top Hat." It was a number that the audience always loved and that now served as a healing process for me. The number is a take-off on all those fabulous Ginger Rogers song-and-dance treats where she's backed by eighty-five men, all in top hats and canes. They never did much . . . but they sure made her look good! It would have been exorbitant to carry eighty-five men with me on the road, but I figured I could coax six kind gentlemen out of the audience, and by teaching them REALLY simple steps, I'd automatically have a spiffy chorus line. I brought the idea to Tony Charmoli, who had choreographed my first act, and he was a bit leery.

"You sure you want six guys? Audience participation is an iffy thing even when you're just singing to one shy or tipsy person, *onstage*. Coping with that many may be too much to handle," he said wisely.

"Let's try it with six. We can always cut it down." I would really have loved sixteen, but practicality won out and we began figuring out the steps. We also needed a foolproof way for them to lift me up and carry me off, with trumpets blaring and lights flashing. It all fell into place quickly. All we needed was four distinct steps and very specific directions as to how to lift me. If my weight was evenly distributed, six men could easily lift me full-press over their heads and walk me off. I stood with my right leg out at hip level and we put one man on my ankle, the man next to him holding my knee, the next my thigh. From the left side of the stage, the man on the end took my left hand, the next my elbow and the last grabbed hold of my waist. With everyone holding on for dear life, all I had to do was push off on my left leg, press down on my ankle and left hand, and I was flying.

When I explained the number to my manager, Harry Romm, he screamed, "For God's sake Carol, have you no respect for your safety? First of all men are too shy to be coaxed to *dance* and, worse than that, you get a smart-aleck drunk up there and we'll need bouncers to get him off the stage! You're begging for trouble!" My agent, the booker, my secretary and the men's room attendant agreed with Harry. Even Tony Charmoli was trying to dig up an alternative song. But somehow I believed in it and we didn't even go out of town to break it in.

At the technical run-through in Las Vegas, naturally there was no audience, so my two boy dancers and Tony ran onstage, dragging a reluctant Harry with them. We needed two more, so in halting Spanish, I recruited two busboys setting the tables in the show room. None of the hats fit anyone well, but Harry's fell way over his eyes and came to rest below his eyebrows. He started to giggle at that; but he was bent over with belly laughs every time one line of men went one way and the other line another, or when no one was on the same foot at one time, or bumped into each other on the kick line. But most of all, he laughed when I said, "Harry, please try to cheer up!" It was the oldest line in vaudeville and he practically wet his pants.

Finally we got to the lift and I reminded everyone to get to their assigned positions. Harry was laughing too hard to even walk over . . . so I yelled, "Come on fellas, we'll have to go without him!" Up I went like a flag at high mast and Harry sat down on the floor hysterical. I'm happy to say "Top Hat" stopped the show cold, and garnished raves from critics who were shocked that the men weren't "plants" we had hired to be in it. From that day on Harry *loved* the number and although he saw it hundreds of times, he would always break into his unabashed high-toned guffaws as if it were tech rehearsal and he were dancing with us.

Of course, the ad-lib quality of such a number lent itself

to questions and free-flowing banter between me and the "chorus boys," like the time I asked Nick to take my knee. Instead of going behind my leg to get it, he walked right in front of me and stood with his back to the audience, holding my knee with both hands. I tapped him on the shoulder and asked, "Nick, in all your years of going to the movies, have you ever seen anyone stand in front of Ginger Rogers?"

He thought hard for a second and then shaking his head earnestly said, "Why, no."

"Well, then would you like to walk around behind me with everyone else?"

He let go of my knee as if it were hot steel, ran around George holding up my ankle and resumed his rightful post *behind* my knee. Everyone including Nick laughed, so at the next show I made sure whoever took my knee grabbed it from in front of me. (The "bit" stayed in.) It was marvelous to see how much natural fun sprang from using men with whom everyone identified and whom some in the audience loved as brothers, husbands or friends.

But the most frantic rendition of "Top Hat" included two Arabs, Yankle and Arafat, who spoke simple English, and a Swede named Swen who spoke no English at all. As I handed each a top hat, I got his name and tried to judge the ones most easily drawn out. The first three, Tom, Dick and Harry (for expedience's sake) were adorable, but then came Arafat, a bit of a flirt, and Swen, a six-foot-four, blond hunk with a willing smile but a really blank stare. When I asked him his name he just kept smiling and put on the hat as all the men had before him. From his table came a lilting woman's voice: "His name is Swen." The melody of her words rose and fell as if riding a roller coaster.

"Where is he from?"

"Sweden."

"Oh, and does he speak English?"

"No."

"And who are you, please?"

"I'm Hilda, his wife . . . I can translate for you though."

The audience cheered approval and I thanked her.

The last man in line was, of all things, "Yankle"—and he kissed my hand as I handed him his hat. I knew I was in trouble.

With canes in hand we all began to learn the first step—"just a sway right and left." Everyone swayed in unison with me. All but Swen, who stood there smiling like a tall, blond, but very dead metronome. I stopped and asked Hilda to give Swen the direction.

"Zuerimmun pleuridi, kruiki prodk"—or that, at least, is what it sounded like. But miraculously, Swen began to sway perfectly. Now it seemed better if I told Hilda and the men the steps. She related them, *"Hermin permin lerlin,"* to Swen, and then we'd all join him. The formula worked, and then we got to who was going to lift what.

I almost broke up when I heard these words come out of my mouth. "Okay, Yankle, I want you to hold my ankle in your two hands." He strode up and took hold of my thigh, smiling all the while. "No Yankle, my *ankle!*"

"But I prrreferr the tigh!"

"Well, I'm terribly sorry but that would ruin the whole picture," I said, disengaging his hands and motioning Swen to stand between us.

Swen was getting good at sign language, and SOS signals, so he was right in position to hold my knee. Hilda sang his instructions and I called Arafat over to take my thigh.

Then started a repartee that was reminiscent of an Abbott and Costello dialogue.

Yankle started it with "Arrrafat, my friend, Hhi'lll give you von toutzand dollarrrs to trrrade places vith me!"

"Okay," Arafat said, letting go of my thigh.

I clutched his sleeve and pulled him back to me. "Oh, no you don't, Arafat!"

"Five toutzan, Arrrafat!"

"You stay on the ankle, Yankle, or you're in deep trouble."

Swen's head was whipping back and forth like an umpire at a ping-pong match.

I instinctively turned into a top sergeant and in double-time commands said, "Tom take my hand, great, Dick grab my elbow, and I saved the best part for you, Harry . . . It's in the back . . . that's right, just grab my waist. Now on the count of three, everybody lift me straight overhead and we'll walk over there, Okay? One . . . two . . . three!"

To my amazement, I was up near the ceiling, floating past an hysterical Hilda, cheering in Swedish. Now I understand why things take so long at the UN.

Every show was different, but it would take another book to tell you all the wonderful things that can go wrong—and that can keep you laughing for years.

In addition, I was exploring another direction. *Tell All the World About Love*, the second album I recorded for Word, had done very well and was nominated for a Grammy Award. I was also doing some concerts of religious music, which gave me a sense of fulfillment I had never known. I was discovering the special joy that comes from performing not only for an audience, but for what you believe. I was learning that talent can do more than please people: it can praise God. That meant more to me than money, more than celebrity status. I hoped that I might be touching people's spirits and giving them the comfort I felt when I first heard that kind of music. I wanted to do more of it, so I stopped searching frantically for one-night stands and any shows that were available. With the International Coffee commercials and a few concerts, I could manage.

One of the most prestigious engagements in the itinerary of religious concerts was to be at the First Baptist Church of Dallas, the largest Baptist sanctuary in the world. Word Records reported that sales of my first album, *New Friends*, were climbing and that my concerts had been well received in auditoriums, theaters and stadiums across the country. My version of a religious concert resembled more a Broadway show or pop concert. I didn't know any better; I just wanted to give my best to God, too. It included some funny stories about *West Side Story*, audience participation, a dramatization of Mark Twain's *Diary of Adam and Eve*, and a forty-five-minute, one-woman portrayal of the life of Mary, the mother of Christ. I also danced. Actually, the one dance number was done to an exquisite Shaker hymn I had recorded, called "Simple Gifts." Since the Shakers worshipped God in song and dance as part of their services, it seemed authentic and appropriate to research and incorporate their real steps into a routine. I wore a soft pink organza full-length gown with high neck and long sleeves. In truth you could see the line of a leg extended or bent, but only now and then a glimpse of the toe of my shoe. I was truly pleased with the reverent pleading my body and words portrayed in unison—reaching to the heavens for answers to relieve the pain I was bearing.

> When true simplicity is gained,
> To bow and to bend will not be ashamed
> To turn, turn will be our delight.
> For by turning, turning, we come round right.

All through rehearsal for the concert in Dallas the emissaries, technicians and clergy were the epitome of Southern charm and hospitality until they saw me run through the dance at rehearsal. A few gasped and sputtered in their halting, most chivalrous drawl . . . "Miss Laaaaawraance, daarlin', aare yoouu shure yoo reeallee waant too daance thaat paarticularr nuuumba heer?"

I knew exactly what they were asking, and Word Records had warned me that Baptists (and many other denominations) were morally opposed to dance—period. But for me, the absolute joy of dancing has always been a gift from God and something inside me insisted I share that as well as my testimony wherever I could.

I had a brainstorm—or maybe a hint direct from heaven—as to how to introduce this controversial three-minute number and soften the blow. I remembered a gospel concert I had done in Albion, Michigan, at the fiftieth anniversary celebration of a complex for so-called incorrigible delinquents very similar to Father Flanagan's Boys Town. The founder was in his late nineties and a fragile shadow of the dynamo described by his athletic staff. In his homespun wisdom he had built small houses where specially trained foster parents lived and nourished eight to ten youngsters from ages six to eighteen, the old-fashioned way. As John Houseman said in his television commercials, "they earned it"—the children's love and trust, that is. The rolling hills were covered with autumnal trees, forming a flaming palette of color. The grounds were immaculate and full of young people laughing, chasing each other and playing. It was Saturday. Their anticipation and curiosity drew about fifteen of them, seven-to-ten-year-olds, to where my conductor and crew were setting up our show.

What a madhouse. The gymnasium was a beehive of volunteers, some cooking, some setting the long party-decorated tables. Technicians were hurriedly trying to set up a stage and sound equipment for our luncheon concert just an hour away. I'd gone through as much preparation as time would allow, but I suddenly realized that I hadn't warmed up my voice. I used to have something akin to a phobia about subjecting anyone to the cacophonous agony of listening to the boring scales and verbal exercises I had to do before every performance. I was never one of those lucky devils who could roll out of bed and sound like Caruso—I rolled out of bed and sounded like Jimmy Durante.

Back at the gym I frantically asked one of the sound men where I could privately warm up, and he said to go to the choir practice loft in the church next door. I figured if I snuck away quickly no one would notice. But as I entered the lovely chapel, I heard trotting little footsteps close behind. As I quickened my pace, I saw a sign with an arrow pointing up and the words "Choir Room," and scaled the stairs two at a time. It became a cowboy and Indian chase and the boys' giggles were almost contagious. I opened the door to a large room with bleachers but there was no lock on the door—I had one second of panic and then spied a tiny door across the room. I hoped it wasn't to the men's room, for in seconds I was through it and grateful to turn the handle of the lock shut—safe at last. It took a few moments to adjust to the dim light, and then I saw I was in the music closet, a three-by-four-foot room lined with shelves. There was barely room to stand. I listened as the boys rushed in to the empty room and, finding no one, left to explore the rest of the top floor.

I didn't think it wise to start singing yet, so I looked at some of the hymnals and organ accompaniments on the shelves. Right at eye level something jumped out at me. It was a homemade blue cover to a songbook. The drawing was a stick figure of a little choir boy, book in hand, mouth wide open and eyes rolled to heaven. In bold print over his head were the words: "For God's Sake, Sing!" The book had been opened to a page, and I began to read lyrics I had never seen before.

> The Lord of the Dance
> I danced in the morning when the world
>   was begun.
> I danced in the moon and the stars and the sun.
> And I came down from heaven and I danced
>   on the earth.
> At Bethlehem, I had my birth.
>
> I danced for the scribes and the pharisees.
> But they would not dance and they would not
>   follow me.
> I danced for the fishermen, for James and John.
> They came with me and the dance went on.
>
> I danced on the Sabbath and I cured the lame.
> The holy people said it was a shame.
> They whipped and they stripped and they hung
>   me high.
> And they left me there on the cross to die.
>
> I danced on a Friday when the sky turned black.
> It's hard to dance with the devil on your back.
> They buried my body and they thought I'd gone.
> But I am the dance and I still go on.
>
> They cut me down and I leapt up high.
> I am the life that'll never never die.
> I'll live in you if you live in me.
> I am the Lord of the Dance, said he.

Dance then where ever you may be.
I am the Lord of the Dance, said he.
And I'll lead you all wherever you may be.
And I'll lead you all in the dance, said he.

Well, that made me feel better about *my* dance—a lot
better. After finishing my warm-up, I hurried off to ask if I
could keep the songbook. Of course my hosts were gracious
and said yes. At the concert I told them how I'd found it. I
read the lyric right before my dance number to everyone's
delight, especially the little boys to whom I had given the
goose-chase of their young lives.

What occurred to me in the Dallas church was that
maybe the touch of God had guided me to that text, had
given me permission to use every fiber of my being to worship Him, and just might free all these Southern Baptists
into at least sharing my joy. I relayed my Albion adventure
to the packed house in Dallas, which sat in pin-drop silence.
Then, without a second's delay, I began my dance. It was
as if special wings were attached to my ankles, for I floated
across the floor. On the last pose, I reached my hands over
my head, crossed my hands below my neck and bowed my
head, and the spotlight blacked out the stage. When the
lights came up, so did my head, and so did the entire
congregation—leaping to their feet, screaming and cheering. Thank God—*again.*

~∽∽ Chapter Thirteen

$\mathscr{B}$y cutting back on my schedule I'd hoped to be able to spend more time at home. I certainly didn't expect to go to Africa, but that's what happened.

For a few years I had been cohosting some of the World Vision telethons, trying to raise money to help the poor in Third World countries. But I was always in the studio. Along with the rest of the audience, I would watch filmed documentaries of anguished mothers holding emaciated babies in their arms, looking at the rest of the world for compassion. Then I would appear live on camera, perfectly coiffed, flawlessly made up, fashionably dressed, well fed, in very good health—and ask the viewers to help us fight hunger throughout the world. We always raised a lot of money, but I was convinced that we could do more.

The first time I asked Stan Mooneyham, World Vision's international president, to let me go to Africa with a documentary team, he didn't take me seriously. "Carol, it's dangerous," he said, as if I were a child asking to go out and play in the midst of a hurricane.

"I know that," I said.

"Look, just keep on doing what you're doing. It's terrific!" he told me.

"Stan," I said, "if I went to some of those countries with one of your teams, if the viewers could see me there, if I could hold one of those dying little children in my own arms and talk to some of the mothers about what they need, wouldn't that mean more than my standing there all dressed up in the comfort of the studio?"

"Sure," Stan agreed, "but you still can't do it."

"Why not?" I persisted.

"Because you're a woman!" he said.

"Well, who do you think is left out there?" I asked him. "All the men are either dead or gone!"

Stan didn't have an answer for that. He had been there himself. "Okay," he said. "But it'll be rough."

I knew it would be, but I had my own reasons for wanting to go. I had been deeply moved by the suffering caused by years of drought and famine in places like Ethiopia and Somalia. I was frustrated by the certainty that so many children would die. How would I feel, as a mother, if my two sons faced that probability?

My other reason for going was one I couldn't share with anyone. If, by going to Africa, I could be a more effective spokesperson for the people who were trying to help starving, diseased infants, then maybe God would forgive me for taking the life of that unborn child. I know, I know—I had been told so often that the loving God I had come to know would never withhold his forgiveness, but somehow I couldn't bring myself to ask for it without offering something in return.

If someone had said to me then, "Do you realize you might get killed?" I would have answered, "Yes, and I still want to go." I wasn't eager to give up my life, but the urgency of my desire to save a helpless child was greater than any fears I had.

I had never been to Africa before, but beginning in 1980, when Stan gave me the green light, I made several journeys to the Eastern Horn countries to make World Vision documentaries. I will always have vivid memories of them. Stan was right, the trips were rough, but they also were glorious! I saw disease and deprivation that broke my heart, but I also saw the courage, dedication and sacrifice of some of God's gentlest warriors.

World Vision is a wonderful organization that is always one of the first to respond to human need anywhere in the world. Its efforts are especially effective because it delivers food, medicine, tools, teachers and doctors directly to the people who need them. It doesn't go through middlemen either here or overseas: it works with missionaries and others who are right there in the midst of the suffering and know where the need is greatest. I had known all that before, but being there where it was happening was an enlightening experience.

We traveled in small groups of five, six or seven. Sometimes Stan Mooneyham went with us. Jim Davies, our director, usually brought two crewmen with him. We also had a pilot, and Lee Mimms, my manager, accompanied me. Occasionally, we were escorted by an interpreter provided by the host government or World Vision.

Like most other people, I had seen photographs and films of Africa, but they didn't prepare me for the real thing. You cannot possibly depict the size of the landscape on film; nor can you show, in two dimensions, how different the earth appears when you're standing along the equator.

The first thing that impressed me when I got off the plane in Nairobi, Kenya, was that I could see for miles because the curvature of the earth isn't as obvious there. Then I saw—and felt and was overwhelmed by—the flies! They were everywhere, all the time, in your eyes, your ears, your mouth, your nose, your hair, your clothes. Newcomers swat at them frantically, but the people who live there don't bother. The dust that constantly blew in the air indicated how serious the drought was. I was warned to conserve every drop of water, what little there was of it. Any water we drank had to be boiled for a long time. The intense heat, along with the lack of moisture, was cruel.

The beauty of the land was awesome. The blue sky seemed to reach higher here than at home. But I was stunned by the unpleasant odors in that clear air. Most of them came from various forms of camel fat and dung, which are used for cooking and for fuel. And because there is so little water, people didn't wash themselves, or their clothing, without good reason.

I never got accustomed to the way the sun behaved in that part of the world. At six o'clock in the morning, the sun popped out of the darkness and suddenly it was day. At six o'clock in the evening the sun said "Bye!" and was gone for the night. There were no sunrises or sunsets.

Usually we would start from Nairobi, fly out into the bush for a few days, and return to Nairobi to get ourselves and our clothes clean before going out again. That was one of the reasons Stan said the trip would be rough on a woman. "What'll you do about your makeup?" he asked me before my first trip.

"Forget it," I said.

"But how will you look on film?" he said.

"Probably I'll look real," I said, laughing. And that's exactly what happened. Makeup, as well as being difficult to keep on, would have been out of place where we went.

On the days we were filming, we always started early in the morning so that Jim Davies and his camera crew could make the best use of daylight hours. Even so, we had to work efficiently because it took us so long to get anywhere and set up our equipment. Then we had to face the tragic possibility that the people we had come to film might not be available—because they might have died.

Most of our filming took place in camps where refugees from the drought and from local wars came to get food, shelter and medical treatment. The camps were flat stretches of land cluttered with huts that sometimes were nothing more than a piece of discarded plastic or cloth held up by sticks. A handful of doctors and nurses in white tents treated thousands of people, mostly women and children, who came to them only as a last resort, frequently too far gone to be helped.

I think that was when I really became aware that life is fragile. We were preceded at the camps by a team of writers who went out a week ahead of us to find patients who were in special need of the kind of medical aid World Vision provides. Most of the patients were children, which was typical of the camp as a whole, and the writers would carefully document their illnesses and the treatment they were receiving. A few days later, when we arrived with our cameras, we would film from the script the writers had prepared. But all too often, by the time we arrived at the camp just days later, we were unable to locate the patients we were there to film. Besides children dying, there were instances of parents taking their children away because they had given up hope and didn't understand what was being done for them.

I remember one tragic case of twin sons brought into a camp by their young mother, whose husband had been killed in the Somalian-Ethiopian conflict. The infants, we were told, were almost dead from starvation but they could have been helped by careful, gradually administered doses of liquefied nourishment. The mother was told this, but she had never been to a doctor before, and couldn't comprehend the process. She was told to bring both infants in for treatment four times a day, but she kept bringing only one child. In the crowd of patients, it took the nurses some time to become aware that only one child was being treated, and by then the other little boy was dead. The mother said she had allowed him to starve to death. She didn't understand what an intravenous injection was, and she knew that in her malnourished condition she had only enough breast milk for one child. What an agony it must have been for her to decide which child she would feed. I met the mother, and I saw the surviving infant, and I broke down in tears because I couldn't even begin to imagine how I would feel if I had to choose between my two sons.

"Cut!" Jim Randall snapped when he saw what was happening. "We can't have you crying all over the place!" he said to me. "When you look into that camera and ask people to dig down in their pocket and help these children, we've got to hear what you're saying!"

He was right. An actress has to walk a tightrope between her feelings and her control of them, and for a few seconds I had forgotten. Jim was too good a director to allow that to happen. As firm as he was with me and the rest of our documentary crew, he was the soul of patience and compassion with the people we were filming, and I could see that very often he had to struggle to control his own tears. Only once did I see him give way to his temper—very effectively.

We had been out in the bush for three days and were on our way to a small airfield where our helicopter was waiting to take us back to Nairobi. In so many of the countries where we worked, the bureaucracy was our greatest obstacle. People in uniform were proud of their authority and most eager to flaunt it, and we were constantly delayed by unreasonable requests to show our credentials, explain the purpose of our presence and allow our baggage to be examined. On this one occasion, our four-wheel-drive vehicle was loaded down with canisters of film which had to be kept tightly sealed until they were processed in Nairobi, but that was nothing unusual. However, we were stopped at the gate to the airfield and told we couldn't go in.

"Why not?" we asked Rebecca, our wonderful interpreter.

The guard, who was about seven feet tall, scowled down at her and bellowed something in words we didn't understand.

"We have to go in by another gate, he says," Rebecca told us. "He doesn't have the authority to let us in."

So we drove three miles to another gate, which was much farther from where our plane was parked, only to be told by the seven-foot guard at that gate that he couldn't let us pass. He told us we had to go back to the first gate. When we did that, the first guard was highly annoyed, but he scribbled something on a piece of paper and gave it to Rebecca.

"We have to go back to the other gate," Rebecca said.

We were hot, tired, dirty and furious. Jim, especially. He wanted to see what was on those films. But we drove the three miles back to the other gate—and again we were delayed. This time the guard insisted on looking through our equipment. Through Rebecca, he ordered us to open the film canisters.

"Not on your life!" Jim said, and Rebecca obediently translated.

The dialogue between Rebecca and the guard became heated, and although we didn't know the language, we could certainly understand the gist of what they were shouting at each other. Rebecca shook her fist and glared up at the tall, thin giant who stood with his hands on his hips, not about to let us anywhere near our helicopter.

"He says, if you don't open cans, he will have water truck come and shoot you," Rebecca said. She pointed to a large, heavy truck parked some distance away. It was fitted with fire hoses. "That's very strong stream of water," Rebecca explained to us. "If he shoot you close up, you get killed."

Jim had had enough. "You tell him," he said, stepping forward, "that he can go ahead and kill me, but I'm not going to let anyone open those canisters!"

When Rebecca passed on the message, the guard signaled to the driver of the truck and sure enough, the monstrous thing began rumbling toward us. It came to a stop a few feet away. I thought, "This is it—I'm going to die of drowning in the middle of a drought!"

Once more the guard issued his order to open the canisters, but this time Jim refused to wait for Rebecca to translate. Stepping up to the guard and looking straight up at him, Jim roared two words: "Fuck you!"

No translation was necessary. The guard backed down and waved us through.

There were so many small wars and skirmishes along the borders of African countries, and occasionally when we were on our way to a refugee camp we had to turn around and go back to avoid being caught in the fighting. But once when we were flying to an orphanage near the Ethiopian-Ugandan border, our pilot didn't turn on the radio and we missed a warning.

Stan Mooneyham and the camera crew had gone on ahead of us in another helicopter, which had already landed, and they were trying to tell us to turn back. They had come down near a group of nomads who were trying to keep their cattle from being stolen by uniformed men with automatic weapons. The nomads had nothing but spears. Stan couldn't get through to our helicopter, but he used his radio to summon help from the local militia.

Our pilot was a skillful, courageous Vietnam veteran who didn't like to use the radio because, as he told us later, "It's always trying to keep me out of places where I want to go." As we came down for a landing he said something like "Hey, there's a raid going on down there." I couldn't hear him over the roar of the copter rotors, but as soon as he turned off the engine I heard the gunfire. By then the militia had arrived and were chasing the intruders and the stolen herd.

When we were told it was safe enough to get out, I looked around cautiously, not knowing what to expect. It was very quiet. Too quiet. We started walking toward Stan's helicopter some distance away, and halfway there we saw the body of a man lying in the dry grass ahead of us. Nothing I had seen of the Vietnam war on television had prepared me for this. The man was naked and half his head was blown away. Apparently he was one of the attackers and his companions had stripped him of his uniform so that it couldn't be identified. Lee Mimms told me not to look as we walked past, but I had to. I saw the decorative scars on his body, each one indicating a kill—not always a man, perhaps an animal. Now he was dead, and I wondered who would be mourning him.

The militia had set up a first-aid tent, and a woman who looked very, very old was sitting in the dirt next to a boy lying on his back. There was a wound the size of a man's fist in the boy's stomach, but he made no sound. In his culture, the slightest whimper would have been unmanly. I knelt down next to the woman and put my arms around her. Her face was expressionless as a nurse began to examine the boy, and I sensed that she wasn't allowed to cry either. I could feel her agony and I borrowed a little of her strength so that I would not embarrass her with my tears.

"Please let me help," I said to the nurse through an interpreter. She pushed a roll of gauze at me and motioned for me to unroll it for her. "Thank you," I said, "thank you." I was grateful to do anything.

The herd was gone and all but a few of the herdsmen were dead. It was just another day of suffering in a tormented land. A group of renegades had raided an arsenal in Uganda, and they came to steal the only wealth the herdsmen had, their cattle. Fighting, conquest and retaliation were age-old customs in Africa, and victory depended upon skill and courage. But in this skirmish, the scales were tipped in favor of modern automated weapons. Against them, spears, leather shields and all the courage in the world didn't stand a chance.

I don't believe there is anything as heartbreaking as the sight, the touch and the stench of a starving child. Did you know that a child's hair turns bright orange from lack of nutrition? And that its tiny face, perhaps only a few months old, looks ancient? There is no sound because the child is too weak to cry, but you know there is pain in the swollen body and in the matchstick-thin arms and legs that move restlessly in your arms, seeking a position of comfort and never finding one. There is no baby smell; there is diarrhea and fear, and when you conquer your squeamishness and bend close to whisper words of hope, you see that the child's eyes are begging you to let it die.

I didn't need to act when I held such children in my arms and looked into a camera. My anger and frustration spoke for me. "This doesn't have to happen if you care." I said. "So—do you care?"

"You were right," Stan Mooneyham said after the first of our many documentaries was shown on a World Vision telethon. A lot more money came in, and a lot more help went out. But those of us who were there knew that much more was needed and we began to plan the next time I'd be free to return to Africa.

In such dire depression, the human spirit is forced to grasp any fragment of humor for mental release. As always, it was the children who saved our sanity. The remote locations seldom had a runway for our small aircraft and the barren horizon afforded no shade or shelter. I carried my one outfit, so my costume would match the previous shoots. So each time I had to change out of my traveling shorts. The only private structure was a tiny, squat cinder-block storage hut for medicines. I could barely stand in the windowless hot-box so I left the door open a crack for air and light. About twenty naked little boys had hovered near the plane in wonder and curiosity. They became the noisy clatter behind us, like a can tied to a dog's tail. We were the closest thing to a circus they had seen. The funny white-skinned woman with *red* hair was the side-show attraction. Our translator shooed them away constantly. Maybe that's why they followed me.

As I began to undress, I saw two, then four, then eight little wide-eyed faces peeking through the door. I'd learned their tribal greeting before we landed, so I waved and said "*Idiock!*" and hurried to get changed. In a twinkling all twenty were squeezed inside, all giggling and pointing as if they had crawled into a monkey's cage. They stared in innocence while I squirmed in embarrassment.

"Let's not just stand here, fellas," I smiled, knowing they couldn't understand a word. "Why don't we sing something?"

Africans sing together by mimicking a leader's improvisations. So I sang a simple melody.

"Da dee da dee dum dum," I led. "Da, di, da, di, dun, dun," they chimed in. Close enough, I guessed, but we could do better than that.

"Let's sing a real song. How about"—and by some unfathomable quirk *this* song rose to my lips at 115 degrees in equatorial Africa—"Jingle Bells, Jingle Bells," I sang.

"Jeedo Baas, Jeedo Baas," they responded.

"Jingle all the way."

"Jeedo oh ti bay."

We all laughed and sang together until I was dressed and the director was calling me to the first setup.

My precious choir was chased from the off-limits hut and scattered like windblown sand. But the wonderful link we had established kept cropping up all day. Whenever we got the whole place quiet and the camera rolling, off in the distance we'd hear a familiar strain from a cluster of children: "Jeedo Baas, Jeedo Baas, Jeedo al ti bay." The director would yell "Cut!" and look at me with a wistful sigh, saying, "I wonder where they picked *that* up?"

No matter how intolerable it got in Africa—somehow the survivors, strong enough to voice their thanks, spoke for *all* . . . and always in song and dance, the universal language. As we joined them in their music and danced with our arms linked around each other, the universal language became transformed into the most miraculous gift of all communication—love.

And now, ten years later, we are finally becoming aware that hunger and disease are still rampant in parts of this earth. When will we start thinking of this as one world, interrelated and interdependent, instead of one where we need only take "a little" responsibility, and have "a little" compassion, because we cannot look beyond the borders of our own nation to see the needs of others? One donation, or even one every year, will help some of the children, but not all of them. If we loved hard enough, we would be able to help all of them. They aren't someone else's children. They belong to all of us. You can see why some of my favorite experiences have come from telethons. World Vision gave me the opportunity to go global, but the telethons benefiting children and victims of diseases here have had powerful moments also.

One of my happiest lessons in courage was taught to me by a five-year-old, doll-like child we'll call Suzie. She was a Shirley Temple lookalike, chosen to be the poster child for the Cerebral Palsy telethon I was hosting. It was my first time cohosting the entire show and I wanted it to be successful. I sent personal letters to all my performing friends and, as usual, if they were in town they promised to come and help. Among the celebrities asked was Frank Sinatra, although it was known that he had *never* appeared on any telethon before. I had enclosed my own special plea—I promised to make him lasagna.

In the middle of rehearsing the band for "The Tonight Show" I got word that "he" called, and just wanted me to know that he would be there for me. Everyone was ecstatic at the CP office and we slated his appearance to be in the last crucial hour. I announced it on "The Tonight Show," and knew that we were assured a full live audience at the studio and millions more TV viewers than before. With all the other actors' acceptances we were really cooking.

Meanwhile, I wanted to establish a real rapport with the children I'd be interviewing and I spent a lot of time at the therapy center meeting parents and doctors. I wanted them to feel at ease with a familiar face instead of being thrust in front of three peering cameras, rows of bright lights and absolute strangers shoving microphones into their faces and asking painful questions. I was bowled over by the cheerful radiance of children and therapists making miraculous strides and by the camaraderie in the circle of parents and patients cheering simple tasks most children take for granted. No pity was tolerated and the lyric "Pick yourself up, brush yourself off and start all over again" took on new meaning for me.

Suzie was wearing heavy steel leg braces all the way to her hips and they made her a load to carry, especially for her petite mother. But because her attempts to walk were frustrating failures, and the pain excruciating, like falling in a suit of armor, for more than a year she had absolutely refused to try. Her parents and friends could still manage to carry her, but that couldn't go on much longer.

Since she would be featured at every station break and I would be singing to her several times, I thought we should be real friends by the time we went on the air. I invited her and her mother for lunch at my home: a main course of spaghetti and a dessert of cookies with "Happy Un-birthday" favors. Then we went into my costume closet and tried on feather boas, hats, muffs and tiaras. She laughed, we sang songs, played with the dogs and picked flowers in the garden. By the time the telethon started, Suzie and I were buddies.

Dennis James, the cohost, had done the telethon for

many years. It was great to have such a wonderful pro to lean on when the unexpected turned up.

Hour after hour I sang, made pitches, interviewed patients, parents, doctors and entertainers, and talked and laughed with Suzie. Then came a number that changed everything for that adorable child. I had just done a long tap dance which was a tribute to Bill Robinson. The marvelous trademark of Robinson was tap dancing up and down a platform of stairs in intricate rhythms. Since Suzie had never seen anything like this, I could see her just out of camera range, mouth open, wide-eyed and smiling ear to ear. After I finished, her mother rushed over to me with Suzie in her arms. We were off camera.

"Suzie wants to tell you something."

"What is it, sweet face?" I asked.

"I want to do that dance," she said pointing to the stairs that were being carted offstage.

"Okay, love, as soon as you learn to walk without those braces, I'll teach you to tap dance."

Suzie looked me straight in the eye and asked, "Promise?"

"I promise, Suzie!"

Things started to roll faster and faster; donations were steadily coming in. Suddenly I noticed uniformed security guards everywhere. The audience sensed a new excitement in the studio. Every house seat was filled, people squeezed into every available corner, and the line to get in went all the way around the building outside. The magnetism of Francis Albert Sinatra has long caused this kind of stir, but I had never stood on *his* side of the footlights with him until now.

We were told that he wouldn't be able to sing anything because all of his music was being rehearsed for a benefit that night in Beverly Hills. "No problem," we said, "just come on and speak to the audience for the kids." We welcomed him and he walked on camera. Mount Vesuvius erupted around us—or at least it sounded that way! Cheering, applauding, whistling, stomping; "Frankie, Frankie, Frankie," the audience chanted. Motioning for quiet, he showed such class and concern, for he didn't just walk on and wing it. No, no. He had prepared a tender, heart-rending speech, filled with vital facts and statistics, knowledge of the disease we were fighting and his own personal feelings about what should be done. He had more than researched the subject. When he finished, the audience shouted their love again with gusto.

"Sing, Frank," yelled a woman in the back.

"Sorry, darlin' I don't have any music with me."

And then my fabulous conductor, Joe Parnello (who had also been Sinatra's conductor) called out from the piano, "How about this one, Frank?" And he started to play what everyone recognized as one of Frank's big hits, "The Way You Wear Your Hat." The audience screamed.

Frank jumped in, "Okay, Joe, but do it in this key," modulating higher. "That's so you can sing it with me, Carol."

"But I don't know the words," I said.

"Don't worry, I'll feed 'em to you," he grinned, taking my hand and the mike. I was dumbfounded, starstruck and in love. For the moment, anyway.

He started the first eight-bar phrase and held the mike for me to do the next. When I needed a word he softly anticipated it as if he were telepathic. He harmonized, tantalized and charmed every breathing soul in hearing range. When the song was finished he gave me a big hug and waved goodbye.

In the pandemonium, we called for a count on the tote board, and with a half an hour to go we needed nine thousand dollars to beat the all-time record. We started to really put on the pressure and then the floor manager handed me a note. It was from Mr. Sinatra and it said, "I pledge $10,000, so you've got it!"

Wow! In about ten minutes, he had stopped the show three times and he wasn't even breathing hard. But that didn't surprise me, for I have known how generous he has always been in countless ways. Out-of-work comics, aging performers, friends in bad times, terminally ill children, even strangers in crisis (whom he reads about in the papers) are sent checks to pull them through for as long as they need it. His only demand is that he remain anonymous. Thankfully, that kind of love can never be completely secret. I am truly proud of and inspired by him. (And you can bet, I sent him the best lasagna I have ever made!)

As we got to the last few minutes of the telethon, I was to sing "You and Me Against the World" to Suzie. She could stand easily if you knelt beside her for support, so that's how we had planned to stage it. I began that touching song with a special lyric I had written for Suzie. Suddenly there was total silence. I was in the final bars when Suzie tightened her little arm around my neck and whispered, "I want to walk."

I couldn't believe it. We had all tried to get her to walk a million times to no avail. I stopped the music and said right into the lens, "Suzie just said she wanted to walk. Isn't that great?"

She nodded but hadn't let go of me yet.

"Okay, Suzie," I said, holding her out from me with both hands. She clutched my arms and looked apprehensive. I caught a glimpse of her mother beside the camera and her eyes were wide open and filling with tears.

"You're fine, Suzie. You can let go now, you're on your own." We both disengaged at once and she just stood, swaying slightly.

"Come on," I urged. "First, your right foot."

The brace scraped against the floor and lifted off, one step, scrape, two steps, and on the third she fell into my arms and we were all crying. All but Suzie, that is. She was laughing that delicious, child's sound of triumph.

After that, Suzie went through many, many difficult surgeries, treatments, training sessions and frustrations. She came to see me at the theater one time in a double leg cast to the hips but managed to come backstage and try on most of my capes and hats and jewelry.

Then one day, I got a call from Suzie asking if I still remembered my promise.

"Of course I remember, silly. But does that mean that you are walking without braces or crutches or even a cane?"

"It certainly does," she chimed.

"Well, then get on down here, so I can teach you how to tap dance!"

It had taken seven years to struggle up those stairs to independence, but she made it. I was thrilled to see her. We worked in the sun porch, tackling the basic, fundamental first steps. I don't know if she's worn out any patterns on her mom's linoleum, but I do know she's going to a regular school like every other kid in her neighborhood. I also know that I've learned more about self-discipline, sacrifice, delayed gratification and courage from Suzie than from any other source. Thanks, Suzie!

Chapter Fourteen

I was quite surprised when, early in 1979, Bobby agreed to meet me to discuss what we could do to help Michael bring up his grades. Bobby was working in New York and I had to be there on business, so in a rush of sentimentality I suggested that we meet for dinner in the restaurant we used to frequent before we were married. Perhaps, I thought, the bitterness was over and we could proceed with a civilized divorce.

Bobby was more than civilized. He was sober, attentive when I spoke, deeply concerned about Michael—and, frankly, I had forgotten how utterly charming he could be. He looked wonderful. His eyes were clear, he had lost weight and his manner was gentle.

"I think the problem with Michael is that his mother and father aren't together," he said after I told him how Michael was changing. "He's a lot like me—and I feel that same way." He seemed to be telling me that he missed me.

I did exactly what I did years ago: I let my guard down. He looked so remorseful. And when he told me he was attending Alcoholics Anonymous meetings with Gordon

McRae, I felt that familiar flutter of hope. Maybe he could change! Maybe he really did love me. I knew I still loved him.

"I'm not drinking, Carol," he told me. I reached for his hand and pressed it hard. I was so proud of what he was doing. "I miss you," he said. "I miss my home, my kids. Can't we call off this divorce?"

"We can try," I said, a bit wary but thrilled.

"Fair enough."

Later that night he called the boys from my hotel room. He insisted on giving them the good news that we were back together. Chris and Mike hadn't known I was going to see their father, and when Bobby got through to them he didn't say I was with him. He just said, "Listen, guys, I want you to talk to the lady I'm going to marry!"

I got on the phone immediately. "It's okay, fellas," I said. "It's me."

They were so happy.

The reconciliation was a disaster. Bobby moved back into the house—and brought all his old habits with him. He stopped going to AA and resumed drinking. "He's worse than ever," my mother said when she spent a few days with us. I had to agree. I assume it was the alcohol that made him do peculiar things such as occasionally projecting his own self-critical thoughts onto me. For instance, when we were driving through a beautiful canyon where the mountains rose steeply on each side of the road, he suddenly turned to me angrily and said, "Why don't you think I could do that?"

"Do what?" I said, wondering if I had missed something.

"Climb those mountains. You think I can't, don't you? Well I could if I wanted to!"

He may have been referring to the time I had climbed the Grand Teton with a party of other amateurs and an instructor. Bobby never forgave me for doing that because he couldn't stand heights.

"I know you could do it," I said.

"You don't mean that," he said. "You always think you're so much better than I am, don't you?"

"I think we both need help, Bobby," I said, starting to cry. "Can't we please go and talk to somebody?"

"I don't need any damned shrink!" he shouted, pressing his foot down on the accelerator. "You're the one who's sick!"

Even I couldn't go on hoping any longer. When we returned to Beverly Hills, I asked Bobby to leave and he refused. "No," he said. "This time you get out."

"I won't do that," I told him. "I want our children to stay in this house. It's the only home they know."

Thankfully he did care about the boys' needs too. As I got ready to leave for New Orleans the next day, I found he had left a note on my dressing table: "By the time you come home, I'll be gone."

I couldn't allow myself to feel anything. I went to the phone, dialed my attorney and told him to start the divorce proceedings all over again.

I think that the most difficult thing we have to do is to be honest with ourselves. I still have a long way to go because there are so many levels and layers. But I'm working on it. When I asked Bobby to leave, I really didn't want him to move out right then. I wanted him to help me face what I could see coming. My father was dying of cancer, and my mother was losing her poorly fought battle against diabetes; her heart and liver were deteriorating.

Aside from my family, Bobby had been the only source of strength I'd ever known. So while on the one hand I wanted him to leave, on the other I wanted him to stay on long enough for me to deal with the approaching deaths of my parents. I still had the fantasy that Bobby and I could face anything together.

We all have unresolved feelings about important relationships that have stymied every attempt at healing. The paramount one in my life was my feeling of never pleasing my father. I had refused his counsel at choosing my life's goal and subconsciously I think he felt disrespected and without value in my eyes. Now he was in a bitter battle with cancer and mere words of love, or hugs and kisses, seemed to stiffen and stifle him. He would not accept pity or special treatment. He would stubbornly do things for himself as long as his iron will could drive him.

From the time he was told of his condition, he did a personal study of cancer wards and saw people screaming in their last days because morphine could no longer squelch the pain. That degradation would never be his fate. He took fewer painkillers than the doctor provided so that he would never diminish their effect by overindulgence.

"I don't want to be a dope addict!" he told the doctor adamantly.

"Mike, I'm afraid you won't have that much time," his longtime friend confided.

Nevertheless, he always carried a little black pen and book in his pocket. In his meticulously beautiful script were the exact time and dosage of each capsule of painkiller he took.

The endless court procedures yanked me up and down like a tired yo-yo in between the concerts, commercials, television shows and nightclubs that paid the bills that were now my responsibility. I had purposely booked a symphony concert just outside of Chicago in hopes that Dad would still be well enough to attend. He had never seen me with a hundred-piece orchestra nor seen me conduct, which was part of the show.

Joey had warned me that Dad was losing ground in his stubborn fight. He was woefully thin, could only walk short distances with help, and it was painful for him to sit too long. For the concert, I reserved the first row for my family and got cushions taped to the back and bottom of his seat in the center. Prior to that date, I wrote him a long letter. It was very personal and into it I poured all the love of the skinny little kid I used to be. I told him how I'd idolized him and followed him around like a puppy because he epitomized patience, wisdom, understanding and uncompromising truth to me. Dad always had the answer I needed or knew how to mend whatever I had broken. To this day, I love the smell of gasoline from a pump because he'd take me with him to do the accounting for a gas station on Saturday mornings, and that was my special time alone with him. I told him that I marveled at his struggle from the poverty of immigrant status to the success of a highly respected official and businessman. I thanked him for the bountiful life he had given his family, and for the windows of enlightenment he opened for us physically and mentally. I told him I was profoundly proud to be his daughter, and that because everybody else knew how much I really loved him, I merely wanted *him* to be aware of that fact as well.

When I called to let my parents know our time of arrival in Chicago, and all the particulars about the symphony concert, I asked Dad if he had received my note. He said yes, and thanked me for "a lovely letter." That was high praise from him and I accepted it happily.

I was doubly nervous as the concert began. Somehow I felt six years old and performing for the very first time. I could see his frail frame slightly bent forward right in front of me. The rest of the audience was mere window dressing—that night I was singing to and for my father, period. All the funny numbers were the breathing spaces for me— the ballads and sad songs were too close to home.

But the hardest was my encore. It was created to be a final kiss, blown to an audience as a forget-me-not. The speech that preceded it began, "Thank you all, you've been wonderfully kind, and I hate to say goodnight. But one of the magical things about live theater is that it happens just like this, only once. Nothing was recorded or filmed, and so the experience belongs to you and me alone. It has been a special time I'll always cherish and keep deep within my heart, and so until next we meet, please remember that"— then there was a music cue and the orchestra began to play—"you will be my music." As I began the phrase, I saw my father look straight into my eyes and nod his head *approvingly.*

"You will be my song." He nodded again.

"You will be my music, to fill my heart with love my whole life long." And then he brushed away a tear and I had to look away.

Somehow, and I don't really know where the strength came from, I did finish the song and people were on their feet applauding. I saw Joey help my father to his feet, and I saw him applauding and smiling and letting the tears fall down his face—unashamedly. Daddy had fixed what had been broken all these years. I threw him a kiss and felt my heart whole again, at last.

The sweetest confirmation came when my sister-in-law, Mary Lou, called me one day. My dad was in his final weeks and had been sent home from the hospital to die in the arms of his family. Joey rented a hospital bed and put it in the living room so his loved ones could be near him. Joey, Lou and Mom were administering his morphine, and although he had been slipping in and out of consciousness he still kept track of the dosages in his little black book. Only now behind the little black book in his pajama pocket was my letter, well worn but always over his heart.

It seems that in her rush to keep everything immaculate, Lou had thrown the pajama top into the washer without emptying the pocket. The letter and book were ruined and she called to apologize.

"I'm so sorry, Carol, because I knew how much the letter meant to him. He was so proud and would read it to us over and over again. In truth, he had it memorized long ago."

They were happy tears I was crying, but I think she knew that.

A few days after Bobby'd left, my brother telephoned me in New Orleans and told me to come home as soon as I could. The Sunday during the engagement of my nightclub act—Father's Day—was my only day off, and I flew back to Chicago with a watermelon in my lap because that was the only food my father was able to swallow. Joey drove me from the airport to his home, doing his best to prepare me for the sight of my father's emaciated body. He had been in a coma and might not be able to acknowledge me, Joey said.

I was shocked by my father's appearance. He was hanging on to the overhead handle of the hospital bed that was set up in Joey's living room. His eyes looked dazed. I took his limp hand in mine as tears ran down my cheeks.

"Daddy, it's me, Carol," I said. "I just got in from New Orleans, and I brought you a fresh watermelon right from the French Market."

He opened his eyes and smiled at me. "Oh, isn't that wonderful," he said, shaking his head in approval the way he did when one of his racing pigeons came in first. Then he closed his eyes and never uttered another word.

Although we took turns sitting with him throughout the night, we all lay down for what we thought would be a few hours of sleep around four o'clock in the morning. And at six, when Joey got up to go to work, he found that Dad had died alone.

I had no time to mourn my father properly because my mother was so distraught.

"He never said it," she kept repeating.

"What, Mom? What didn't he say?"

"That he loved me. Even at the end, when I asked him, he wouldn't say it."

"Oh, Ma, he did!" I said, putting my arms around her. "He just didn't say it in words—but everybody knew how much he loved you."

Her fists were clenched and her body was rigid with anger. "Not me!" she said. "I never knew it—because he wouldn't tell me!"

My mother was very good at covering up her own disability. But I could see how fragile her health had become. "Come home with me, Mom," I said. "Don't stay here all alone." To my relief, she agreed.

Now I can look back and be grateful that I had my mother with me for the final months of her life. She loved the California climate and the view from our house. She did her best to spoil Chris and Mike, and they cherished her. Sometimes she went to church with me on Sunday, and she enjoyed the informality of the service almost as much as I did—something my father never allowed himself to do because he thought it was a sin to worship God anywhere but in a Catholic church. I only wish that I could have spent every moment of those days with my mother, but I had work to do.

We tried to have a cheery Christmas but Mom was catching a cold and we put her to bed and pampered her with soups and hot tea. But by New Year's Day, she was not responding to her medication and I was getting worried. She hated hospitals, so it was difficult to persuade her to submit to the treatment she needed. And once she was in the hospital, she just seemed to give up living. I could see her dying minute by minute, and it took all my strength to control the anger I felt because she wouldn't fight to stay alive. I was extremely selfish about her. I knew how sick she was—but she was only sixty-one years old, and I needed her! She had loved me more than anyone else in the world and I didn't know how I would survive without her.

I didn't want to think about the divorce, which was still held up by Bobby's refusal to sign a reasonable settlement. He wouldn't talk to his own lawyer, let alone mine. Strangely, the only person he seemed to trust was my brother Joe. "He's agreed to meet with me and his lawyer on his boat next week," Joey said when he called, as he did every night, to ask how my mother was doing.

"Oh, Joey," I said, "I'm sorry you have to come all the way out here."

"I want to come anyway," Joey said. "I want to see Mom—and I think maybe you could use a friend."

"Thanks, Joey. I didn't want to ask."

"You didn't have to. I'm your brother."

Joey arrived the day he was going to meet Bobby. He and I spent the afternoon sitting by my mother's bed in a private room. There were wires connected to many parts of her body, all of them hooked up to a bank of machines with dials and lights and soft, methodical sounds. She was in a coma, but we prayed that she could hear our words of love and hope. Then the line on one of the dials stopped moving and another gauge started whining a thin, high-pitched ay-y-n-n-h-h.

I screamed, but the room was already filled with nurses and doctors. My mother's heart had stopped. Joey and I waited in the corridor while the medical staff did everything they could to revive her, and then finally they told us she was dead.

"Do you want to see her?" one of the doctors asked.

"Yes," I said, not yet realizing what had happened.

When they told us we could enter her room, I knew it was a mistake. My mother was blue, and to this day I can't forget how she looked.

The show of strength I had always put on in front of the doctors and nurses was over. I couldn't control myself; I started to scream and cry.

"Please, Miss Lawrence," one of the doctors said, "try to calm down."

But my brother understood. "It's okay," he kept telling me, "Do whatever you feel like doing—I'm here for you."

Joey drove me home, but he didn't get out of the car. "I'm still going to see Bobby," he told me.

"No, Joey, you can't."

"I have to. You shouldn't have this divorce over your head any longer."

When he came home later that night he gave me a copy of the settlement. Bobby had signed it. In a few weeks the divorce would be final.

I had lost too many people in too short a time, and I couldn't stop crying. Weeks went by and still I would burst into tears when I least expected it. I tried not to let the boys see how depressed I was, but they knew. They were considerate, but much too quiet. I wanted to assure them that I was going to be all right, but I didn't really believe I would be. I wasn't sleeping and I was exhausted. With a change in my spiritual needs, I had joined a new church, the Church on the Way. I had been attending one of their prayer groups, for women who had lost loved ones. But even after my work in Africa I couldn't seem to feel God's presence the way they did. Most of them spoke of the comfort Christ was bringing to them. How I wanted that kind of comfort!

Where did my responsibilities begin and end? Which were the nudgings of the Spirit within that I was asking to teach me, and which were anxiety attacks that destroy? I blamed myself for not spending more time with my mother. I should have made her take care of herself. I should have gone home to see my father more often. I should have appreciated more of what my husband was, rather than driving him to become someone he wasn't. How much of his drinking was my fault? Was I unable to communicate love? How much of his gentle laughing side could I have drawn out? At the worst of times I would relive the abortion, going back over all the reasons for it and telling myself that there should have been some other way. I felt so very far from God.

Then I got a call from the account executive at Young and Rubicam. He had trouble getting to the point, which was that the new people at General Foods were reviewing the entire International Coffee account. "Don't worry," he said, sounding terribly worried. "I'm sure everything's okay. But you know, new people come on board and sometimes they have different ideas."

"But the commercials are doing so well," I said. "Why would anyone want to change them?"

I had done the commercials for about six years, and we went so well together that people would stop me on the street and tell me how much they liked "my" coffee. Truck drivers would honk at me and yell, "Hey, Carol, how about a cup of coffee?" It was work I enjoyed doing, and the people involved with it, both at Y&R and at General Foods, had been wonderful.

"Now they don't want it associated with anybody," he explained. "They want it to be everybody's coffee."

"What are you telling me? That I'm out?"

"No, no. Not out." He couldn't bring himself to say it.

"What you mean, then, is that I'm not in any longer, right?"

"Well, what I really called about, Carol, is to invite you to a lunch we want to give you. We appreciate all you've done—and we want you to know how much we love you."

Sure. It's always nice to know people love you. "Okay," I said. "Let's make it easy. When do we do lunch?"

It was a lovely, extravagant lunch, but you never saw

such a gloomy group of celebrants. And why not? We were gathered to put to rest an ad campaign that was nothing but successful. After each of us said a few words about how great it was to have worked together, I was presented with a delicate Limoges cup and saucer on a platform of polished wood encased in Lucite. It looked like a glass coffin. On the front was a brass plaque engraved as follows:

IN APPRECIATION TO CAROL LAWRENCE
SPOKESPERSON FOR GENERAL FOODS INTERNATIONAL COFFEES
NATIONAL INTRODUCTION FOR SWISS MOCHA 1974—75, CAFE
VIENNA 1975—76, CAFE FRANCAIS 1974—75, ORANGE
CAPPUCCINO 1976—77 AND IRISH MOCHA 1978—79.

It sits in my office at home. And when people still tell me how much they enjoy "my" coffee, I just smile and say, "I'm glad you enjoy it. You have good taste."

My instinct was to run in six directions at once, looking for work. "Anything!" I reminded my manager. "It costs a fortune to run this house."

I hadn't been able to stop crying. I managed not to cry in front of anybody, but the moment I was alone—in my car, at home, in a ladies' room—the tears would start. I sobbed from so deep inside myself that my ribs ached. I was afraid that one day I would cry onstage, or even backstage, and that would be the end of everything. Producers put a lot of money into a show, and they want performers who aren't going to fall apart. Sometimes I wondered if anyone ever died from crying.

One night, alone in the blackness of my bedroom, sadness overwhelmed me and grew into a crescendo of heart-wracking sobs. I was out of control and unable to stop. *This is dangerous!* I told myself. *You've got to do something. You can't let yourself get sick! Your kids need you.* But for the first time in my life I couldn't fix something. I didn't even have the strength to try.

Then I remembered something a woman in my prayer group had said when I thought I couldn't go on living after my parents died. "God never burdens us with more than we can carry," she said. "That's his promise to us, so if your grief is too heavy, ask Jesus to help you carry it."

I had been praying for help for a long time, but never in specific terms. I didn't feel I knew God that well, and I guess I was afraid He might turn me down. But I didn't care. I had no one else to cry to but God. I couldn't breathe. I felt like a baby gasping in desperation, unable to stop. I felt as if I were drowning!

I slid off the bed onto my knees. "Dear Lord Jesus!" I sobbed. "Take these tears from me—or I'm dead. You said you'd never give me a burden I couldn't carry, but I'm going under with this one. *Help!*"

Then I did something I had never had the courage to do when I prayed. I thanked God for answering my prayer before I even knew it was answered. I dared to believe that He loved me enough to ease my pain—because He understood that I couldn't take it anymore.

Very gradually I started to feel better. I could breathe, and my ribs didn't ache as much. After a while I stopped crying. A beautiful kind of peace came over me, and I knew that I never had to be alone again. I thought of Christopher and Michael asleep in their rooms. I wanted to give them what God had just given me. For the first time—ever—I felt that someone loved me even though I couldn't fix anything or live up to anyone's expectations. Now if I could only learn how to love Chris and Mike in the same way, we'd be okay.

We weren't going to have an easy time of it. I would have to learn how to get along without Bobby, but Chris and Mike would have a much more difficult adjustment to make. Eventually Bobby would no longer be my husband, but he would always be their father. I would have to cope with my own feelings of loss without involving my sons in them or expecting them to make up for that loss.

I needed to learn how to feel good about myself again. I had to recapture that huggable feeling I used to have when I was a little girl doing time steps while my mother applauded so hard her hands must have stung. Being loved made my life an adventure. I had lost that sense of adventure, and with it much of my self-confidence.

But I was getting occasional moments of deep calm. Finally I was able to realize that there was no barrier between God and me, unless I put one there. (As Meister Eckhart said, "God is at home, it is we who have gone out for a walk.") I didn't have to go looking for God because He had already found me.

I felt like I'd finally been reconnected to my source after a long separation. An awareness kept surfacing that God was inside and that everything I had and was, and everything that surrounded me, was His gift.

I breathed a giant sigh of relief and gratitude for feeling this complete. "Thank you," I prayed," and please let this enveloping sense of wholeness come back often." Just being alive filled me with wonder.

Chapter Fifteen

I remembered saying I'd hold on to our house and our lifestyle even if I had to scrub floors to do it. I meant it—but where do you scrub floors in show business? I was about to find out!

I needed money. I was working frantically, traveling all over the country doing one-night stands, filling in for sick and injured performers, and breaking in a new nightclub act. I wanted to change with the times, and I needed an act that didn't require a supporting cast of male dancers and musicians, because nobody could afford to travel that way anymore. I also wanted to be flexible because I knew I wouldn't always be performing in clubs.

As hard as I worked and as much money as I made, our living expenses ate up everything. We weren't careless or extravagant, but all we had to do was stand in place and the money just went out the window. Or, rather, into the canyons around us. For instance, bees can do a lot of damage to old houses, so we needed the regular services of an exterminator to keep them away. We needed someone to clean out the fast-growing brush that crept up the canyons

223

and threatened to catch fire and burn out the neighborhood. We needed a full-time live-in housekeeper because I was away so often. Besides the normal expenses any family has, we lived in an affluent neighborhood, and Chris and Mike had wealthy friends. If they were invited to go off and ski for a weekend, that meant they needed the outfit and gear. I also had professional expenses: my manager, agent, costumers, arrangements, choreography, accompanist, secretary, accountant and press agent.

I thought I was doing well financially because I was so busy, but one day my accountant got up the nerve to tell me that I was operating at a loss. He didn't want to upset me, he said, so for a long time he had borrowed from one account to pay another, and, oh, yes, I was behind in my income taxes. That's when I learned an important lesson: stay on top of your financial situation. Know how much money is coming in and where it's going. Don't assume that someone else, no matter how qualified, will look after your best interests. You're the only one who can do that, and if you don't know how, you had better learn.

I was very happy with my new nightclub act. Though it was filled with new songs and arrangements, I had kept what now had become my signature number, "Top Hat."

"I've got you a booking in a condo tour," my agent told me.

"What's that?" I asked.

"It's something new," he said. "Instead of playing the nightclub circuit, you play in the Florida condos."

I wasn't so sure it was a good idea. "Who's my audience?" I asked him.

"The condo residents," he explained. "They subscribe to a series of performances, and you go from one condo to another for a couple of weeks. It's good money."

"I don't know," I said.

Then he began to twist my arm. "Look," he said, "you'll be in good company. A lot of great performers are going this route."

"Name a few."

"Okay, let's see . . . How about Sergio Franchi . . . Vic Damone . . . Anna Maria Alberghetti . . . Shirley Jones . . . Donald O'Connor . . ."

I was impressed. "All right," I said, "I'll try it."

"Great!" he said. "These people will love you! They all remember you."

What he'd neglected to tell me is that a condo tour is the pits.

You do two shows a night for ten nights, and often you have to travel as much as a hundred miles by van from the first show to the second. Your first show starts at 5 P.M. but you arrive much earlier because you and nine musicians have to set up your equipment on the stage. Did I say "stage"? That wasn't always true. Sometimes, you performed on the floor of the condominium recreation room, which generally wasn't large to begin with, and which you had to share with the musicians because there was no other place for them to go. The audience was right on top of you.

There weren't enough overhead lights, and there was only one small spotlight a few feet in front of you, so you had to do without the magical illusion that professional theatrical lighting creates. Everything looks different: your makeup, the color of your hair, your costumes. The audience knows something is missing, but they don't know what. So you work twice as hard to give them their money's worth because, after all, they came to see you, and you appreciate it.

"You can't do that routine where you take six men from the audience," the tour manager told me shortly before my first performance.

"Why not?" I asked, astonished. "That's the best part of my act."

"Our insurance doesn't cover it," he said matter-of-factly.

"But what could possibly happen?" I asked. I could see ten minutes of my act disappearing right in front of my eyes. What would I substitute for it?

"You don't understand, Carol," he said. "These are old

people. Some of them are in wheelchairs. Some have walkers. You can't ask them to get up and dance. Suppose they fall and break a hip. Or have a heart attack?"

"That's ridiculous!" I said. "All they do is take a few steps."

"And lift you up."

"I'm not that big. Besides, there are six of them."

"Okay, okay, but if anything happens, you're responsible."

About an hour before my first show I was arranging my costumes behind the flimsy screen where I was supposed to change. It was in full view of the audience, but what could I do? There wasn't a dressing room. Besides, I made six or seven changes during my act and I had to move fast. I wore some of my costumes layered to save time.

I was dressed in a robe and my hair was up in rollers, which is typical of the way I look backstage in the theater. Only I was now onstage all the time and some of the audience were arriving.

"Hmmmm, so that's Carol Lawrence," I heard a woman say to another. I smiled, but they didn't smile back. "She's not so much in a robe, is she?" her friend answered. I was off to a great beginning.

At least we had a full house, and that didn't always happen. Sometimes only a handful of people showed up, but still the show went on. Donald O'Connor told me that once he performed for only two people. "But—I got a standing ovation," he said, with that wonderful grin of his.

I had been inspecting the floor and it wasn't in good shape. I'd have to be especially careful to avoid certain areas where I might trip during some of my fast dancing. I'd have to keep my six men off to one side.

As I waited behind the screen for the show to start, I began to feel depressed. There were so many performers just like me, doing the same kind of thing all over the state of Florida, and probably in a few other states as well. We had worked very hard for a long time to develop our talent, to keep getting better and better at what we did. And now that we were better than ever, we felt unwanted. Ten years ago we wouldn't have believed it if anyone had told us we would be doing our act in the rec room of a high-rise condominium for an audience of people who had nothing better to do.

But as my agent had said, my audience knew me, and they expected a good show. I was going to give them the best I had.

If I had been opening in a new show on Broadway I couldn't have given them more than I gave that night. And they gave me their enthusiasm. They applauded wildly after each song and dance. I knew they would love the routine with the six men.

As I worked, I was scanning the men, looking for the younger ones. When I started my routine, I approached one man who looked pretty healthy, and reached for his hand. Before he could get out of his seat, his wife reached across and hit me on the arm with her program.

"Take your hands off him!" she screeched at me. "He's got a pacemaker and you'll kill him! What kind of idiot are you?"

I was stunned, and the poor man sank back into his chair, shrugging his shoulders apologetically. I smiled at his wife and moved out of her range. "I wouldn't dream of hurting your wonderful husband," I said. "He's too cute."

Well, the tour manager had tried to warn me. Nevertheless, I refused to give up the best part of my act, so I moved on quickly to another man, but this time I didn't touch him. I simply held out my hand, and kept one eye on the woman sitting next to him.

I got my six men, and they were terrific. Naturally they didn't walk very fast, and when they lifted me up they barely got my feet off the floor, but they had no shortage of spirit. The audience cheered!

As soon as the show was over, the nine musicians and I packed our equipment into the van and off we went to the next performance. I touched up my makeup and reset my hair along the way.

After ten nights of a condo tour, you're exhausted. But the act had been a success, and the tour manager wanted to sign me up for another series. It was the last thing I wanted to do, but I needed the money. Before I said yes, I called my agent.

"Good news," he said, "You've got a role in a 'Murder, She Wrote' if you can get right back here."

"You bet I can!" I told him. Thank you, Lord!

Gradually I was offered more shows and better roles. For five months I toured with Mickey Rooney in *Sugar Babies*, and I had a great time singing, tap dancing and doing comedy routines. I was feeling confident about my future.

Chapter Sixteen

My greatest concern was that I wasn't home very much, and I didn't like being an absentee parent. Mike and Chris were fifteen and seventeen years old, and both of them were over six feet tall. It was hard enough for me to be a firm parent when I had to crane my neck to look them in the eye, but it was impossible to convey any kind of authority by way of long-distance telephone calls.

The first sign of trouble was the way they looked. Their eyes were often bloodshot and unfocused, and they were always tired. Then I began getting calls from their teachers about their failing grades. "Mike doesn't hand in his assignments," one teacher told me, "so I can barely give him a passing grade." "Chris is cutting up in his classes, and he has mood swings," another said.

All along I'd thought Michael was handling the divorce quite well. When I tried to get him to talk about it, he kept telling me it didn't bother him. "It's all over, Mom," he used to say. "It was a long time ago." I wanted to believe him, but he wasn't the same sweet, playful, hard-working boy, and I could trace the change to the time of my separation from

229

Bobby. Sometimes when Michael looked at me, I saw anger in his eyes. And blame. During the years of our court fights Michael had gained a lot of weight. He was convinced he was ugly, which wasn't true. He was gorgeous; they both were.

Until Bobby and I broke up, Michael and Chris got along well. Not anymore. Now there were arguments and violent confrontations.

Chris later told me that Michael felt the separation deeply even though he didn't talk about it, and there were many nights when Michael cried himself to sleep. Chris had foreseen the divorce for some time, but when I told them that their father wasn't coming home anymore, Michael was stunned and badly wounded. I can understand why: Michael didn't want me to be hurt, but he didn't want to hurt his father either. That it was Michael who ran for his knife on the climactic New Year's Day in 1976 was typical of him. He immediately sized up the situation and decided that something had to be done about it—but he couldn't be the one to do it. He loves his father very much.

So does Chris, but in a different way. As the first son, he took the brunt of Bobby's insistence that a boy had to be tough, strong, and fearless and must never cry. He wanted so much to please his father, yet he feels that he never succeeded. He's extremely sensitive to other people's needs, and is eager to win their approval, so a lot of his time and energy go to helping people do things they really ought to be able to do for themselves. That includes me. Sometimes I catch myself counting a little too much on his generosity and good nature because he seems to know, without my telling him, when I need a shoulder to lean on. He learned early in life how important it is to please. It is the natural behavior pattern for the "oldest adult child of an alcoholic." Now I wish he could unlearn a bit of that and learn to please himself.

If you come to our house, Chris is always the one to greet you, take your coat and make you feel at home. When I used to come home from being on the road, Chris was always at the door waiting for me. Michael was there, too, but Chris was always ahead of him, so what else could Michael do but stand off to one side? It got to be his way of life. Chris was more verbal; he could tell me how happy he was to have me home. He could say, "Mom, I love you." Michael may have needed my attention and my love as much as Chris did, but he didn't know how to claim it. He's too much of an individual to copy his brother, and he wasn't going to compete with him, so he said nothing. I was full of guilt for having been away, and felt responsible for any problems my sons were facing. I thought Chris missed me and Michael didn't. Lack of time, energy and strength in those frantic days blinded me from seeing they both had needs.

I knew that both Chris and Mike were experimenting with pot, and like so many teenagers, they were drinking, too. And they were old enough to drive. All of their friends had gotten a car for their sixteenth birthday, and I didn't know how to say, "No, Chris and Mike, you can't have one!" It wouldn't have kept them from driving; they would have driven a friend's car. So when Chris turned sixteen, I gave him my father's old Chevy. I purchased a used car for Michael when he came of age. Unfortunately, my worst fears were realized—both of the boys were involved in accidents and I'm only grateful that no one was ever seriously injured.

When I was home, I couldn't sleep until I heard each of them drive up the hill into the garage. When I was away I worried about them constantly. I just didn't know what to do. I told them they were not allowed to drink in our home, but while I was away they got into my wine cabinet. I told them drugs were absolutely forbidden, but I still could smell pot. I begged them not to drive when they were drinking. "Call me," I said. "I'll come and get you wherever you are, and I promise not to say a word." They didn't call.

I didn't know how much children act out their pain, loss, fear, insecurities and anger. Like most grown-ups, they haven't learned to express their emotions and needs in a safe, verbal way, so like steam leaking through a loose fitting, they get belligerent, rebellious, withdrawn—whatever. How much more compassion I could have had for them if I had understood their behavior as their way of expressing their agony over our breakup. *Not more leniency*, mind you—just more compassion. And maybe I would have known how to talk to them better, to listen.

For the first time in my life, I felt so alone that I began to admit defeat. My mother and father were gone. I could always count on my brother Joey, but he lived so far away.

I have a dear friend named Arlene Hunnicutt who listens to me when I'm not making much sense and who somehow understands what I'm trying to say. I was wondering out loud if there was something I could do to help my sons solve their problems. "I've tried psychiatrists," I told her, "and they don't have an answer. I've tried to bring Chris and Mike into the church, but they think I'm a Goody Two-Shoes. Is there anything else I can do, any place I can take them?"

"Maybe," Arlene said. "Have you gone to Al-Anon?"

"Yes. When I was married to Bobby. It helped."

"Well, they have a program for adult children of alcoholics. They're called ACAs."

"Mike and Chris would never go to anything like that," I said. "They don't want to remember that their father was an alcoholic."

"That's typical of an ACA," Arlene explained. "We try to deny that there ever was anything wrong with our alcoholic parents." She smiled at the question on my face. "That's right," she said, "I'm one of them. And Al-Anon sure helped me."

"How?"

"When you grow up with an alcoholic parent, you carry some scars around with you. The trouble is, you don't know it. You think you're normal, but you don't know what normal is."

"What kind of scars, Arlene?"

"They show in the way you relate to people. You're afraid to trust them because you think they'll hurt you if you let your guard down. You're afraid of your own feelings, so you don't dare let anyone find out what's going on inside you.

And you don't want to talk about the way you grew up because you were taught to pretend that everything was okay."

I remembered all the years we'd pretend to be the perfect
family. Did we do it to fool the public? Or ourselves?

"The ACA program helps you get in touch with the real
you," Arlene said, "the person God meant you to be before
all the trouble started."

Chris and Mike didn't want to hear about ACA or go to
any kind of meeting where alcoholism was discussed. "We
don't have a problem, Mom!" they said. So I went to a six-
week course at Bel Air Presbyterian Church.

I sat in a group of people who seemed to be doing very
well with their lives. They had families, they worked hard
and had all kinds of careers—there was a nurse, an en-
gineer, a copywriter, an actress, a nurseryman—yet they
had a lot of trouble feeling good about themselves. Most
of them felt they weren't doing enough for their families,
especially their parents. I learned that it was typical of
adult children of alcoholics to miss out on childhood because, even as children, they felt responsible for the ir-
responsible parent. Quite often these people were abused
as children and many of them couldn't recall long stretches
of their early years.

One woman, a nurse, said, "Anytime I'm in a group of
people and someone raises his voice, I want to scream and
run out of the room." Then, amazingly, some of the others
said they felt the same way. All of a sudden they were like
brothers and sisters, sharing a common experience, reaching out and hugging each other, giving each other the love
and support they never had as children.

I attended the entire course because it gave me insight
into myself as well as my sons. I could identify with many
of the feelings they expressed: the compulsion to be perfect
in order to win a parent's approval, the longing to be loved
by a parent who didn't know how to express love, the conviction that I was to blame for whatever went wrong and
was never the cause of anything good.

My sons had a much more complicated experience of

parental love. For them, it was either feast or famine. When Bob and I were home they were overwhelmed with affection and discipline. Because of our own problems, we were inconsistent: sometimes strict, other times permissive. And then Bob and I would be on the road again, leaving the boys in the care of a nanny. Understandably, Mike and Chris weren't sure they were loved. Children want proof, and they want it constantly.

Hearing the experiences of adults who had grown up as my sons had, I could understand much more clearly how I had shaped their lives—and their problems. Oh, yes, I loved them. And I wore myself out trying to prove it. But the truth is that I was totally preoccupied with Bobby.

Even when I took Michael and Christopher to museums and went off on picnics with them, my mind was at home, wondering how much Bobby was drinking and what he might do to hurt himself, or what kind of mood he might be in when we returned. Loving an alcoholic is a way of life. There isn't room for anything or anyone else, and my kids knew that better than I.

I was an "enabler." I was always trying to save Bobby. I covered up for him when he couldn't give an interview. When he couldn't remember the lyrics to a song, I said he was tired. When he accused me of thinking I was better or more talented than he, I tried to be less than I was. I told myself he was discouraged and worried about his career. Never once did I allow him to suffer the consequences of what he did or didn't do. I "enabled" him to go on drinking and destroying not only himself, but the rest of us. I have to share the blame.

I never made a conscious decision to look for a new husband. I certainly wasn't going to be one of those women who married on the rebound. But I wanted to be in love and I needed help, and that's all it took.

In 1981 I met Greg through Vince, a colleague who had gone into the real estate business when Los Angeles property values were booming. I thought it might be a good idea to invest in a condominium, so I called Vince for advice.

"You ought to meet Greg," he said. "He taught me the real estate business."

"Fine," I said. "How do I do that?"

"Greg's staying with me for a while. I'll tell him to call you."

Greg called and then came to the house. He was on his way to play tennis and apologized for wearing tennis shorts. But he looked good in them and I enjoyed his easygoing manner. He gave me a short course in buying a condo and made an appointment to show me a few of them later that week.

I was looking forward to seeing him again. He picked me up and we spent a wonderful day together. He was much more interesting than the condominiums we saw, and it felt good to spend time talking with a man who wasn't trying to prove how strong he was.

I told him I wanted to give more thought to buying a condo.

"That's being smart," he replied. He wasn't trying to tell me what to do, either. I appreciated that.

I went on the road again, and when I came home there was a message from Greg. "I wondered if you'd have dinner with me sometime," he said when I called him.

"Sure."

"You will?" He sounded so boyish, I had to laugh. "How about Saturday?"

I looked at my calendar, which was a joke. I hadn't been on a date in years. I never had time for a social life.

It was a delightful evening. Greg had made reservations at an excellent restaurant in Pasadena, and when we arrived everything was "Good evening, Miss Lawrence," "How are you, Miss Lawrence?" "Right this way, Miss Lawrence!" I hadn't been fussed over in a long time and, as phony as I knew it was, it felt good. I guess my ego was at the point of starvation.

Greg was exactly the kind of company I needed. He wasn't handsome. He was slender, his height was average and he had dark wavy hair. I wasn't able to see it then, but he reminded me of my father, although only in appearance. His behavior was completely different. He didn't tell me much about himself, other than the fact that he and his wife were getting divorced. He was the kind of man who makes you feel like talking because he knows how to listen. You feel interesting. It's easy to laugh. You think of funny things to say, and you both laugh.

He was interested in Chris and Mike. He told me his former wife had been married before and had three teenage boys. "I know what a rough time that is for parents," he said. "I went through that with our boys—the drugs, the rebellion, the drinking."

"How are they now?" I asked.

"I think they're going to be okay," he said. "We're very close, even with the divorce."

How refreshing! I thought. *There really are decent people in the world.*

"Next week Chris has a birthday," I told him. "This would be a lovely place to celebrate. Will you join us?"

"I'd like that," he said. "And I'd like to meet your boys."

Chris and Mike didn't take to Greg at all. Chris at least was sociable. Michael didn't say a word.

I can look back to that time now and wonder why I was so thrilled that a man had taken me out to dinner. I had been in some of the finest restaurants in the world. I had sat at good tables in the company of exciting, creative, powerful men. What was so special about Greg? I think it was the way I felt when I was with him. I didn't feel owned. I didn't feel that I was being used to make money for someone. No one was out to conquer me and then forget I existed. There wasn't anything for me to fix. In fact, I felt as if I were with someone who wanted to fix something for me. I wasn't an actress; I was a woman, a person, a mother.

I knew very little about him. Like my mother, he was a diabetic, but he paid attention to his diet and he used insulin. He told me that he had been in the hospital, and when he came out he went to live with Vince, an old friend. He also sold his business, a school that offered courses in real estate sales. He said it had been successful, but he wanted to get into something else because the real estate boom was over. He seemed to have a good business sense, and even though he had no experience in the theater, he took an interest in my career. I needed someone like that in my life.

Vince didn't agree, and that surprised me. "He's your friend," I said.

"I know, but he's wrong for you. I don't think I can stand by and let you do this."

"Do what?"

"Fall in love with this guy. It's a mistake."

Well I guess fear and loneliness have their own power —such enormous power that it deafened me to my own instincts. I refused to listen to trusted friends trying to help. I rationalized away every glaring clue, and melted into dependency on what I thought was a wise, strong, caring man. He said, "I don't want anything from you, Carol. I just want to be here for you in any way I can."

Greg meant what he said, or at least part of it. He was there all right. He was ready to help me with anything. He gave advice about my sons. He said I was too indulgent with them and he encouraged me to reinstate the rules I had allowed them to ignore. There would be no smoking, no drinking and no drugs in our home. When they went out with their friends, they were to be home by midnight. If they were going to be late, they were to call me by eleven o'clock and let me know where they would be and for how long. If they didn't like the rules, out they went. I balked, but Greg insisted it was the only way to make my point.

Greg persuaded me to invest in some real estate, and he gradually began to know more about my financial situation than I did. When he questioned some of the things my accountants did, I let him take over that part of my life. Then he found fault with the way my career was being handled. He thought he could do better. He thought I could be a superstar. Oh, that encouragement felt good from someone who believed in me fully.

It was inevitable that Greg would move in with me. In fact I was the one who said, "I will live with you, but that's all," when he said that he wanted to marry me. He looked so hurt. "I'm just not able to make more of a commitment yet," I told him. "It's not you—it's me." I was terrified that something would happen to this marriage as it had to Bobby's and mine.

Greg even went to church with me and seemed to enjoy it. He talked about becoming a member, although he never did. I was happy to be with someone who could understand how important my spiritual life was.

But I still had a lot to learn about that spiritual life. I had assumed that once I became aware that God loved me, I was going to be all right. But I forgot that with all growth, it takes time and effort. Before I'd become acquainted with the Bible, I'd expected it to be a rather forbidding, difficult book. While it isn't always easy, and it can and should mean different things to different people, it is anything but forbidding.

I signed up for Bible study classes, but I couldn't attend most of them because I was out of town so often. I bought books, and read them when I could, but I didn't have time to discuss them with a group, which always helps to get more insight into their meaning. When I was away I listened to tapes of inspirational messages, and wherever I was I tried to attend church services. But there was no continuity to my religious education, and I had so many questions that needed answers.

I didn't feel right about living with Greg. I knew commitments of any kind were terrifying to me at the time, and I knew the fear that gripped me was getting in the way of trusting God and taking life's risks again.

Whenever I felt uneasy, I told myself that I wasn't hurting anyone. What Greg and I did was our business and no one else's, which is a great way to bury your head in the sand. I discovered that the day Christopher asked me if he could bring his girlfriend home for the night.

I wanted to say no, but I choked on the word. How could I tell my son that he had to follow the rules while I didn't? Greg, who was always telling me that I wasn't strict enough with the boys, took Chris's side. "This is the way kids are today," he insisted. "If you say no, they'll go somewhere else, and do the same thing." *Maybe he's right*, I thought. *Maybe I don't know enough about these things.* I gave in. I even convinced myself that I was an understanding, "with-it" mother.

Eventually, I married Greg to make peace with my warring conscience. Being on the road is very rough on a woman alone. When you're performing, you don't simply play your part and call it a day. People want to meet you. Producers want you to come to parties and promote the show. Local citizens' groups want you to help their causes and launch their crusades.

I reasoned that if Greg and I were married, he could travel with me. He was already such a help and delight that when I wasn't with him, I missed him. I had a big tour coming up. It would be wonderful to have his company and to stop hiding our relationship.

I knew I didn't love Greg the way I had loved Bobby, but I thought we both might be better off that way. I cared about Greg and I was comfortable with him. Instead of competing with each other, we might be able to build a good life together, and that was more important than passion. I no longer had to please my parents, but how I wished I could take Greg home to Melrose Park to meet my mother. She would have loved him!

We were married on March 7, 1982, and on our way home from the ceremony I began to have the uneasy feeling that something was wrong. The helpfulness, the sensitivity, that caring manner, seemed to fade. Now he was in charge. As we sat back in the limousine, he began to plan what we would do with my future and my money. He offered some convincing reasons why he was the one who should manage my career—and wouldn't it make sense for me to authorize him to sign my checks?

I fell into an old familiar pattern: I blamed myself for my uneasiness. Maybe I just wasn't accustomed to this kind of man. Maybe I shouldn't be so suspicious. If I didn't let him know that I trusted him, what kind of marriage would we have? He was so devoted to me, what more did I want?

I said yes, be my manager. Yes, sign my checks. And he was happy.

He became my manager, my secretary, and my accountant. But he had no previous knowledge or experience in a business at which lifetime veterans fail daily. He orchestrated my social life, what there was of it. At his suggestion, I changed my will so that he would inherit a third of my estate, and I took out a million-dollar life insurance policy naming him the sole beneficiary.

Our marriage lasted about a year and a half, and the best thing I can say about it is that I'm learning to call things by their right name. If something is a "mistake," then learn from it, cut the losses and move on. And this had been a giant mistake, for which I take full responsibility—for being vulnerable, needy, lonely, gullible and too anxious to have a strong male to help guide and befriend my sons. That does not mean divorce is a light issue to me. To the contrary, I would have done almost anything to stay married, but in this case it would have permanently jeopardized my sons' future.

It was my sons who brought me back to reality. Had I been overprotective, or made too many excuses for them? Had I showered them with too many gifts, or at least the wrong kind—the material goods instead of the emotional encouragement to grow and follow their own paths with confidence? Was there still time for me to create order, mixed with love and security, for them? I loved the line Matt Fox used once, "One of the things we know for sure about Jesus was that his parents raised him as though he were the Son of God."

Now that we were alone again, I took a good look at the boys, their needs, the malady that psychiatrists call "adjustment reaction to adolescence," and I knew I was in way over my head. The only other thing I knew for sure was that I loved them and that if they could get past this period with the same confidence in themselves that I had in them, they were going to be fabulous. Clearly that was not enough to base sound decisions on.

For the first time, I got livid at the educational system

of the greatest country in the world, that had allowed me to go through sixteen years of school without ever teaching me how to raise children. There is typing for secretaries, accounting for business majors, hosts of wonderful things to learn, but for the most important thing—the appropriate rearing of our children to equip them to wisely rule the world—there is no required course! Boy, did I need one now.

Both boys were wary and mistrustful. Michael was at best uncommunicative. Otherwise, he was belligerent and angry. When I tried to talk to him about his life, it was like trying to talk to Bobby. No wonder I felt so much pain when I saw what Michael was doing to himself. He was throwing his life away: drinking, shifting the blame, showing a self-destructive will to fail. And he knew exactly which one of my buttons to push. In one argument, I slapped him across the face as hard as I could, and he smiled. "You hate me because I remind you of my father," he said. He knew how to hurt me, too. I sank back and fought against my tears. "You're wrong, Michael," I told him. "Oh, in some ways, you're right. You do remind me of your father, but I don't hate you for that. I loved your father. He had wonderful qualities I wish you would remember."

"I love my father," he said, as if he were making a declaration of war.

"I want you to love him."

"And he understands me," he said. "He doesn't always pick on me the way you do."

"Really? How do you know that, Michael?"

"He says I'm fine the way I am!"

"Failing school? Doing drugs?"

"That's the way you see it!" Michael shouted. "Dad says I'm just a kid with growing pains, trying to have some fun! What's wrong with that?"

I could have said it was life-threatening, not only to him but to anyone else whose path he happened to cross. I could have told him that he was wasting the precious years of his youth. But it wouldn't have done any good. Bobby's words seemed so much more loving to Michael. They were so easy to accept. To tell Michael that I loved him even though I

didn't like some of the things he did was much too complicated.

Chris was not as overtly self-destructive, but I could see
the lethargy and the lack of direction and initiative. Both
were over eighteen now, and neither was getting any better.
I knew that parents' "sins of omission" (doing nothing)
could be more destructive sometimes than their "sins of
commission" (doing the wrong thing), so I went for help.

I had heard about the Toughlove organization, and I
went to one of their meetings. I was surprised to see so many
people there, because I thought I was the only parent in
trouble. Then my heart broke when I heard some of the
parents struggle to talk about their children. They told of
drug addicts, child alcoholics, kids who stole from them and
some who threatened them with bodily harm. Some of their
children were in rehabilitation centers, some were in jail.
Some had run away, their whereabouts unknown. These
were parents who loved their children and wanted to help
them, but didn't know how. Some suffered terrible guilt
because they had beaten their kids or punished them more
than they deserved. And we all had the same question: what
can we do to save them?

The answer we got from the people at Toughlove was
hard to take. They told us we couldn't save our kids; they
had to save themselves—or go under. The decision was
theirs. Our job as loving parents was to confront them with
their unacceptable behavior and let them know we weren't
going to tolerate it in our homes.

I went to several Toughlove meetings because what I
heard there made sense. If I loved Chris and Michael, then
I had to find the courage to insist that they begin to stand
on their own two feet. Sometimes it was hard for me to
believe that they were over eighteen, but they were quick to
remind me that I no longer had authority over them, and
they knew their rights! Well, maybe until the day we die, we
will be learning lessons about rights and responsibilities
going together. Just trying to discuss it was awful. After
two minutes I'd turn into a raging mother, telling them that

they had to keep their word and do what they said they were going to do, that they had to become self-sufficient and either go to college or get a job, and that I would no longer support them. Screaming has never made me effective, and my sons knew that—and they knew how to start me screaming. Then they'd leave the house to get away from the sound of my voice, for which I couldn't blame them, and I'd be left feeling guilty for all the things I'd said.

The people at Toughlove understood why I had cold feet, because many parents do. But they were willing to help. They offered to be with me when I spoke to my sons. They showed me how to draw up a contract spelling out the kinds of behavior that I would not tolerate in my home.

You'll notice I said "my home," an important distinction. Toughlove made me aware that the house we all lived in was *my* home. I paid for the mortgage and the maintenance. I furnished it and supplied our food. It was my right to establish rules for the way people behaved in my home. My sons, however much I loved them, were guests there.

The boys were not to drink. I would lock up any alcohol and I would have the only key. Chris and Mike were not to take drugs at home or to be home under the influence of drugs. They were to be home at a specified time. They were not to smoke or swear, or invite friends to my home without my knowledge. The rules would apply whether I was home or on the road, and the contract was to be signed by all three of us.

"Wait a minute!" Chris said when I finished reading the terms of the contract out loud. "What's this about setting a curfew?"

I had expected Michael to object, but he said nothing. Chris surprised me with his outburst. But I remembered how I had been coached at Toughlove, and tried to be calm. "It's the way I want things to be in my house, Chris," I told him.

"You expect me to sign this?" he said.

"If you want to go on living here in my house, yes," I said.

"No way! I refuse to be treated like a prisoner in my own home!" He stood up. "I'm leaving," he said. It was a threat. He knew how much I depended on him.

But it was time for me to grow up too. "That's your decision," I said.

Chris was shocked. "Evidently, it's yours as well," he answered, as he headed for the stairs.

I wanted to go after him. It was normal for me to do that. I couldn't understand how I could sit there and let my son go. But something was changing in me.

"Michael," I said, "how about you?"

Michael is good at masking his feelings. His face told me nothing, but he reached for the contract that I held in my hand. "I'll stay," he said quietly. "Got a pen?"

I looked over at the two men from Toughlove who were sitting silently through our meeting. They nodded. I knew what they were trying to tell me: you win some, and you lose some.

Chris left home and shared a small apartment with a former classmate. He got a job as a busboy in a restaurant, which he said was a fill-in until he got something better in the music world. We kept in touch, but when we spoke on the phone or when I took him to dinner we were like strangers, afraid to talk about our feelings, always smiling and telling each other we were fine, thank you. So many times I wanted to tell him to come home. I worried about him—how was he paying his rent? What was he eating? Who were his friends? I even wondered if the people at Toughlove knew what they were doing, but something told me they did, I just wanted it to be easier to let go of Chris, and it wasn't.

Michael lived up to the terms of the contract, to the letter. He didn't break any rules, but he wasn't home any more than he absolutely had to be. He came and went without saying a word, and the only way I knew he was home was the sound of his bass upstairs in his room behind the closed, locked door.

Then one afternoon several months later, Chris called me. "Mom, I'd like to talk to you," he said. "Got some time?"

"Of course, Chris," I said, trying not to show how eager I was to see him. "As much as you need. When?"

"How about now?" he said.

An hour later I sat in the den listening to him explain why he'd decided to come home, even if it meant signing the contract he loathed. "It's a rough place out there," he said. "Being a busboy is as far as I'm ever going to get. Do you realize I can't do anything?"

I nodded. I was too close to tears to say a word.

He sank down on the sofa. "Gee, it feels good to be here!" he said. "What a great place this is."

I agreed with him. From where we were sitting we could look out into the walled garden in back of the house. The lemon trees were heavy with fruit and their leaves glistened in the sun. You couldn't hear a sound.

Michael felt that school was a waste of time. Playing in a band was all that counted. He rehearsed so diligently and for so many hours that he couldn't even think about getting a job. Eventually I had to give him an ultimatum. "If you want to go to school," I told him, "I'll pay your tuition. And I want you to live on campus because it's time you were on your own."

"No school," he said emphatically. He had already taken a year's study at a music-recording engineering school, but no job materialized.

"Then you'll have to find some way to support yourself because I won't support you any longer," I said.

For a long time Michael made ends meet by selling some of his guitars. Then he told me he was moving out.

I felt the old panic rising in me. He didn't have any money. What would happen to him? Who would look after him? But if I really respected and believed in him I had to let him go.

I thought back to those creative, hilarious and talented babies as they grew into distinct personalities with specific gifts. I remembered when I first realized Chris's natural ear for music.

He was about three years old, and I watched him on the lawn, lying on his stomach very still with his eyes wide open and his head raised. I thought he had hurt himself. But when I went over to him, I could see he was smiling. I bent down and asked him if he was all right. "Oh yes, Mommy," he said, "but you know, when I hold very, very still I can hear the most beeeeauuuutiful music."

That same music still pours out of him when he sits to improvise at the piano today. That same year I realized that he could reconstruct melodies by ear on the piano. The afternoon he had seen a "Peanuts" special on TV, I heard a lovely Beethoven piece being played, yet I knew we were at home alone. I went in and found Chris at the piano, and asked him where he had learned to play that. Very matter-of-factly, he said, "I just saw Schroeder playing it for Lucy on TV."

I said, "Well, what's the name of it?"

"I'm not sure, but I think it's called the 'Moonlight Sinatra.' " I smiled because I knew *sonata* was a word he'd never heard, but *Sinatra* was.

Like Chris, Michael was born with music in his bones, too. Both of them had been composing since they were three. Their sibling rivalry became the accepted norm from the time they were two and three years old, and I often felt like warm taffy being pulled in at least two directions at all times. There were quieter times, though. After the boys had bathed in a toy-dotted tub filled with Mr. Bubble, we settled on one of their twin beds to read their favorite stories over and over again. It was a delicious exercise in dialects and cartoon-character voices for me and for them, as the adventures of Babar, Dr. Seuss, Old Yeller and Peter and the Wolf raced across their fertile imaginations. One on each side, they'd intensely stare at the pictures and hold tightly to my arm or grab hold of a strand of my ponytail as an anchor to reality.

But one particular jousting for my undivided attention was actually tape-recorded and remains my most prized memento of their childhood antics. Michael was three and a half and Chris was almost five; and I wanted to tape a dear song Michael had improvised while accompanying himself on the ukulele I had brought him from

Hawaii. They both had had ukes, but Chris had "analyzed" and "dissected" his into pieces while Mike guarded *his* with understandable pride. I sat on a low chair near the coffee table where the tape recorder was turned on, and Michael stood playing and singing his opus one, "The Woolly Mammoth." I guess it was too much for Chris, for he immediately crawled over on all fours, growling and pawing my knee with little animal sounds. I put my free arm around him as though he were a puppy, and said, "Be quiet now, Chris. Michael is singing for me."

In a thin falsetto he softly purred, "I'm not Chris, I'm Simba, king of the jungle" (a well-known animated favorite of his).

"All right, Simba. Sit right here and listen with me. This is a wonderful song."

Michael began with four strong "open string" strums—a perfect introduction . . .

(ukulele) Brrrung, Brrrung, Brrrung, Brrrung . . .

(Michael) "There once was a woolly mammoth *(sorrowful sigh)* who lived in the cold black swamps."

(ukulele) Brrrung, Brrrung.

(Michael) "He played in the water with the frogs and fish, and he leaped on a green lily pad."

(ukulele) Brrrung, plink!

(Michael) "Then one day in the dark dark swamp—"

Quickly, Chris pawed at my knee and roared softly, "Reeeoow, Simba needs water—reeeow arg."

"Yes, Simba," I whispered. "We'll get it soon. Please listen."

(ukulele, with new verve) Brrrung, Brrrung *(open-hand slap) (Silence)*.

(Michael) "Then one day in the dark dark swamp—"

(Simba) "Simba's thirsty, reeow . . . cough . . . cough!"

(Me) "Shhhh, please."

(ukulele) BRRUUUNG, BRRUUNG!!!

(Michael) "*Suddenly*, the wooly mammoth died!"

(ukulele softly) Brrruung. . . . brrruuunng.

(Michael) "But don't be saaaad—"

(ukulele) Brrrruuunnng . . .

(Michael) "Because all things die . . . all . . . things . . . die."

(ukulele) Plink.

I was not prepared for such a profound statement from the wee angel face smiling at me. I was touched to tears and full of pride. I jumped to my feet and threw my arms around Michael and congratulated him on his fantastic song. Simba (Chris) growled and reminded me that Simba was still thirsty, and so we all turned toward the kitchen for milk and cookies.

Now that they were grown, and bursting with talent, I begged them to let me pay for voice and piano lessons, begged them to take seriously the tools of their craft and develop their potential. Michael refused, basing his decision on the lists of his favorite, and very successful, rock stars who prided themselves on not being able to read a note of music. Although he wasn't communicative at home, he had a lot of friends. He had lost about sixty pounds and was tall, slender and handsome. He was serious about getting a rock band together.

A year ago, while I was reading manuals on how to raise children, Michael started maturing. Since then he has been studying voice, and working. Recently, like an answer to my prayers, he called and told me he had enrolled in college to study the beginning music courses. What a giant step forward. He's also enrolled in a class on marketing and advertising which I'm going to attend with him. Won't that be fun!

The maturity shows in his motivation to develop his gifts, his increasing dependability, and the warmth and helpfulness that have come back into his attitude. He's still trying to make it in the rock world, and I hope he succeeds because he wants it so much. I've seen him perform, and he comes to life when he's onstage. He looks so much like Bobby . . . and he has so much charisma . . .

As for Chris, he too has had a variety of jobs in the marketplace, and has learned a lot about getting along with people and the need for discipline and priorities. He has discovered again that the world is not an easy place to negotiate, so he'll continue his training as a music composition major at UCLA.

Now, both Michael and Chris are living in apartments in the same complex. I'm grateful that they've grown up to appreciate and love each other. Watching them together is like a comedy routine, but you've got to be quick on the uptake, or they're way past you! Those years in the bathtub with Mr. Bubble, doing Dr. Seuss in voices and dialects, are paying off—Monty Python, move over! They are old enough to determine their own lives. They're entitled to make their own mistakes and to learn whatever they can from them. This is their birthright, and I have no business keeping them from it, no matter how much I want to protect them.

I've had some help with Chris and Michael. After my marriage to Greg ended, and Bobby made it clear that he didn't think the boys had a problem, I ran smack into a limitation I had tried to ignore for a long time: I couldn't help my sons. I couldn't change the fact that they had grown up in a family that was far from normal. Hopefully, they will recognize their problems and solve them someday. But in the meantime I have to let them know that I love them and always will. Not, however, in the same way I used to love them when I was trying to fix them.

In some ways I'm grateful they can't remember some of the ugliness that went on between Bobby and me. But in important ways, I wish they could. We all have many feelings that have to be acknowledged instead of denied before they can begin to heal.

I want to reach out and hold both of them and keep them from hurting anymore. I want to tell them what they can do to find their way in this world. I want to walk ahead of them and make smooth the path. But I can't.

In many ways I correlate my children and the planet. Both have been terribly hurt and damaged. There is no turning back, no undoing what's been done. Neither is denial or protection of any help. There are no shortcuts to facing up to what is sick and naming it, and then starting the arduous, difficult journey back to health, wholeness and creativity. That takes a lot of courage and strength. But that is what's required to make the shift from further damage to starting the healing process—for all of us. As Brian Swimme says, "We invented our behavior, we can reinvent it."

Letting go of the boys to let them begin their own lives, difficult as it was and is, was only part of the program. The other part was doing whatever it took to put the pieces of my life together in a different and healthier way than before. Because I had so many whys and what-happeneds, I went everywhere for information. I asked therapists, ministers, historians and professors, thinking I'd somehow find the missing part of my puzzle. Some of the more interesting and comforting information was ferreted out by Dr. Anthony Friedson, editor of the prestigious quarterly, *Biography*. It helped me get a larger, more historical perspective on the traditions affecting all of our lives and relationships in ways of which we're unaware. The following is what he had to say about the cultural conditions relating to Bobby and me. I thought it might interest you as well.

> I suspect youth—which goes with the vigor—was a major problem in your marriage. You loved each other, and you thought you knew each other. I suspect that both of you have many times wished you were aware then of the complications which lay behind what seemed an ideal love.

When you were married, you thought that you understood the implications of your social and religious backgrounds. Surely, they were similar. You came from minority families—Roman Catholic and recently immigrated to America. You were an Italian-American Catholic girl. Bobby was an Irish-French-Canadian lad. Surely you understood, and sympathized with, the problems which went with those factors. And to some extent you did. But what you didn't realize was that those similar backgrounds were also very different, and that even where they were similar, there was some bad as well as good news.

The typical Catholic of your generation was raised an idealist. The church imposed earnest demands—standards which, if not observed, haunted the guilt-ridden mind of the sinner. Nowhere was this more true than in sexual relations. Bobby was typical. Like most Catholic lads he approached women as ideals. And if on intimate acquaintance they failed to measure up to the wondrous vision, they descended from an angel to a witch.

And perhaps you had a similar innocence. If Bobby was seeking a mixture of the Holy Virgin and Mary Magdalen, you were insisting on a combination of Jesus and John the Baptist. Neither of you, of course, was fatuous enough to consciously expect these impossible creatures, but each of you had been raised with the ideal, which persistently mocked the real, mere human you were stuck with. Looking back, it's impossible to decide which of you was most responsible for the disillusion. In the Catholic societies from which you both came, disappointed men had their ruthless weapons of dominion, and rueful women had their less crude, but still powerful counters. Most of us would prefer to be de-dignified or disempowered rather than beaten or killed, but neither is a pleasant choice.

And failure to understand the sexual complexities (which needless to say are not exclusive to a Catholic upbringing) was probably equalled by your failure to fully realize the social wounds which you imagined you had in common, but which were in fact different. You were both descendants of recent immigrant families. The comedy here is that all Americans are descended from recent immigrant families. But as sociologists have pointed out, that makes us the more wary of today's immigrants who are more recent than we are.

If you thought about such matters, both of you probably fed them into your computers as a unifying empathy. In fact, your differences in this matter were probably as great as the similarities. Certainly, those of you raised in an Italian district of Chicago were victims of social prejudice—not only by others from different ethnic backgrounds, but also in an odd neurosis you imposed on yourselves: your extravagant Italian pride warred with the poverty which your families had suffered.

The Melrose Park Italian from a close, upwardly mobile family, however, was a "yuppie" compared to the son of French Canadian-Irish immigrants who had been scornfully beaten out of *their* ethnic pride in one migration, and then worked in factory squalor in a second move. Bobby probably never talked much about the inherited anger of being a French Canadian. He may not have been that conscious of the anger. It may have been a secondhand complex which came down from suffrants who were too numb to be aware of the lead chip they carried on their shoulders. These ancestors, so my Canadian friends tell me, had been put down as perverted Papists and their private lives, even their sexual and social lives, summed up in the most scurrilous terms by an English-speaking Protestant ascendancy. The anger, still noticeable in the politics of Quebec and of Canada as a whole, was probably remote to Bobby, but the hurt probably came with the crib.

Chapter Seventeen

A few summers ago I walked into Harrah's in Atlantic City, where I was scheduled to star in a summer production of *Sugar Babies* with Rip Taylor. Right there in the lobby, opposite the registration desk, were two enormous photographs of Rip and me, with our names on the marquee above them. You couldn't miss the display.

At the desk a young woman stapled some papers and put them on a pile as she turned to me with a courteous smile. "Yes?" she said.

"Hello, I'm Carol Lawrence," I said. "I think you have a reservation for me."

"How do you spell that?" she asked. "Carol with a *C*? or with a *K*?"

It had been a long time since I'd been flustered. "With a *C*," I told her, turning and pointing behind me to my picture and my name in rather large lights. She didn't look. She was busy with her computer.

"And Lawrence?" she said. "Is that L-a-w? or L-a-u?"

I surrendered. "L-a-w," I said meekly. I remembered the

first time I had seen my name up in lights when I was in *West Side Story*. It had seemed so important to me. But many years later I was learning something else about having your name up in lights: it isn't important to anybody else. I try to remember that.

Getting into a Broadway show used to be the most vital thing in the world to me. It isn't anymore. I love being on-stage and I always will. To me it's a vacation, and I never grow tired of it. I even thrive on the repetition of all those performances. But now I know that there is more to life than the curtain going up. There is more to me than the role I play.

In my personal life, I often found myself playing a role to please people. And every now and then I would wonder, "Who am I? And why don't I play me?" That's what I'm beginning to do now: play myself. And God is the only critic whose review matters. Because "God is love," I'm making a serious effort to learn all I can on the subject. I'm beginning to understand that I can't love anybody in a healthy way until I learn how to love and accept myself. I think that's what Jesus meant when he told us to "love thy neighbor as thyself." There is such a comfortable balance implied in that—no conceit or martyrdom, just an easy exchange. The interdependence that emerges out of giving to and receiving from each other is as necessary as breathing in and out in order for us to achieve a balanced fulfillment in our rela-tionships. Doing one is no good without the other. But the unexpected joy of giving begins to outweigh our own selfish needs, and a deeper fulfillment is experienced. To nourish another human being with a personal sacrifice of time, ef-fort, comfort, understanding or support brings me closer to realizing my purpose in being alive. It's a special form of ecstasy I seek everyday.

Ten years ago these ideas, of needing fulfillment or of somebody not knowing my name when it's in bright lights above my head, would have made me suicidal if not homi-cidal. What has happened instead is an incredible change of my perception and perspective of myself and those around me. And this came as a gift. It is not something I learned.

It came out of my desperation to figure out what was wrong with my life, marriage and family—and what I could do about it.

As I write this to you, I'm drinking a cup of coffee—why don't you get one, too? And I'll tell you some of the steps of my journey. And just maybe it will encourage you in yours. The biggest obstacle to starting mine was the fear of being found out, of being my real self, when I had spent so much time on my/our image. (Have you noticed how easy it is for our egos to prevent us from experiencing the happiness and health that is available?) So, taking my fears and ego in hand, because I didn't know how to get rid of them, I took them with me to that first AA meeting. The next place I took them was to Al-Anon. The love and support that those people surrounded me with made the rest so much easier. That doesn't mean "easy," you understand—just easier. Their warmth made fear and ego no longer an issue, so I could deal with the next layer. Taking a hard look at yourself, especially if you've been pretty demanding all your life, is painful. That's where the love and support get powerfully important. I wanted to learn everything I could from any source available.

As you read earlier, the ACA and Toughlove programs were especially relevant and helpful to my needs, as was John Bradshaw's new program called CoDa (for Codependents Anonymous: people who are addicted to feeling needed, to helping, which applies to about 98 percent of the population). What you need, or what is available in your community, I don't know. What I do know is that there are dynamite resources out there for every problem, and for worthwhile causes that need our support and enthusiasm. And what each of us needs, let alone our children and the planet, is for us to come alive, look around, and see what we can applaud, enjoy, be grateful for, or contribute to.

Other resources that have been helpful to me are the host of wonderful books and tapes available on practically every subject. I have been thrilled at the range of information I have gleaned that is fascinatingly written, from physics and botany to social history, psychology and theology. No more are "heavy" subjects only discussed in textbook language that it takes a Ph.D. to understand. Now the world around us can come excitingly alive through authors like the ones I've mentioned throughout the book.

At each of these meetings, workshops or seminars, I would meet new people with new suggestions of books to read or workshops to attend. They also told me about tests that were available—personality, psychological, and aptitude tests—which would tell me specifically who *I* was. I found these to be invaluable. I was no longer dealing with a set of priorities that was supposed to apply to everybody. Instead, I embraced the knowledge that every human is different from every other human, with different needs. It is in those differences we find our destiny and delight. The best favor I have done myself and my children was to give us the head start of knowing what gifts and interests we should develop, and at the same time freeing myself from that horrible feeling that I should be a finished, perfect example of whatever I was striving for. It is in the painful learning process that the adventure of creativity is born!

Instead of thinking in terms of limitations, deficiencies and faults, I'm trying to think in terms of uniqueness, variety and the richness of diversity. I'm trying to see that oak trees aren't supposed to have the colors of snapdragons. That grass isn't supposed to have the fragrance of roses. And that gazelles aren't supposed to fly like eagles. But most of us seem to feel that we should all look like Venus or Adonis, have the brains of Einstein, the heart of Mother Teresa and the stamina of Tarzan. Most of us are made to feel we are somehow deficient if we are only brilliant but not beautiful, only athletic but not straight-A students, only creative but not rich. When can we learn to celebrate who we are, and encourage each other in our gifts, rather than wishing we or other people were something or someone else? Then we could come together not to envy or judge, but to enjoy and to help make a better world.

My experiences are easy to write about, but they have taken time and tears to live through. They have resulted in a new ability to stand here embarrassingly naked, saying,

Hey world, this is the mess I've made, the choices I've chosen, the life I've lived—with all of its wonders and horrors. I wish I could undo and unsay things that I regret still. But that is not possible. What is possible is to say, "I'm sorry, I blew it," and let it go. And then to let those mistakes that embarrass or haunt me serve as a basis for understanding and compassion, comfort and forgiveness, for other people who make the same mistakes I have.

While I was going through these major transitions, I began to discover a "Pattern of Priorities." I share them with you, hoping that they will enrich your search for a balanced life.

1. Acknowledge the glory of God and remind yourself, "He loves me and has a purpose and plan for my life here."

2. Learn about God from as many sources as possible. Start with your home church. Get involved in Bible study classes, workshops, seminars and retreats sponsored by your church.

3. Be physically accountable; maintain the magnificent gift your body represents. That means a daily, conscientious schedule of exercise, proper diet and an ongoing commitment to good health habits.

4. The same commitment applies to mental health. Seek a psychological balance based on the wisdom and the word of God. Stay mentally stimulated, but on guard to stress, insecurities, fears and problems in personal relationships. Face problems early, knowing they can be resolved.

5. Be a friend. Find ways to participate in and contribute to your friends' and loved ones' lives and growth—without trying to fix them. Love as our Lord showed us to.

6. Stay on top of responsibilities and new projects. Make sure the things on your "to do" list get done. Laziness eradicates the joy of achievement.

7. Be gentle with yourself and others. Seeds don't grow overnight. Be encouraged by small, ongoing improvements.

8. Allow yourself recuperative periods of relaxed enjoyment and appreciation of what pleases you. You deserve it! Drink in the Lord's blessings and give thanks.

9. Stand up for what you believe and get involved in organizations for ecological, educational, ethical, environmental and political concerns. Speak out, take risks, stay in balance and be responsible. The survival of our planet depends on all of us contributing our parts.

Church has become a tremendous source of inspiration and comfort to me, as have temples, synagogues and mosques to many of my friends. I am a member of The Church on the Way, and I feel at home there. In the lobby, before the service begins, I see familiar faces, many of them actors and actresses looking for the same spiritual environment as I am: a place where we can be real, where our needs can be fed, where we can be loved and accepted. Our needs aren't any greater than anyone else's; we just have a harder time admitting them because we keep confusing real life with the roles we play.

I don't want to give the impression that The Church on the Way is a celebrity church, because it isn't. The rest of the congregation, the people who really make it work, know that performers aren't special. We're people.

In our Sunday services we sing for a long time, mostly contemporary gospel songs that put feelings into words. And even if we don't know the people next to us, we talk to them, hold hands and share our needs in prayer for each other. Sometimes we run out of words and just hug. But we know that in that circle of love are God's power and blessings, and our strength.

One of the results of my faith, and of all the books I've read and the seminars I've gone to, is my increasing ability to trust and let go. I found that out by accident when I was in a shop on Rodeo Drive looking at some shirts for Chris and Mike, and I saw Ken Trevor, the man I'd been involved with years ago, standing at another counter. "Why not?" I thought, and I went toward him. Ken looked up and smiled. "Carol!" he said, "You look wonderful!"— as if nothing had changed in all the years since we had seen each other.

"How are you, Ken?" I asked.

"Right now, I'm happy, because I'm looking at you," he said. He still had the charm. "You know you're the only woman I ever loved."

"Ken, you really don't have to go on like that."

"But we have to have lunch!" he said.

I laughed. "No, we don't have to have lunch. Old friends don't have to make a fuss over each other."

He seemed relieved. Motioning to a tall young man across the store, he said proudly, "This is my son," and he introduced us. For a long time after that we talked about our children.

As I drove home, the old pain from an old love was gone, and I wondered what had caused the pain to last so long: Ken's rejection of me, or my inability to forgive him? I sensed that something was different. No wonder they say the person who does the forgiving is the one who benefits the most from it. I'm learning a lot about that now from Dr. Gerald Jampolsky's books and tapes, such as *Love Is Letting Go of Fear*.

Recently, when I was in New York, I picked up a telephone book and looked up Gus Allegretti's name. I dug out a quarter, dialed the number and got an answering machine. I was about to hang up when I simply had to say what was in my heart. I realized that I didn't have to be there when Gus heard it.

When the tone sounded, I said, "Hello, Gus, I know you'll find it hard to believe, but this is Carol. I'm in New York and I'm about to go home, but I just wanted to call and say hello and how are you. I hope you're okay, and that you're happy—and, well, God bless you, Gus!"

Bobby wasn't as easy to forgive. When I'd pray about him I felt like I was really saying, "Lord, I want to forgive him but first let me punch him out, or belt him one for destroying all we could have had together." I loved him, so I couldn't seem to get past the chaos of emotions: hurt, rage, confusion, sadness and the never-ending whys.

Two years ago, Bobby was touring in *South Pacific*. The show was scheduled to play in Costa Mesa, forty-five minutes south of Los Angeles, in January 1988, and suddenly I knew that I wanted to see it. I wanted to see *him*.

I had been angry with Bobby for so long because he'd dashed the hopes and dreams I'd had for us.

We hadn't seen each other in nearly ten years. Only rarely did we speak on the phone, and then only about the boys. How many times I had told myself I'd forgiven him, but I knew I hadn't. I hated him. And I knew he hated me. I didn't want it to be that way, especially when I saw the damage it was doing to Chris and Michael. It was forcing them to take sides.

Then something in me changed. Maybe it was all part of letting go. Maybe I was allowing God to write my script instead of insisting on doing it all myself.

When I called him to ask if I could come backstage after the performance, he was startled. But he agreed.

Chris had already seen the show in San Francisco, but he came with me. As we drove down to Costa Mesa, he was a little too cheerful, and I knew he was nervous. He wasn't sure how the meeting would go.

I didn't know what to expect either, so I was nervous, too. I remembered how easily Bobby could switch from sweetness to fury, and I hoped I wouldn't say anything to upset him. I hadn't met Vera, his wife, but we had talked on the phone many times and we were polite.

Bobby had reserved our seats, and we arrived only a few minutes before the lights were dimmed. Chris squeezed my hand and I smiled at him. "I'm okay," I assured him.

From the moment the show began, I felt as if I were seeing Bobby for the first time. It was like watching him in *Camelot* so many years ago, when I could see what was wonderful about his performance, and how I would have envisioned it differently. But amazingly, I felt no need to change what he was. Like all of us, he was getting older, but he looked terrific. I hoped he wasn't drinking. He had to work harder, but he still had the magic in his voice. At one point, when he sang "This Nearly Was Mine," there were tears in his eyes. He seemed to touch the hearts of the audience in a way I had never seen him do before. I was sad, thinking back over the past, but not angry. I was letting Bobby go.

After the show, Chris and I went backstage. We spent a few minutes with Vera, who was cordial, and then I met Bobby in his dressing room. We didn't argue. We didn't shout. We said nice things about each other and wished each other well.

On the way home that night, Chris said, "It was so good seeing the two of you together without hurting each other." I couldn't have said it better.

When I woke up the next morning, I looked out my bedroom window at the view I had loved for twenty-three years, and I knew I was ready to give it up. The house, the lifestyle and all the mementos in it had been a heavy burden for me to carry, and at last I realized why I had held on to it for so long and at such cost to me as a person.

I was able to face something I had been hiding for years: somewhere deep inside of me, I was hoping that Bobby would come back. I was keeping the house for him. Of course, I was nurturing a fantasy, but when had I ever been realistic about our relationship? He was married again, and I had been married and divorced again. What made me think we could ever get back together? Nothing, actually. It was a fairy tale that I was trying to make come true. But I know now that a fairy tale is a very unhappy place for anyone to live. I prefer the real thing.

I called a real estate agent and put my house on the market. I will always love it, but my needs are different now.

I need a home that I can lock up and leave at a moment's notice, because I want to be available to do a play, a musical, a television show, a documentary or a concert anywhere in the world. There is so much more I want to do with my talent that sometimes I feel as if I were nineteen again, living in a New York loft.

As I write this, I am in Lake Tahoe, starring in *Sugar Babies*. Some people, with disgust, have asked how I can tolerate the "off color" jokes and skimpy costumes. I just smile, because what they don't know is that every week, everybody in the cast who wants to comes to my dressing

room to study *The Road Less Traveled* by M. Scott Peck
and to share our stories and our love. This time together,
with its openness, vulnerability and closeness, has bonded
us into a support system. People who ordinarily would never
have really known one another are now friends for life. None
of us are teachers, ministers, seminar leaders or therapists.
We don't have any degrees or training. We just have the guts
to reach out and say, "Here's what I need and want, how
about you?"

And the love that has strengthened us as individuals
and as a group is especially needed now, for one of our
dancers, a delightful, whimsical, talented man, just died.
He went from fine to depressed to a case of the flu to cardiac
arrest in two weeks—a total shock. But in the brief span of
one summer, he and the rest of us had become a family
through our little dressing-room seminars. Tomorrow, we
will have a memorial service here at my place on the lake to
say goodbye to our dear friend.

When Lou Phillips, the head of Harrah's, heard about
our discussion group, he was generous enough to offer a
few other enlightening sessions for us. He had been in
charge of "human resources" at Harrah's in Reno, and he
loved people—that was obvious! Between shows, and long
after his full day of work was done, he would meet with us
to administer psychological tests.

One test had been developed by a mother-daughter
team of psychologists, Jacquelyn Wonder and Priscilla Don-
ovan, in their book, *The Brain Preference: Right/Left Brain
Indicator*. It revealed great differences in how men and
women usually think from using the right or left side of
their brains. The whole group was a buzz with endless questions and had a new hunger for understanding themselves
and the person next to them.

Another well-respected and long-used test was called
the "Myers-Briggs Psychological Test" and is based largely
on Carl Jung's theories of personalities. It was exciting and
encouraging, and the cast floated through the second show
the night we heard about it.

I was truly touched by Lou's warmth, enthusiasm and

expert insight—not to mention the outlay of funds to have the twenty-seven tests processed and the follow-up meetings he conducted to explain and clarify our results. All of us were stimulated, enhanced and, best of all, nurtured and loved. Well, Lou Phillips, we love you right back!

My new dream at the moment is to have a women's center where we can come together to empower and encourage each other to discover and become all we are capable of, to learn to meet our needs—mental, spiritual and physical, and to share our problems, joys and solutions.

Can you imagine, if we got together in little groups all over America, what we could accomplish, individually and collectively? Can you imagine if we were using our gifts and talents to their fullest, the incredible things we could accomplish for our communities, our children and ourselves?

Any caterpillar dies if it stays in its cocoon too long. However secure that cocoon feels and terrifying the great unknown seems, we are each butterflies. We must fly out to our own destinies or die. Whatever our gifts, our talents, our backgrounds and our interests, we have to give of ourselves not only for our own survival, but for the planet's. And if in some way I can encourage you, as I have been receiving encouragement from everybody I've met (whether it was meant that way or not!), then you, in turn, can pass on your encouragement to your neighbor.

As I told you earlier quoting from Stewart Emery's book *The Owner's Manual for Your Life*,

> The very qualities about us that are magical as
> children . . . the ability to wonder, to love, our
> passionate curiosity, all fade unless we are given
> the opportunity to contribute them to others . . .

We each have to get out there and give what we have to give. And if you don't know what to do, just go to your local convalescent home, botanical garden or animal shelter. They will suggest ways to keep you happily busy. All creation needs our love and attention.

The Assistant Secretary-General of the United Nations, Robert Muller, gives us a call to which I pray we all rally.

Let us all coalesce with all our strength, mind, heart and soul around a New Genesis, a true global, God-abiding political, moral and spiritual renaissance to make this planet at long last what it was always meant to be: the planet of God.